# DISCOURSE ON METAPHYSICS AND OTHER WRITINGS

## DISCOURSE ON METAPHYSICS

## THE PRINCIPLES OF NATURE AND OF GRACE

## THE MONADOLOGY

Gottfried Wilhelm Leibniz

*edited by Peter Loptson and*
*translated by Robert Latta and George R. Montgomery,*
*with revisions by Peter Loptson*

broadview editions

Library and Archives Canada Cataloguing in Publication

Leibniz, Gottfried Wilhelm, Freiherr von, 1646-1716
[Discours de métaphysique. English]
    Discourse on metaphysics and other writings : Discourse on metaphysics, The principles of nature and of grace, The monadology / Gottfried Wilhelm Leibniz ; edited by Peter Loptson and translated by Robert Latta and George R. Montgomery ; with revisions by Peter Loptson.

(Broadview editions)
Includes bibliographical references and index.
ISBN 978-1-55481-011-6

        1. Metaphysics—Early works to 1800.  I. Loptson, Peter
II. Latta, Robert, 1865-  III. Montgomery, George R.
IV. Title.  V. Title: Discours de métaphysique.  English.
VI. Series: Broadview editions

B2572.E5M66 2012          110          C2012-902636-0

**Broadview Editions**

The Broadview Editions series represents the ever-changing canon of literature by bringing together texts long regarded as classics with valuable lesser-known works.

Advisory editor for this volume: Martin Boyne

Broadview Press is an independent, international publishing house, incorporated in 1985.

We welcome comments and suggestions regarding any aspect of our publications—please feel free to contact us at the addresses below or at broadview@broadviewpress.com.

*North America*
PO Box 1243, Peterborough, Ontario, Canada K9J 7H5
2215 Kenmore Ave., Buffalo, New York, USA 14207
Tel: (705) 743-8990; Fax: (705) 743-8353
email: customerservice@broadviewpress.com

*UK, Europe, Central Asia, Middle East, Africa, India, and Southeast Asia*
Eurospan Group, 3 Henrietta St., London WC2E 8LU, United Kingdom
Tel: 44 (0) 1767 604972; Fax: 44 (0) 1767 601640
email: eurospan@turpin-distribution.com

*Australia and New Zealand*
NewSouth Books
c/o TL Distribution, 15-23 Helles Ave., Moorebank, NSW, Australia 2170
Tel: (02) 8778 9999; Fax: (02) 8778 9944
email: orders@tldistribution.com.au

www.broadviewpress.com

Broadview Press acknowledges the financial support of the Government of Canada through the Canada Book Fund for our publishing activities.

This book is printed on paper containing 100% post-consumer fibre.

PRINTED IN CANADA

# Contents

Acknowledgements • 7
Introduction • 9
Gottfried Wilhelm Leibniz: A Brief Chronology • 53
A Note on the Texts • 55

*Discourse on Metaphysics* • 57

*The Principles of Nature and of Grace, Based on Reason* • 103

*The Monadology* • 115

Appendix A: From Anne, Viscountess Conway, *Principles of the Most Ancient and Modern Philosophy* (1690) • 135

Appendix B: From Antonie van Leeuwenhoek's 1699 Letter to Antonio Magliabechi • 143

Appendix C: From Pierre Bayle, *Historical and Critical Dictionary* (1695-1702) • 147

Appendix D: From G.W. Leibniz, *Theodicy* (1710) • 155

Appendix E: From David Hume, *An Enquiry concerning Human Understanding* (1748) • 209

Appendix F: From Voltaire, *Candide* (1759) • 213

Appendix G: From Thomas Reid, *Essays on the Intellectual Powers of Man* (1785) • 219

Further Reading and Select Bibliography • 227

Index • 229

# Acknowledgements

I have had considerable input on my thinking about Leibniz, over many years in the past and for this specific project. For direct and extremely helpful comments on earlier drafts of my introductory material I would like to acknowledge with deep thanks Richard Arthur, Martha Bolton, Thomas Lennon, Brandon C. Look, Pauline Phemister, Nicholas Rescher, and Catherine Wilson. Their comments contributed in different ways, but in all instances substantively, to making that material better—clearer, more accessible, and more accurate—than it had been. Remaining faults or infelicities will be due to my sometimes resisting what was probably good advice. I would also like to acknowledge conversations with Daniel Garber, as well as the stimulus of his many exceptionally scholarly and lucidly argued publications on Leibniz, and editions of his texts.

I would also like to thank Padraig O'Cleirig for his invaluable assistance with translations of some of Leibniz's quotations, chiefly in the *Theodicy* (Appendix D), and in some instances with tracking down a source.

For technical assistance I am extremely grateful to Kathy Hanneson, at the University of Guelph, as well as to the team at Broadview, notably, Martin Boyne, Leonard Conolly, Leslie Dema, and Marjorie Mather. Their input contributed immensely to the fine-tuning of details of translation, formatting, and other aspects of the production of the volume, and is much appreciated.

# Introduction

## Birth and Early Life

Gottfried Wilhelm Leibniz was born on 1 July 1646 in Leipzig, Germany.[1] At that time Leipzig, with Dresden, the capital, was one of the two primary cities of Saxony, one of the constituent states of the Holy Roman Empire. (Its ruler was one of the electoral princes of the Empire.) The Empire was a huge, central European, chiefly German-speaking federal state, formally ruled by its (Catholic) emperor in Vienna; the hundreds of states that it comprised were variously of Catholic, Lutheran, or "Reformed" (Calvinist) religion, chiefly determined by the denominational allegiance of the state's ruler. Saxony, and Leipzig in particular, were of a very emphatic and conservative Lutheran stamp, and Leibniz was raised in this denomination and remained so throughout his life. Electoral Saxony[2] had no fewer than three of the major German universities in Leibniz's day—those at Jena, Leipzig, and Wittenberg.[3] Leipzig was the oldest, founded in 1409.

---

1   For a full biography of Leibniz, see Maria Rosa Antognazza, *Leibniz: An Intellectual Biography* (Cambridge: Cambridge UP, 2009). See also the Chronology, p. 53f below.

2   The Holy Roman Empire was nominally an elective monarchy, its emperor "elected" on the death of his predecessor by a body of electoral princes, some of them of hereditary princely status, some ecclesiastical. In the period of Leibniz's earlier life there were five hereditary electoral princes (Saxony being the territory ruled by one of them), and three electors who were archbishops. Unlike other German territories, the lands of the electors passed without partition to the next holder. Leibniz himself was to have a role in bringing about the elevation of a ninth prince (his employer the Duke of Brunswick-Lunebourg) to electoral status.

3   Subsequent Saxon territorial losses were to deprive the electorate of all but Leipzig.

Leibniz was the son of Friedrich Leubnitz, or Leibnütz[1] (1597-1652), the professor of moral philosophy at the University of Leipzig, and his third wife, Catharina Schmuck (1621-64). Friedrich died when Leibniz was just six, and this was to have the unexpected but fortuitous result that Leibniz was given free rein of his father's very extensive library. His formal schooling was primarily centred on Latin, at which the young Leibniz proved exceptionally adept. This pair of pedagogical developments together played a very significant role in the formation of the interests and the rapidly acquired academic breadth of the youthful scholar. It helped as well that Leibniz was of quite exceptional intellectual gifts.

Leibniz was admitted as a student at the University of Leipzig shortly before his fifteenth birthday. He graduated with a bachelor's degree, in philosophy, in December 1662, at sixteen. Like many a talented graduate in philosophy in the present day, he then faced the question of whether to go on to acquire further degrees in philosophy—or to go to law school. (In Leibniz's case, theology and medicine would also have been options.) Leibniz opted for both: he obtained a subsequent master's degree in philosophy, and all three degrees—bachelor's, master's, and doctorate—in law.

Leibniz's career thereafter was in a central way a function of his status as a doctor of law. His formal employment was as a legal scholar in the employ of sovereign princes of the Empire. The first of these was the Archbishop-Elector of Mainz; thereafter, he worked for the rulers of Hanover. On the side, as it were, he involved himself in the intellectual culture of Europe, especially in the sciences, philosophy, mathematics, and theology. He was an enthusiastic advocate throughout his adult life of unificatory and reconciliatory projects, both political and sectarian as well as in the commonwealth of learning. The latter included schemes of universal encyclopedias, learned societies, and a symbolism

---

1  Leibniz adopted the spelling of his surname that is now standard at some point in his twenties. The spelling "Leibnitz" became common during his lifetime, and frequently in subsequent centuries, though he himself never used this spelling. He did, though, sometimes style himself Gottfried *von* Leibniz. Possibly it was this "appearance" of nobility that led to his being styled, posthumously, "Freiherr [i.e., Baron] von Leibniz." There is no conclusive evidence that any such title was conferred on him, and he himself does not appear to have claimed this rank. However, see Nicholas Rescher, "Was Leibniz Ennobled?," in N. Rescher, *On Leibniz*, 2nd ed. (Pittsburgh: U of Pittsburgh P, 2012).

for the whole of knowledge.

We are given a vivid sense of Leibniz's personality and talents at the beginning of this career, in a description—a job reference, in fact—provided by a friend and advocate during those early years (the Baron von Boineburg):

> He is a young man, twenty-four years old, from Leipzig, a doctor of law, and a more learned one could scarcely be imagined. He understands the whole of philosophy thoroughly and is a productive thinker in both the old and the new. He is furnished above all with the ability to write. He is a mathematician, hard-working and ardent, who knows and loves natural philosophy, medicine, and mechanics. Of independent judgement in religion, he is a member of your [Lutheran] confession. He has mastered not only the philosophy of law but also, remarkably, legal practice.[1]

Thus Leibniz, in 1670. He went on to a distinguished public career, with two primary facets: the official and formal career, as diplomat, courtier, legal officer, and mining engineer, and the equally prominent parallel life of one of the foremost philosophers and mathematicians of his age.

## Leibniz's World

The western European world of Leibniz's period was in a great many ways the modern and contemporary world. A single trajectory may be seen from that time to our own, very markedly in the spheres of scholarship and the sciences. Like ours, Leibniz's world was characterized by regularly appearing academic journals,[2] in which the (typically provisional) results of research, and of speculative hypothesis, were published and received the scrutiny of a sizeable international community of fellow-scholars and fellow-scientists, who would in turn be

---

1 Letter from Boineburg, 1670, quoted in Antognazza, *Leibniz*, p. 86.
2 The earliest of the scientific journals, the *Journal des sçavans* (subsequently the *Journal des savants*), began publication in January 1665, followed shortly afterwards by the *Philosophical Transactions of the Royal Society of London*. German Europe's first scientific journal, *Acta eruditorum*, appeared from 1682. Leibniz was to publish in the first and third of these journals (he had played a role in the foundation of the third).

prompted to bring forward some of their own advancing work. It was a world of learned societies and associations, whose membership rolls included prominent public figures, many of them sponsors, private or officials of the state, as well as mutually recognized and honoured workers in the developing fields of research and science.[1] The period also saw the flowering and expansion of the experimental laboratory, and the practice of what, ideally at least, was the publicly observed and repeatable empirical test. It was punctuated, certainly, by wars among or between the several European national societies, as modern history continued to be until at least 1945. It was an international world, and fundamentally a secular one.[2] As was only somewhat problematically the case earlier, Catholics, Protestants, and other thinkers and investigators of no particular religious persuasion consulted, corresponded, employed each other, and generally conducted their business in the work of the mind with spirited animadversion (as of course one finds still now), but in a shared cultural and work environment characterized, mostly, by mutual toleration.

## Leibniz's Works

Leibniz was a rich, indeed, a magnificent, exemplar of these patterns. His first published philosophical paper appeared in 1684, in *Acta eruditorum*. His work appeared frequently thereafter in the scholarly journals of his day. He also developed a network of correspondence and other contact with leading thinkers of his time. Indeed, Leibniz was an astonishingly active and prolific letter writer. The surviving body of his papers includes over

---

1   The Royal Society of London for Improving Natural Knowledge (usually called more briefly the Royal Society) was founded in 1660, with an official charter two years later. The French Académie des sciences followed shortly thereafter, in 1666. Other European scientific societies and associations, usually state-sponsored, ensued. Leibniz was in fact to be the first president of Prussia's Berlin Society of Sciences, in 1700.

2   Throughout the period from 1640 to 1815 the greatest of the European powers, militarily and culturally, was France, with Great Britain a close and steadily rising second. Leibniz's life almost exactly coincided with the reign of Louis XIV (1643-1715), the resplendent and often belligerent leading sovereign of the age. Another curious alignment with the span of Leibniz's life was the fact that "the years 1645-1715 were bitterly cold across much of the Old World. From London to Guangdong, diarists and officials complained about snow, ice, and cool summers" (Ian Morris, *Why the West Rules—For Now* [Toronto: McClelland & Stewart, 2010], p. 450).

fifteen thousand letters from over one thousand distinct correspondences.[1] A great many of his ideas and arguments are set out and defended in this body of material. Several volumes of the correspondence were published, beginning with the exchange with Samuel Clarke (1675-1729), Newton's ally and advocate, in 1717, the year following Leibniz's death. A collection of some five hundred of Leibniz's letters were subsequently published in a four-volume set between 1734 and 1742; particular correspondences followed, among them the correspondence with Johann Bernoulli,[2] in 1745. A good deal more has been published since.

The majority of what now is given highlighted attention in Leibniz scholarship in fact appeared in print only posthumously. Some of it, including two of the treatises included in the present volume, the *Discourse on Metaphysics* and *The Principles of Nature and of Grace*, had some very limited circulation during Leibniz's lifetime, but what is probably the most famous and now most widely read of his metaphysical works (indeed, of any of his writings), the *Monadology*, came to attention, and publication, only a few years after the philosopher's death. In Leibniz's lifetime, apart from papers in learned journals, the philosopher's primary publication was a 1710 book, the *Theodicy* (see Appendix D). He was otherwise especially famous—controversially famous—as inventor of the calculus. The controversy stems from the fact that, most remarkably, Isaac Newton (1643-1727) made the same fundamental mathematical discovery around the same time. This led to a spirited dispute, with advocates of the two great mathematicians accusing the other of plagiarism. Eventually it was determined that the discoveries had been independent. Newton's was slightly earlier, though Leibniz's notation has been the one subsequently adopted.

## Leibniz's Personal Life and Later Years

Leibniz never married. In fact, very little is known of his private life.[3] He was amiable, tended to dress well, and had the manners

---

1 Paul Lodge, ed., *Leibniz and His Correspondents* (Cambridge: Cambridge UP, 2004), p. 1.
2 Johann Bernoulli (1667-1748) was a Swiss mathematician.
3 That is to say, of his inner life. In spite of the great detail of his correspondences, and of his well-tracked intellectual and public projects and activities, the psychology of the man himself remains in some ways enigmatic.

and personal style of a courtier and diplomat. His enormous correspondence involved relationships with a great many individuals, famous and otherwise, and some of these epistolary relationships may reasonably be described as friendships. Life at the court of Hanover, where the greater part of his time was spent over the final three decades of his life, was isolated and provincial. It was intellectually enriched for Leibniz, however, by the presence there of three very intelligent and philosophically and scientifically minded women in the ruling family, all of whom took an interest in Leibniz's work, and in discussing it with him: the wife of the Elector (Ernst August), Sophia (1630-1714);[1] Sophia's daughter Sophie Charlotte (1668-1705), subsequently queen of Prussia (1701-05); and the wife of Sophia's grandson, Caroline of Ansbach (1683-1737)—subsequently queen of Great Britain (1727-37).

Leibniz's last years were a period of diminished acclaim. His employer had become George I, king of Great Britain and Ireland, and when he left Germany for England did not invite Leibniz to accompany him, to Leibniz's disappointment.[2] Leibniz died, in Hanover, on 14 November 1716.[3]

**Leibniz's Metaphysical System**

There are disagreements about minor (and *some* major) issues in the interpretation of the metaphysical system that Leibniz developed by stages and with some modifications over the course of the last 35 years of his life. These include questions of consistency that some of those details pose. There are also

---

1   She was in fact a younger sister of Princess Elisabeth of Bohemia (1618-81), the celebrated friend and philosophically acute correspondent of Descartes, whom Leibniz met toward the end of her life.
2   The reasons for this neglect and disfavour probably had most of all to do with Leibniz's failure to deliver on the principal task that his princely employers had set him, namely, a detailed historical account of themselves—a scholarly record of the origins and history of the house of Brunswick, or Guelph. Leibniz had spent many years on this research (he was originally charged with undertaking it in 1685), with much travel and archival sleuthing, but had managed by the end of it, and of his own life, to get no further than the eleventh century.
3   In his last years Leibniz had been plagued with gout and arthritis. Succumbing to what was described as colic, he died peacefully in his sleep.

issues of periodization. Leibniz had begun to develop his philo-sophical ideas before he was 20. He lived to 70, and a variety of changes in his views, certainly in the terminology he adopted or preferred and in topics or emphases that came especially to concern him, may undoubtedly be noted. Nonetheless, on the whole it is meaningful and appropriate to speak of a single sys-tem, mostly formulated by the mid-1680s.[1] That system, with its postulates and principles, given its mature or final articula-tion in the philosopher's last decade, is strikingly cohesive and unitary; it is also reasonably straightforward. It is, to be sure, in its extensive detail somewhat *complicated*; that is to say, though the individual components of the system are—with a few impor-tant exceptions—mostly clear and readily intelligible, there are quite a few of those components. For many observers and critics the system provokes incredulity; it will seem to some, in fact, a kind of phantasm. But a formal account of what makes up the world as Leibniz describes it may fairly readily be given. So too can a structure of rationale be supplied. Given various basic principles, the system will be generated from those principles, together with a few foundational postulates. Apart from fun-damental logical ones, these principles chiefly include a very strong version of a principle of sufficient reason—according to which, for every truth, and every existent, there is a sufficient reason (logical, causal, or some other) why it should be so, or should exist, rather than not—and a principle of perfection. In fact the latter may be understood as our simply having a clear and distinct concept of complete or absolute perfection. From our having that concept, Leibniz argues, the existence, then the nature, and in consequence the activities of a unique, absolutely perfect being will follow, by an ontological argument (an importantly novel one, it should be said). At least one fur-ther principle also is necessary for Leibniz's system. This is the postulate that there are individual substances, understood as

---

1   In fact a body of notes on metaphysics intended by Leibniz to be incorporated into an exposition of his system (like so many of his other projects, unrealized) shows that the majority of its essential principles were already in place in 1675. (He called the projected work *Elementa philosophiae arcanae, de summa rerum*—the work is now usually abbreviated as *De Summa Rerum* ["on the totality of things" or "on the highest of things"]; the notes were written, in Paris, over the period from December 1675 to April 1676.)

(metaphysical) atoms of the world, which the perfect being—God—creates.

An immediate set of consequences of these postulates, as Leibniz understands both of them, independently and in their conjunction, should be seen and made explicit. In virtue of being *perfect*, God cannot *act* capriciously; the supremely and wholly rational being will always have sufficient reason for the resolution of any set of alternatives he might confront, in the particular way that it is resolved. Furthermore, perfection will imply complete knowledge of all possibilities and all actualities, as well as power and will to effect the latter from the former. And in virtue of their metaphysical atomicity, the existence of substances will be a feature of any scheme of things that will have been possible; moreover, each substance will have a complete nature and history, which will constitute and, so to speak, define the substance. This will comprise a complete concept of that substance, in itself and as itself, apart from any other substance. God will have had that complete concept in view, in determining whether the substance concerned will be real or actual.

It would be question-begging to give the matter much further content, at least at this stage, but Leibniz has throughout his philosophical career a basic and fundamental concern also with *bodies*. His aim is to ensure that his metaphysical system should encompass a correct, accurate *philosophy of material nature*. He may or may not successfully realize that aim; scholarly interpretation of this matter differs. What is not in doubt is that there is to be a thoroughgoing treatment of body, and that in that treatment body will be found to be in some manner *subordinate* to the substances that are the bedrock of the system. Also not in doubt, and affirmed in all three of the texts of Leibniz's included in this volume, is Leibniz's holding a thesis he sees as part of his philosophy of material nature, in its intersection with the account of (simple) substances. He was later to call this the thesis of the *pre-established harmony*. Like some other aspects of his account of material nature, or body, this thesis has been interpreted in different ways. The thesis *seems* to say that both thinking substances and bodies are real, and they operate systematically in separate spheres that involve the appearance but not the reality of contact between them. I will say more on these issues below.

Discourse on Metaphysics

The first of the works included in this volume, the *Discourse on Metaphysics* (*Discours de métaphysique*), was written (in French[1]) in late 1685 or early 1686.[2] Although a summary of the work was sent to the great French philosopher Antoine Arnauld (1612-94), the work itself would not achieve publication until 1846; and it was not until 1907, in a critical edition, that a fully integrated text of its variants appeared. It thereafter became and remains a very well-known and much-studied treatise. Two things may be noted immediately about the work. First, though Leibniz lived long, this was not a work of his youth, or an early stage in the formation or articulation of his thought; he was 39 when he wrote it. Second, although it describes itself as a discourse on metaphysics, it begins, and continues at least for its first eight sections (and frequently for the sections that follow), with an account almost entirely focused on God, and on issues of theodicy (the subject, and title, of another of Leibniz's well-known works, from 1710[3]). The more general character of the system of substances that Leibniz formulates in the *Discourse* appears gradually or by stages as the work advances.

I have remarked that the *Discourse* plunges immediately, without preamble, into an account of God. The *Theodicy* (*Théodicée*) also has much to say about the deity, of course; but in *Discourse* he is immediately the sole focus of attention and discussion. The heading of the first of the *Discourse*'s 37 sections reads, "*Concerning the divine perfection and that God does everything in the most desirable way*," and the

---

1   In the course of the seventeenth century French had become the primary European language among the educated. It was the language of diplomacy as well as of scholarship (even if much work continued to be written in Latin, or in the several national languages). German in particular was only to come into its own in the later eighteenth century; in Leibniz's time it was viewed, regularly also by those whose first language it was, as provincial, the speech of a cultural backwater.

2   In a letter of 11 February 1686 (to the Landgrave Ernst von Hessen-Rheinfels), Leibniz says, "Being in a place where I had nothing to do for a few days, I recently wrote a little discourse on metaphysics, on which I would like Monsieur Arnauld's opinion." Leibniz goes on to explain in the same letter that he has been unable to have a full copy of the *Discourse* made and so encloses "the summary of the articles which it contains." It was this text that reached Arnauld and was to be the basis of their subsequent very extensive correspondence.

3   It was Leibniz in fact who coined the term *theodicy* (*théodicée*) in this work.

sentence immediately following declares: "The conception of God that is the most common and the most full of meaning is expressed well enough in the words: God is an absolutely perfect being" (I). I will have more to say presently about Leibniz's account of God. We may note also as distinctive features of the *Discourse*—i.e., features missing from *The Principles of Nature and of Grace*, and from the *Monadology*, or of minor or muted significance there—a repeated set of references to what Leibniz calls "our new philosophers," meant pejoratively, or at least dissentingly. He rarely provides names to go with this negative characterization, though Descartes and his followers are included among them. "Our new philosophers" are, evidently, primarily philosophers of nature, and physicists; they are mechanists, or are drawn to and affirm purely mechanical analyses and explanations in the study of nature. Accordingly, they reject final causes in the study of nature,[1] as well as incorporeal postulates; they also view with contempt, even derision, the intellectual contributions of medieval theorists and most of the ancients (except, apparently, the ancient atomists, and, with qualifications, Aristotle). Leibniz makes it clear that he dissents from all of these stances. He embraces modern developments and affirms some of his own contributions to them, but he claims that the real truth will unite modern results and assumptions with decried older views and principles (suitably interpreted). Leibniz particularly valorizes, in the *Discourse*, Plato. He thinks highly of the scene with the slave boy in the *Meno*[2] and asserts that at least a modified version of the doctrine of reminiscence is correct (XXVI). He expresses admiration for the *Phaedo*, too, indicating his accord with the anti-mechanist convictions Socrates affirms in that dialogue (XX). Leibniz expresses high regard for Plato for his own ideas, and, relatively, in contrast to Aristotle. Of the latter's conviction that the soul is a blank slate, Leibniz says, "This position is in accord with the

---

1   Final causes are the ends or goals for which some act or event was carried out or exists. In Aristotelian philosophy every type of object or event has a final cause.

2   In this dialogue Socrates elicits responses from a slave boy—intended to be understood as the epitome of an uneducated person—that are held to show that the boy has, and hence all human beings have, extensive implicit—in fact, a priori—mathematical and other conceptual knowledge. For Socrates and his interlocutors, this knowledge is concluded to have been acquired in a life prior to the individual's present life, and to be able to be recovered through the right sorts of stirrings of memory—thus, the so-called theory of reminiscence.

popular conceptions, as Aristotle's approach usually is. Plato thinks more profoundly" (XXVII). Of the early church fathers, whose thought Leibniz values, he says that they "were always more Platonic than Aristotelian in their mode of thinking" (XXVIII).

Leibniz also writes several times in the *Discourse* of the contrast between modes of thinking and speaking that are appropriate and peculiar to metaphysics (above all, of course, to the truths of his own metaphysical system), and the modes of thinking and speaking of everyday life; more precisely, he writes of a need for, and his confidence about his success in, "reconciling the language of metaphysics with that of practical life" (XV). Thus, for example, "if to act is to determine directly, it may be said in metaphysical language that God alone acts upon me and he alone causes me to do good or ill" (XXXII). And there will be the attributions we make "in the ordinary uses of life" that we need to and will revise when "we are dealing with the exactness of metaphysical truths" (XXVII).

I will address the issue of idealism[1] in the system in the later

---

1   Given the importance of the term in interpreting what Leibniz's views may have been, it will be desirable that the term "idealism" be explained with some care. The core idea is that everything that is real is fundamentally *mental*. For many philosophers, including Leibniz, God is a wholly non-bodily thinking substance and exists necessarily. Hence, for Leibniz, as for others, there is no possible or conceivable way in which reality can be that will lack God, or the effects of his power, will, and *thought*. In Leibniz's system, as we learn, there are other *dependencies*. *If* bodies were real, they would be real only in virtue of the accompanying presence of a mental substance (a monad) that confers, in some way, whatever unity the body may have. Metaphysical or philosophical idealism is the theory that everything real is mental in nature, that it is itself a thinking substance, or a mental state of a thinking substance, or a private or subjective or inner (sometimes called a *phenomenal*) item that has no reality apart from the mental states or experiences of a thinking substance. Leibniz himself never used the term *idealism* in this way; but he became acquainted with the idealist theory of Bishop George Berkeley (1685-1753) at a late stage of his career, and seems to have understood it and dissented from it. Matters are made still more complicated in Leibniz's case because, as we will see, he thinks of the "thinking" that appertains to substances as admitting very significantly of levels or degrees, so many states that would not commonly be described or regarded as states of thinking will be seen as being such by him. Also complicating things will be the question whether a *group* or *aggregation* of thinking substances would be viewed, or could be viewed, as a thinking thing; or indeed whether a group or aggregation of unextended thinking substances could intelligibly be viewed as a bodily thing. More on these matters will enter the discussion below.

texts we will be exploring, arguing that there is no trace whatsoever of that view in what we investigate—rather the contrary, in
fact.[1] It is otherwise in the *Discourse on Metaphysics*. At any rate,
that treatise's Section XII does appear to formulate and endorse
an idealist view of body:

> *That the conception of the extension of a body is in a way imaginary*
> *and does not constitute the substance of the body....* he who will
> meditate upon the nature of substance ... will find that the
> whole nature of bodies is not exhausted in their extension, that
> is to say, in their size, figure, and motion, but that we must
> recognize something that corresponds to soul, something that
> is commonly called substantial form.... It is even possible to
> demonstrate that the ideas of size, figure, and motion are not
> so distinctive as is imagined, and that they stand for some-
> thing imaginary relative to our perceptions as do, although
> to a greater extent, the ideas of colour, heat, and the other
> similar qualities that we may doubt are actually to be found in
> the nature of the things outside of us. This is why these latter
> qualities are unable to constitute "substance" and if there is no
> principle of identity in bodies other than what has just been re-
> ferred to, a body would not subsist for more than a moment.

In the famous, and important, correspondence in which he
engaged with Arnauld, Leibniz was to enlarge upon the claims
he makes here, and to try to explain and defend them against
Arnauld's probing and his advocacy of corporeal substance.[2] In
fact at least part of what Leibniz says here can be rescued from the
charge—if charge it is—of idealism. It will be one thing to deny
that bodies are *substances*, but quite another to deny that they are
*real*. It will also fail to be a denial of bodily reality if it is just held
that *without (the fact and presence of) substantial form, in any and*
*every case in which there is a body, bodies would be unreal.* (Any more
than someone who said that without a mother no human being

---

1 At least explicitly, or on the surface of the texts. Some scholars
  think nonetheless that the idealism is there, to be discerned by
  those with eyes to see and ears to hear.
2 See H.T. Mason, ed. and trans., *The Leibniz-Arnauld Correspondence*
  (Manchester: Manchester UP, 1967). A very valuable discussion of
  this correspondence is R.C. Sleigh, Jr., *Leibniz & Arnauld: A Com-*
  *mentary on Their Correspondence* (New Haven, CT: Yale UP, 1990).

would be real would be denying the reality of human beings. That a thing of one sort *cannot* exist without there being a thing of some other sort will not, obviously, imply that the first sort of thing does not exist; nor that the nature that it has is of the same kind as that of the second sort.) Leibniz thinks that there cannot be any such thing as bodily *unity* without a so-called substantial form. The one part of the passage quoted above that is not so easily shown to be wholly compatible with what may be called *body realism* is Leibniz's saying that "[i]t is even possible to demonstrate that the ideas of size, figure, and motion ... stand for something imaginary relative to our perceptions ... in regard to which we may doubt whether they are actually to be found in the nature of the things outside of us."

Leibniz does not in fact provide the demonstration that he says is possible here. He does nonetheless—we must be candid—seem to be saying that these qualities, of size, figure, and motion— which collectively comprise extension—*are* imaginary, and exist only relative to our perceptions. He does also, though, at several places in the *Discourse*, say things that appear to imply the reality of bodies. Perhaps even more importantly, he insists emphatically on the two explanatory systems, and perspectives, of final and of efficient causes, along with making it clear that there are no genuine causal relations between individual simple substances (other than God) and anything outside them. So there *is* an order of efficient causes; it is a reality, and it applies to *something*. Efficient causes are used in "*explain[ing] nature mechanically*" (XXII). There are "*the two methods of explanation*"—the one by final, the other by efficient, causes, and: "Both explanations are good; both are useful ... for discovering useful facts in physics and medicine." Leibniz is especially concerned to reinstate and justify the value and power of final-cause explanation; but he does not dispute the validity of mechanical, efficient-cause explanation in the study of nature—in physics and medicine, for example. It should be noted also that, since there is, as Leibniz makes abundantly clear, no causal contact between created substances and anything beyond them, the *content* of the experiences of those substances can only be phenomenal. Whether or not there are bodies with "primary" or "secondary" or any other qualities, what created substances experience cannot be those qualities, or bodies that supposedly have them, but at best contents that *resemble* or *correspond to* them. Every created substance and its experiential contents will comprise, with God, a "world," which will "mirror" the rest of the universe, but not in fact literally include any of it. Though created substance *a* will have experiences that are *as though* of created substance *b*, they will not in fact be of *b*; *b* might in fact be unreal, non-existent, and *a*'s experiences would not differ at all. *All* of the content of *a*'s experiences will be phenomenal. So it will always be a separate matter, apart from a created substance's experiences, what in fact actually exists, and what it is like. Typically, regularly, *a*'s experiences will include or seem to be of something *b*, and there will actually be a *b*; so it certainly *can* be that there are actual bodies, which may in one degree or respect or other resemble the content of *a*'s (purely phenomenal) experience allegedly of them. So, in an entirely literal and accurate sense, "the ideas" that we actually have of "primary" as well as of "secondary" qualities will "stand for something imaginary relative to our perceptions," and those qualities will not "actually ... be found in the nature of the things outside of us"—even if they may *correspond* to qualities that actually are to be found in the nature of the things outside of us.

Not merely is Leibniz's *account* of God in the *Discourse* fully orthodox, from a Christian point of view, but so too is its *tone*. On its face, this is a work of Christian affirmation, joyous and enthusiastic in its declarations of Christian truth, including (supposed) emotional or psychological truth.

The question of the fundamental *character* of Leibniz's system meets with one of its central aspects in the matter of the nature of Leibniz's theism. More than most other issues, this one, if it could have a fully satisfactory answer, would need to involve the investigation of features of Leibniz's biography and his personal psychology. As we have noted, Leibniz was raised within a very conservative Lutheran family and cultural setting. He never departed from formal adherence to Lutheranism (in spite of "career opportunities," more than once, to abandon that commitment for Catholicism). At the same time, a fundamental characteristic both of his declared approach to intellectual issues, including theological ones, and of what seems genuinely to reflect his temperament and outlook, is a reconciling ecumenicism. This took the form of his active involvement in projects that might lead to reunion among the Protestant and Catholic denominations.

But several other elements of the picture should be added. First, notwithstanding the examples of ancient Epicureanism and varieties of departures from Christian orthodoxy,[1] it is reasonable to hold that genuine opposition to that orthodoxy became a serious option for the overwhelming majority of European intellectuals only in the 1690s, with the publication of Pierre Bayle's *Dictionary* (see Appendix C). Filled with a barrage of sceptical ant-theistic and anti-clerical arguments—and with a lengthy and important article that discussed the philosophical ideas of Leibniz!—the work became a best-seller, undoubtedly one of the most important and influential publications in the history of the West. Leibniz was not by temperament a rebel. Son of an esteemed and very orthodox professor, and raised in a fully conventional Christian setting, he was the recipient of encouragement and honour within entirely religiously established crucibles (albeit of diverse denomination); he would have had no base from which to develop any kind of explicit theological "unorthodoxy." This is not meant in a cynical or diminishing way: from what we know of his upbringing and later life, it would have been in his interest to conform, and he would have aimed to please, and with his great ingenuity would have succeeded in pleasing. We know, in addition, that Leibniz was not much of a practising Christian and rarely attended religious services. We know too that Leibniz had at least modest ambitions as a *literary* philosophical craftsman; at any rate, he set out his ideas, a number of times, in dialogue form,[2] consciously following his much-admired Plato. Striking a note of pious effusion in the *Discourse*, and other writings, can then be seen as the adoption of a literary mode—not necessarily one implying insincerity on its author's part. Literary modes aside, in his heart of hearts, what does Leibniz really think? The answer is unknowable, but

---

1   Some of these had appeared in the widely read, and very controversial, philosophies of Hobbes and Spinoza. There were also humanistic or ethical versions of Christianity, such as Socinianism. For Leibniz—and indeed, *most* of his generation of western European thinkers, raised and acculturated in an orthodox Christian context—any commitment other than to at least formally full orthodox Christianity would not have been, in William James's famous sense, a "live option." Had Leibniz been born thirty years later than he was, things might have been otherwise; at any rate, the live options would have been.

2   Most notably in the longest of all of his works, the *New Essays Concerning Human Understanding* (published posthumously in 1765).

it may not be unreasonable to see him, at least in theological terms, as essentially a deist.[1] He is a determinist: there are no miracles (the events so called being merely instances of infrequently occurring natural laws); Christ has no real role in the system; we live forever, and hence we carry on after our deaths, but then everything—every individual substance—carries on forever. Nonetheless, Leibniz *is* a theist. His system is generated from, and needs, the postulate of a creative God. In fact, though, despite Leibniz's protestations, his God is more the architect and engineer of the vast complex world-system than the embodiment of love of Christian orthodoxy.[2]

## *Principles* and the *Monadology*

Leibniz wrote two short treatises, both in French, in 1714, two years before his death, setting out succinct versions of his system and utilizing the key term *monad* for the simple substances of the system. (The term first appears in Leibniz's writings in the

---

1 Deism was a philosophical current or movement that developed in the seventeenth century and had a special prominence in the eighteenth, in the writings of a number of British and continental European thinkers. Deists held that the world was created by an intelligent, perhaps perfect, being, who left it thereafter to operate on its own, in accordance with the laws of nature with which he had designed it. Individual deists differed on whether there was an afterlife, the precise nature of Christ, and other metaphysical and theological matters. All were strong critics of "superstitious" beliefs, of established religion, and of the public and legal roles of the clergy in European societies. In suggesting Leibnizian theological affinities with deism, I do not mean to imply that Leibniz was a secret or closet deist, but rather that his version of Christianity is not easily distinguished, in theological terms, from deism.

2 A sentiment that Leibniz expresses at diverse times in his career is the equivalence of public service and the worship of God. Thus, in 1671: "To love the public good and the universal harmony, or (what is in a sense the same thing) to understand and, as far as one can, to augment the glory of God." And in 1699: "To contribute to the public good and to the glory of God is the same thing" (G.W. Leibniz, *Sämtliche Schriften und Briefe* [Darmstadt, Leipzig, Berlin: Academy of Sciences of Berlin, 1923-], vol. IV, 1, p. 532; vol. I, 18, p. 377).

1690s.[1] It is to be found in the metaphysical treatise of Anne, Lady Conway [1631-79] posthumously published in 1690, in Amsterdam, which Leibniz read and praised [see Appendix A]. He may have derived the term from her or, perhaps more likely, from Conway's own philosophical "tutor," Henry More [1614-87], who uses a similar formation; or he may have devised it himself as an entirely natural formation from Greek, as he himself says.[2]) The earlier and shorter of these treatises is *The Principles of Nature and of Grace, Based on Reason* (usually just called *The Principles of Nature and of Grace—Les Principes de la nature et de la grâce*), consisting of eighteen numbered sections; the latter is the *Monadology* (*La Monadologie*), in ninety numbered sections.[3] (After some 46 of these sections Leibniz himself provided annotations consisting of references to his *Theodicy*.) Although the two 1714 treatises cover much the same ground, and are sometimes almost identical in wording, there are also some differences, some of them significant. The two works may also be said to have a different style or tone. *The Principles of Nature and of Grace* is more enthusiastically religious, and orthodoxly so, than the *Monadology*. This is not to say that there are genuine theological differences between the two; the reader can find them in general mutually coherent, with perhaps different kinds

---

1  In the "New System of the Nature of Substances and their Communication, and of the Union which Exists between the Soul and the Body," published (in two instalments) in the *Journal des savants*, June and July 1695.

2  Leibniz's first "published" work was his bachelor's dissertation in philosophy at the University of Leipzig (*Metaphysical Disputation on the Principle of Individuation*, 1663). In the standard way at a German university of the day, the thesis was published with a preface by the student's supervisor, in Leibniz's case Jakob Thomasius (1622-84)—one of the important formative influences of his early philosophical development. In his preface Thomasius, formulating Aristotelian doctrine on substances, distinguished between "monadic" and "sporadic" substances—the former held to be substances that are the sole members of their species. It seems highly probable that it is in this context that we should see the earliest root of Leibniz's eventual use of the term "monad."

3  Leibniz seems to have titled the work *Principes de la philosophie* (*Principles of Philosophy*); the title by which the work is now universally known is evidently a posthumous addition, introduced by Heinrich Köhler, the editor and translator (into German) of the treatise's first published presentation.

of focus or emphasis. However, that basic coherence duly noted, the *Monadology* could be read as being compatible with an eighteenth-century deist perspective; the shorter, earlier work (both of course from the same year) not so easily. Some of the phrasing in the *Principles* seems more compressed, and even hurried. That work was evidently composed for Prince Eugene of Savoy,[1] with a view to providing him with an overview of Leibniz's system. Both works were published only after Leibniz's death: *The Principles of Nature and of Grace* appeared in its original French in 1718; the *Monadology* in a German translation in 1720, followed by a Latin translation in 1721 (the French original not appearing in print until 1840). (Unless explicitly assigned to the *Principles*, citations as we proceed are to the *Monadology*.)

Leibniz begins the *Monadology* with a contrast between *simples* and *composites*—more precisely, between simple *substances*—or *monads*—and things that are composite. As he informs us in the *Principles*: "*Monas* is a Greek word that signifies unity, or that which is one" (1). A *simple*, he says, is a thing without parts. Being entirely without parts, a monad will of course, as he tells us immediately as well, be unextended, and without figure (or shape). He does not say, at least at this stage of the *Monadology*, that there is such a thing as a composite *substance*,[2] though that phrase does appear in the *Principles*. The *Principles*, but not the *Monadology*, tells us what a substance *is*: "1. *Substance* is a being capable of action." The definition, if definition it is, is somewhat ironic, since, save for one singular substance, Leibniz's substances turn out to be precisely *incapable* of action, externally to themselves. A composite "is nothing but a collection or *aggregatum* of simple substances" (*Monadology*, 2); a simple substance, moreover, "enters into composites" (1). Further, "what is in the compound can come only from the simple ingredients" (8). These last formulations are undeniably somewhat unclear.

---

1 Prince François Eugène of Savoy (1663-1736) was a successful military commander and companion-in-arms of John Churchill, first Duke of Marlborough (1650-1722) in their wars against the French.

2 In the first sentence of section 61 of the *Monadology* a number of English translations have the phrase "composite substances." This is not in fact found in the French original, where the reference is simply to "composites" ("Et les composés symbolisent en cela avec les simples").To be sure, at *Monadology* 30 there is a reference to substances that may be composite.

At any rate, while a great deal of the *Monadology* consists of what at least on their surface will read as unargued declarations that matters are thus and so, Leibniz gives right at the beginning of the work an explicit argument for the existence of simple substances, or monads: "there must be simple substances, since there are composites" (2). (The same argument, slightly expanded, appears in the *Principles*, Leibniz here drawing the further conclusion that, since there must be simple substances *everywhere*, "consequently all nature is full of life" [1].) Evidently we are to take it as clear and unproblematic that composite things exist. And it follows from this fact, Leibniz says, that simple substances exist.

But in fact this argument does not seem compelling. Why could the composites not be composed of simpler parts, and those of others still simpler, without end? Leibniz himself subsequently says, later in the work, that every "portion of matter is [not only] infinitely divisible ... but also ... actually subdivided *ad infinitum*" (65). Each individual monad, we are to learn, has an infinity of states and qualities, and one very special monad— God—is characterized by several varieties of infinity. So what would be the problem with composites all the way down? And how would even a very large number, even indeed an infinite number, of things that were unextended produce something that was extended—or, if (as some of Leibniz's interpreters have supposed) extension is mere appearance, not reality, how could even an infinite aggregate or accumulation of things without parts produce something that had parts? And, even if we grant that there must be, and indeed *are*, simples, why need they be *substances*?

Many questions, then.

Leibniz goes on to say that the monads "are the veritable atoms of nature, and, in one word, the elements of all things" ("Et ces Monades sont les véritables Atomes de la Nature et en un mot les Éléments des choses") (3). The "one word" is evidently "elements." Although he does not explicitly indicate this, perhaps we would do well to take this claim to be an articulation, and an instantiation, of a more general principle that for Leibniz is itself a primitive and independent postulate—namely, the idea or principle that there are basic entities of the world, out of which are formed or comprised the other things that there are. Contemporary physics continues to forward just such an idea, with its notion of the nineteen (kinds of) "basic particles" of the world. If we think of Leibniz as taking it to be, if not literally self-evident, then a deeply inherently plausible postulate or first principle for the investigation of the nature of the world that there *are* basic entities—i.e., items that are the ultimate items of some nature in the universe, the items in whose terms or by reference to which other things are to be understood and explained—then, given also that there are composite things of some nature, it will make sense and be persuasive that the composite things must be explained by reference to non-composite things. For if being composite is having parts, then if *simpler* items that explained them, and still simpler ones that in turn explained the last, and so on, were themselves composite—had parts—the simpler items would be *more* basic but explanations of the composites in terms of *the* basic items of the world would never be reached. So the basic items of the world—the "veritable atoms" of the world—have to be "partless." At least, Leibniz appears to be reasoning in this way. To be sure, one might suppose—and many would say that this is the actual case of the world as it in fact is—that there *are* basic entities, and while there *could* be more basic or partitioned things than them, there in fact are not. In the actual world, as we now evidently suppose, the most basic items, out of which everything (else) is formed, just *happen* to be, contingently, the "atoms" of the world (in Leibniz's sense).

Even so, if one were convinced, as Leibniz (and perhaps *any* thoroughgoing rationalist) is, of the fundamental soundness of a robust *principle of sufficient reason*, according to which no fact is capricious, and for everything there is an inherent explanatory reason, it will be unsatisfactory that there should just happen to be such-and-such simplest items, even if there could be simpler and more basic ones. One would be driven to "partlessness" willy-nilly. As for *substance*, the term signifies something "standing under" or underlying and since the earliest stages of metaphysics has been used for the basic items or entities of the world. So, given that there are composites, and *some* things that are the basic entities (the "veritable atoms"—not of course the physical atoms of ancient or modern theory), then the latter must be existent simple substances—just as Leibniz says. The "manner of composition" of the composites out of the simple substances, or monads, remains of course to be explained. Leibniz does rather dash off the phrase "nothing but a collection or *aggregatum* of simple substances" (2) as though it were clear, and as though this settled things. But of course it will be anything but evident that if you simply "put together"—and what will this mean, when it is partless entities that are involved?—say, 37 simple substances, you would have something with parts, something composite. So more of the character of the kind of "formation" or "constitution" of composites out of simple substances that Leibniz has in mind will need to be explained.

That task is the more daunting because of Leibniz's analysis of and conclusions about *causation*. Something could only act upon, or be acted upon by, something else, as Leibniz sees it, if there are places of ingress and egress for the things concerned. He puts the matter vividly, persuasively, and famously:

> There is also no way of explaining how a monad can be altered in quality or internally changed by any other creature, for nothing can be transposed within it, nor can there be conceived in it any internal movement that could be excited, directed, augmented or diminished within it, as can be done in composites, where there is change among the parts. The monads have no windows through which anything could come in or go out. (7)

*Windowless monads*: this is the model and metaphor that has resonated in formulaic conceptions and summations of Leibniz's central ontological postulate since the first publication of the *Monadology*.

In virtue of their windowlessness, it will be evident that, as Leibniz says (4-6), monads cannot be created or destroyed, at least in any "natural" way. Beginnings and endings for them, if they occurred, would necessarily be *tout d'un coup*—instantaneous, and apparently, miraculously, through divine agency. The idea, it appears, is in fact that all *created* monads begin contemporaneously, in a single event of monad creation, and thereafter exist unceasingly. At least, that is what Leibniz seems to say at a later stage, at any rate for the created monads with the capacity for reason and the monads that dominate animal bodies. In section 82 we learn "that the animal and the soul begin with the world and end no more than the world." However, in section 47 we read that "God is the only primitive unit or the only original simple substance, of which all the created or derivative monads are the products, born, so to speak, every moment by continual fulgurations from the Divinity...." This appears to imply that there is an ongoing creation of new monads, through creative sparks ("fulgurations") from God. One might hope for consistency between these passages by seeing the sensitive and rational monads as entirely created at "the beginning of the world," and the unending fulgurations as producing only "bare" monads (those without sensation, memory, or rationality)—except that the passage in 47 does refer to "all" of the created or derivative monads.[1] Alternatively, one could understand 82 as meaning that *the first* animals and souls came into being with the coming into being of the world, subsequent animals and souls being created later—which would be more consonant with Christian theology.[2]

Monads, like anything, have qualities or properties. And any alleged pair of monads that had *all* the same qualities would in fact be one and the same monad. They are all also subject to continual change. Since the changes they undergo cannot, as we have seen, be due to any agency external to them, they must be changes that occur as a function of one or more internal principles of change. Some monadic qualities will continue unchanged, just as others will be present and then gone. This seems normal, unsurprising, just as would be supposed for anything. Apparently—and also not particularly surprising—some qualities, or groups of qualities, will differentiate monads into kinds or types.[3] We may note that Leibniz says "that all created beings, consequently the created monads as well, are subject to

---

1 One *could* interpret Leibniz's meaning in section 47 with special focus on his "so to speak"—i.e., as implying that the "birth" of created monads at every moment is not literal birth or beginning, but merely figurative, with the self-same monads being continuously "reborn" by divine "fulguration" (understood now as "sustaining"). Thanks to Martha Bolton for this suggestion, in correspondence. (Leibniz's French: "... toutes les Monades créees ou derivatives ... naissent, pour ainsi dire, des Fulgurations continuelles de la Divinité de moment en moment....")

2 The French text may help encourage this rendering: "l'Animal et l'Âme ne commencent qu'avec le Monde, et ne finissent pas non plus que le Monde"—"the animal and the soul only begin with the world, and end no more than [does] the world."

3 "... il y ait un *detail de ce qui change*, qui fasse pour ainsi dire la specification et la variété des substances simples" (12).

change" (10). So there are created beings that aren't monads; monads do not exhaust what has been created.

It may be noted as well that, so far, there has been nothing said that would point to monads' turning out to be *minds*, or anything like minds. While not, as we have seen, physical atoms, they might be some other sort of particle or entity, which happened to be without parts or extension. But now we learn something that is (apparently) new: "The passing state, which involves and represents a multiplicity in the unity or in the simple substance, is nothing but what is called *perception* ..." (14). *Involves* is not of course a mental term—the French is *enveloppe*, "envelop, include," and indeed *represents* (*représente*) can just mean *constitutes*. We do, however, immediately learn that perception "must be distinguished from apperception or consciousness," and that a signal error of the Cartesians is that they have believed that "only spirits are monads, and that there are neither animal souls nor other entelechies."

In seeking to understand how, and what, Leibniz is thinking, we might compare four cases: 1) an oven timer that goes off when a certain temperature is reached; 2) a heat-seeking missile; 3) a human sun-worshipper who has gone out on a Spanish beach in mid-August to get a desired tan; and 4) a heliotropic plant, which opens up its petals in response to the warmth of the sun.[1] All four can be grouped together under a single conception, which we might call "heat-seeking." If we stressed the first trio, we might particularly be highlighting a distinctive character, or role, of conscious agency, and its extensions or manifestations. If we stressed, or gave special attention to, the cases of the human and the plant, on the other hand, we might be finding a commonality between a thinking being and an unthinking one, where the commonality took the form of thinking, in the one case, and the form of a motile activity that might be regarded as a kind of *cousin* of (this particular variety of) thinking, in the other. Both, we say, are kinds of seeking. Seeing that sort of commonality in the behaviour of human and plant might be seen, from a certain theoretical perspective, as a (very) modest contribution toward what will be called, in present-day philosophy, the *naturalizing* of thought; we can think of this as subsuming

---

1 Strictly speaking, heliotropism is response to the sun's *light*.

thinking under conceptions, other instances of which will be non-thinkings. What label or labels to use when this has been done? Possibly misleadingly (or not, if requisite care has been taken), one might appropriate the mentalistic term, or terms, and apply it to both. One isn't then merely noting analogies or parallels between one phenomenon and another, but achieving (or aiming to achieve, at least) a richer theoretical understanding of a single phenomenon, which can take a number of forms or expressions. One might instead be primarily interested in the first place in thinking, and come to see degrees of it, or approximations to it, in not obviously thought-involving *other* parts of nature—eventually, all other parts. The difference between the two might be expressed in the following rather loose pair of ways. The latter says (something like): if you think about it, everything is a kind of mind. The former says (something like): minds are actually just special instances of a higher genus, which we can call, by a kind of synecdoche, mind (or at any rate characterize as though its generic traits and structures were mental, even though they're not).

Putting these matters in direct relation to the text of the *Monadology*, and Leibniz's terminology and intentions, the issue is this: what does Leibniz mean by *represents*? Is the idea (the *motivating* idea, one may say) that one can discern a continuum across the "animal kingdom," such that humans will have obvious, self-conscious mental states and lives, the states typically "of" objects and states of affairs that are putatively exterior (to them); then other primates, and "higher" mammals (dogs and dolphins, for example), have similar states, which may be *conscious* but not (perhaps) quite "self-conscious"; and as 'descent' is explored in the animal kingdom, comparable adjacent-in-the-continuum states are identifiable? "Primitive" mental lives, or "almost" mental lives found in even the simplest forms of animal life, are then argued to characterize all of them, and then next something still on that continuum is identifiable in and for plants, and ultimately all living things, even bacteria? And then further, that the divide between the living and the non-living being found, or argued, to be *non-basic*, that for what in the living things is "mental"/"representational," and on the continuum of states at one extreme end of which is full rich self-conscious mental life, that continuum can be seen to extend to all objects in nature? The object/substance/monad then would be the possessor of mental or next-to-mental states, or that thing in virtue of which the successively descending creatures in the hierarchical continuum of nature has those states.

An entirely different kind of idea or approach might be taken. We can consider an arbitrary object, and things that might be in some kind of *proximity* to the object—at one degree or other of distance from it. This puts things *spatially*, but perhaps the idea wouldn't have to be limited to spatial or physical relationships. Every object can be seen to have states and qualities that put them into "putative relation" with what has relative degrees of putative proximity (or other sorts of propinquity) to it. In the cases of "higher" sorts of objects, this relatedness or propinquity will include "perceptions" and self-conscious perceptions (apperceptions, as Leibniz will dub them), of items putatively in the "vicinity" of the object. But maybe that would be conceptually, at least initially, an entirely secondary and subordinate "fact of the matter." The root conception, according to this way of viewing things, is of putative (or apparent) relations to items of an object's "neighbourhood," that neighbourhood coming by degrees to encompass the whole of the universe. Nothing even remotely mental (nor "almost-mental" or a primitive or rudimentary form of being mental) would be incorporated in this root conception—even if *very* many particular instances of it would be so, sufficient to merit the appropriation of the term *perceptions* for the entire category of "neighbourhood-apparent-relatedness." There will for this conception be the idea of a *location* of each of the partless substance-atoms—a location that need not be an actual location in real physical space. From the object's location it may appear to be the case that there are other objects with qualities and between or among which there are relations, all relative to the location of the monad concerned. For an entirely mindless object it will be easy enough to conceive how this would work where there actually are objects, qualities, and relations at various distances from the object. (So, relative to some *point* at which we might conceive there to be a partless object, it might be that there is a red tomato four metres away, on the left, and a blue cube three metres away, on the right; we can imagine ways in which the contents of surrounding "fields" might be very much more detailed than this.)

Harder to grasp, for a completely mindless object, will be how this might work where the "neighbourhood" or "field" is only *apparent*. Harder, but not impossible. Think of the heliotropic plant, again, or of a thermostat. Both these objects might behave or register *erroneously*. The plant might open as to the sun when there is no sun present, and the thermostat might register a level of heat that did not obtain. In these cases it will be *as though* a relation were obtaining to a usual stimulus in the "neighbour-hood" of the object. The plant, or the thermostat, may be said to be *representing* something that hasn't obtained, just as it might be said to be representing something that has obtained in the veridical case. So—it seems—representing *can* occur (or can be regarded as occurring) in cases where not even minimal minded-ness (or sort-of or almost-mindedness) has been involved. And perhaps this is what Leibniz has been thinking of. Somewhat ironically, since the *Principles* generally has a marked *biologistic* character, it is in that work that this model finds a particularly explicit apparent articulation: "For the simplicity of substance does not prevent multiplicity of the modifications, which are to be found together in this same simple substance, and must consist in the variety of relations to things that are external. It is just as in a *centre* or point, entirely simple as it is, there is an infinity of angles formed by the lines that meet at the point" (2). Two models then of the fundamental character of what it is to be a monad and what it is to *represent*, for Leibniz.

Leibniz tells us that he will call "the internal principle that causes the change or passage from one perception to another" *appetition* (15). This is of course another mentalistic term. As he has explained it, it won't be clear that it has (or is supposed to have) a mentalistic signification, any more than is the case for *perception*, even if, as with the latter, it is intended to *apply* to mentalistic and mind-like instances, as well perhaps as instances that are neither.

The next new thesis is an emphatic avowal of *anti-mechanism*. It would not be unreasonable to see this stance as stemming from the simplicity (partlessness and indivisibility) of the monads, thought through from considerations like those motivating, and perhaps indeed from the direct influence of, Plato, notably in the *Phaedo*. At any rate, section 17 is another oft-noted passage of the *Monadology*. *Thinking*, Leibniz argues, cannot be explained or understood as a matter of material parts colliding or otherwise interacting; it is something different in principle, and, indeed, something that needs to be grasped as *sui generis*. It is (appar-ently) a fundamental kind of operation within the universe.

This stance might seem to argue against the logico-structural understanding of monadic simplicity and perception discussed above; but it need not so be taken. For that account the primitive objects still are partless and indivisible, and operate in terms of internal principles that generate changed states (some of those preserving properties previously had by the monad). Leibniz can just mean, here, that the operation of mere appetition, as such, cannot be explained by reference to physical parts that "push and move each other." He is not necessarily affirming that something mind-like is to be found at the lowest level of analysis or onto-logical fact. He is, however, rejecting atomistic options advanced and defended since antiquity by Anaxagoras, Democritus, and Epicurus, and many thinkers thereafter.

More terminology is introduced, which is to have technical significance in the account: *entelechy* and *autarkeia*.[1] But these add nothing new. We already know that (created) monads have an internal principle that explains their operations, their changes from state to state; that they have a self-sufficiency, a species of—if one likes—"perfection"; and that they are "the sources of their own actions and [are], so to speak, incorporeal automata" (18). This Greek terminology seems primarily to offer linkage to earlier Greek prototypes, especially in Aristotle. It does also, though, in its explicit self-disclosure, raise questions for the orthodox Christian (or otherwise theistic) reader: what need will these—supposedly "created"—absolutely simple, not-naturally-destructible, self-sufficient "virtual atoms," sources of their own actions, have of a deity? Even Descartes had held to the (Thomistic, and broadly Aristotelian) argument that we selves could not sustain ourselves in being, nor could anything contingent do so, without the ongoing supportive maintenance of God. Once launched into being, though, Leibnizian monads do not seem to need anything to maintain their existence.[2]

---

1  Both are terms in Aristotelian philosophy, signifying full actuality and independence from other beings.
2  Whether consistently or not, in a number of passages, in distinct texts at different times in his later work, Leibniz affirms that God sustains the created monads in being, and evidently that this is necessary to their continued existence. The apparent inconsistency will of course be that Leibniz even more often affirms that the monads could not come "not to be" without a miracle—that, on their own, they would be incapable of destruction or cessation.

Leibniz goes on to unfold the hierarchical gradation among monads. At the lowest level are monads, or entelechies, merely with "perception" and appetition. Then, "but as feeling is something more than a simple perception" (19), there are those that sense. These aren't, as such, given a name; those that sense and also possess memory are to be called "souls" (*Âmes*). The *Principles*, putting things in its life-focused way, says that "there is not only life everywhere, accompanied with members or organs, but there is also an infinity of degrees among monads, some dominating more or less over others" (4). (We are not of course to understand this as literal dominance or power that one monad will have over another, since no monad other than God has literally *any* power over another; it is relative internal power, or clarity of perception, comparatively, that is intended.) It is in this context also that Leibniz makes a case for *unconscious perception* (in humans as well as in monads low in the hierarchy of thought), an idea that he will know to be at odds with the views of both Descartes and Locke.

What is involved in the specifics of the monadic internal principle is enlarged upon. "[E]very present state of a simple substance is naturally a consequence of its preceding state, so its present is pregnant with its future" (22). This will affirm, a little picturesquely, the principle of determinism—at any rate for monads. One may note that determinism is affirmed not just for created monads, but for all monads (i.e., including also God). Perhaps, we should say, still more than determinism is affirmed with this claim. It is not just that a monad's later states will be ineluctably causally produced by those that precede. The later states are actually present in the earlier ones. Some of the *content*, then, of an occurrent monadic state will be future-referencing. So, for example, not just (something like) "there is apparently blue 3 metres to the left of orange, 8 metres from point of observation," but also "there will be the appearance of red 5 metres above purple, 9 metres from point of observation, 11 total-quality-states from the occurrent one." And so on.

Another note advances the picture—and returns us to the non-monadic. We learn that "one perception can come in a natural way only from another perception, as a motion can come in a natural way only from a motion" (23). We are focused of course just on what may happen "naturally." But only perceptions can produce perceptions—hence, it appears, something taking place exterior to a monad (even, it seems, something in the monad's perceptual field) cannot produce a perception. And—evidently—monads aren't things that move. This may not be completely obvious. The monadic universe doesn't preclude—hasn't yet precluded, at any rate—an independent space and time within which they operate. Even if partless and indivisible, monad *a* might be *at* one spatial location (a *point*, one will suppose) at one time, and at another at another time, and—presumably—have traversed a trajectory of points between the one and the other to eventuate at the second location. This might seem to be a matter of a monad's moving. At any rate, Leibniz appears not to be thinking of such hypothetical motion as this, but rather of movement as something that happens to composite things, extended things, with parts. We have again, then, seen their reality implied. This is immediately reinforced in the sections that follow, where Leibniz refers to the organs of animals, light rays, air waves, sticks, and the sun, all without qualification or indication that mere appearances or natural objects or items only so called are being discussed, or that theoretical developments to follow will show that these were *façons de parler* requiring more accurate redescription.

Further pieces of Leibnizian psychological theory are introduced. Monads, at least those of sufficient complexity, have imaginations, think by association, and form habits. And the highest group of monads, those with reason, are called *spirits*. Beyond just being able to reason, spirits can think of necessary truths, and of God. By virtue of the powers of abstraction this involves, spirits—*we* ourselves are among the spirits—"rise to *acts of reflection*, which make us think of that which calls itself '*I*,' and observe that this or that is within *us*" (30).

Leibniz next presents six sections of what for him are the fundamental principles of rational inquiry. Presumably these could well have appeared at the very start of the *Monadology*. At any rate, itemized are the principles of contradiction and sufficient reason; the distinction between truths of reason (necessities) and of fact (contingencies); mathematical concepts including analytical method, speculative theorems, practical canons, definitions, axioms, and postulates; and the concept of simple or primitive ideas and propositions. In this very context, in a discussion of sufficient reason, Leibniz (again) refers, without comment or qualification, to the "immense variety of the things in nature and the division of bodies *ad infinitum*" (36). We find affirmed also the Aristotelian contrast between efficient and final causes; Leibniz's own act of writing the present work will have both efficient and final causes, he says.

We may note independently that uniquely in the *Principles* appears a question that no philosopher before Leibniz seems explicitly to have asked, and that subsequently is taken by many philosophers to be perhaps even the most basic—indeed, the most important—of all the questions or problems of philosophy: "*Why is there something rather than nothing?*" ("For nothing is simpler and easier than something," Leibniz goes on to remark) (7).

Next follows a series of arguments for the existence of God. These should be examined with care—not so much for the cogency of the arguments themselves as for what precisely Leibniz takes them to show, including more specifically the ways in which Leibniz's God will turn out to differ from Spinoza's, or from the God of seventeenth- and eighteenth-century deism. The first argument purports to establish the reality of a "sufficient or final reason" for "the sequence or series of this detail of contingencies" (37). Leibniz hasn't in fact previously referred to a succession or series of particular substances, but rather to infinite series of efficient causal events, and to others that contribute to the final cause of an event. At any rate, what he affirms is "a necessary substance, in which the variety of particular changes exists only eminently, as in its source" (38): "this supreme substance is unique, universal, and necessary; there is nothing outside of itself that is independent of it, and its existence is a simple consequence of its being possible" (40). This last is a succinct formulation of Leibniz's—highly original—contribution to ontological argumentation, his implicit grasp and utilization of what we now call the S5 modal principle that if something is possibly necessary, then it really is necessary (hence existent, or true).[1] (Leibniz sets it out a little more explicitly in 45.) God "must be incapable of limitations and must contain as much of reality as is possible" (40); "God [therefore] is absolutely perfect; for *perfection* is nothing but amount of positive reality" (41). We may note once more Leibniz's appropriation of a term with a more usually

---

1   The S5 modal principle is so called as it was the fifth (and most powerful) of the systems of modal logic developed prominently in the early twentieth century by the philosopher C.I. Lewis (1883-1964).

wider, in this case *normative*, signification, to express a narrower, or at any rate different, non-normative conception. For earlier theology perfection does often include or imply a maximum of positive reality—more precisely, disposition to *create* a maximum of positive reality. But it includes or implies also having various normative, especially moral qualities—goodness, mercy, justice, love—to maximum degrees. Not so for Leibniz, at least in the declared sense or intension of the term, in this context.

Others of Leibniz's pronouncements about God also seem carefully phrased. For example,

... [I]n God there is not only the source of existences but also of essences, so far as they are real, or of that which is real in the possible. For the understanding of God is the region of eternal truths, or of the ideas on which they depend, and without him there would be nothing real in the possibilities of things, and not only would there be nothing existing, but nothing would even be possible. (43)

But Leibniz makes it clear that God has not created the eternal truths (as Descartes had wrongly supposed); they do not "depend upon his will" (46). Leibniz seems to be thinking of a sort of co-dependence for God and necessary conceptual contents, whether they be concepts or propositions. He is a necessary being, and concepts of possibilities as well as necessarily existing ideas and eternal truths "reside" in him, as eternal and necessary as he is. Saying that *in* God is the *source* of the existence of other things— specifically, of the existence of the (other) monads—seems a somewhat anodyne way of saying that he has created those other things. The vigilant Christian would presumably like to hear Leibniz say outright that God has created, brought into being from nothing, those other monads; and Leibniz doesn't, at least here, seem quite to say this—any more than Spinoza does. Even classical early modern deism assigns a creation of the world and its constituent substances, without qualification or circumlocu-tion, to God.

Still, we do hear much that appears wholly orthodox. God is a (simple) substance, hence a monad: "God alone [of monads] is wholly without body" (72). He has an understanding and a will: "In God there is *Power*, which is the source of all; also *Knowledge*, which contains the detail of ideas; and finally *Will*, which effects changes or products according to the principle of the best" (48). And indeed Leibniz does come to a forthright enunciation of the model of divine creation among modal options for which he is famous:

> 53. Now, as there is an infinite number of possible universes in the ideas of God, and as only one of them can be actual, there must be a sufficient reason for the choice of God, which leads him to select one rather than another. 54. And this reason can only be found in the *fitness*, or in the degrees of perfection, that these worlds possess, since each possible thing has the right to aspire to existence according to the measure of perfection that it possesses. 55. And this is the cause of the existence of the best, which wisdom makes known to God, which his goodness makes him choose, and which his power makes him produce.

The theology of the *Principles* is more explicitly orthodox, including its formulation of what it is for this to be the best of all possible worlds. God has "perfect power, knowledge and will: that is ... supreme omnipotence, omniscience, and goodness. And as *justice*, taken very generally, is nothing but goodness in conformity with wisdom, there must also be supreme justice in God" (9). Leibniz continues:

> 10. It follows from the supreme perfection of God that in creating the universe he has chosen the best possible plan, in which there is the greatest variety along with the greatest order; the best arranged ground, place, time; the most results produced in the simplest ways; the most power, knowledge, happiness, and goodness in the creatures that the universe could permit. For since all the possible things in the understanding of God claim existence in proportion to their perfections, the result of all these claims must be the most perfect actual world that is possible....

How much more could the orthodox want? Well, of course, quite a lot. There is nothing here suggestive of a trinity, or of divine interventions in history, or of other doctrines of theology held or known through revelation. (Granted, the *Principles* does refer to "the details, reserved to revelation, of the great future," which "reason cannot teach us" [16].) Most critically, Leibniz's doctrine of the absence of causal interaction between created monads makes biblical historiography, as well as standard Christian conceptions of moral psychology, appear pale, bloodless, and certainly in need of drastic redescription. Leibniz is more than prepared to provide the last. His doctrine of the pre-established harmony is set out by that name, briefly, in section 78 of the *Monadology*.[1] As he explains it, it is intended above all to "solve" the so-called mind-body problem: to show how a total system of physical or bodily objects, events, and interactions can subsist alongside a system of mental or psychological realities, the two systems appearing to interact with each other on a daily basis, frequently with very significant consequence. Leibniz proposes then

> a way of explaining naturally the union or rather the conformity of the soul and the organic body. The soul follows its own peculiar laws and the body also follows its own laws, and they agree with each other in virtue of the *pre-established harmony* prevailing among all substances, since they are all representations of one and the same universe. 79. Souls act according to the laws of final causes through appetitions, ends, and means. Bodies act in accordance with the laws of efficient causes or of motion. And the two realms, that of efficient causes and that of final causes, are in harmony with one another.

This mutual harmony is such that all apparent psycho-physical interaction is mere appearance; no psychological or mental state is ever cause of or caused by any bodily or physical occurrence. Nor, just about as importantly, is any psychological or mental state *within* any created monad cause of or caused by any psychological or mental state within any *other* created monad. God has set up the two large systems of mental and physical realms, *and* an indefinitely large subset of the first of these that will comprise psychological monadic unit-realms, as total systems, which appear to interact on pre-scheduled occasions in a huge, immense pair of event-and-content canvases that are

---

1 Leibniz's first use of the phrase 'pre-established harmony' seems to be in a letter of 30 September 1695 (R.S. Woolhouse and Richard Francks, eds., *Leibniz's 'New System' and Associated Contemporary Texts* [Oxford: Clarendon Press, 1997], p. 137). The phrase appears regularly in his writings thereafter. The *idea* of the pre-established harmony, and Leibniz's conviction that by means of it he has achieved the solution to the mind-body problem, is found fully explicitly in section 33 of the *Discourse on Metaphysics*.

experienced—by the minds, or monads, which are sole subjects of experiences—*as though* real causal contacts were occurring. But the mutual autonomy of the two realms is complete and entire: "... bodies act as if (to suppose the impossible) there were no souls, and souls act as if there were no bodies, and both act as if each influenced the other" (81).

However proud Leibniz may have been of this component of his system, and however ingenious and imaginatively rich it undoubtedly is—and in spite of the fact that, suitably elaborated, it *does* appear to afford a solution to a mind-body problem (if there really is such a problem needing a solution) as well as being a *possible* way things could be—these merits notwithstanding, there is probably no part of Leibniz's philosophy that more readily provokes responses of incredulity. Even his claims of this being the best of all possible worlds, in spite of what seems to be such overwhelming and clear evidence that it is not, will seem to be the soberest of common-sense conclusions compared to the theory of the pre-established harmony and the psycho-physical parallelism (although Leibniz does not use the latter term in the *Monadology*) on which he here rests it. (At least *some* form or version of a best-of-all-possible-worlds view seems a necessary consequence of adopting a standard theist position,[1] and most will regard *that* position as at least not certainly false.) It is important also to recognize that the pre-established harmony does appear to be ineluctably tied up with parallelism, and the latter with affirming the reality of bodies as well as of minds. It has long been recognized that mere *determinism*, as such, will imply, if united with theism, a *kind* of pre-established harmony. That is, the basic theistic idea, if conceived (as it frequently if not standardly is) as involving divine determinations of the events of world history, as of individual human destinies, will imply events coming into conjunctions through physical as well as psychological causes, so as to have moral and religious significance, in ways that will permit human responsibility even if God has known and willed that they will occur. Leibniz's pre-established harmony, that is to say, is more than just divinely orchestrated determinism.

---

1 Unless one held, as Aquinas seems to have done, that magnitude of goodness in worlds is like magnitude in numbers—always able to be extended or augmented. Leibniz discusses, and rejects, that alleged parallel.

This will return us to an issue raised by implication at a number of earlier stages. A number of Leibniz's interpreters have understood his metaphysical system as *idealist*. Subtle distinctions, and the consideration of a very wide body of the philosopher's writings, including important parts of his extremely extensive correspondence, are involved in addressing this issue adequately. Those things noted, it is important to say very straightforwardly that there is not the slightest indication in the *Monadology* that Leibniz is an idealist. Nothing he says in the work implies, or even suggests or hints at, idealism. Very much to the contrary, he says or implies repeatedly that composites are bodies, and that they, and matter, have parts, are divisible, extended, and *real*. He does not say or imply that material things are *substances*. In spite of characterizations, in *The Principles of Nature and of Grace*, of "compound" (or composite) "substances," it appears that all substances, in the strict sense, are monads. (Compound substances, evidently, receive the label "substance" by virtue of having monads "within" them, either with a single dominant or governing monad or with a cluster of constituent monads.) But not everything real is a substance—even if everything that isn't a substance may *depend on*, and only have any unity that it may have by virtue of there being, a substance (a monad) on which it depends.[1] Leibniz has, in fact, a good deal to say in the work about matter and bodies. He tells us that

the world is a plenum, rendering all matter connected, and since in a plenum every motion has some effect on distant bodies in proportion to their distance, so that each body is affected not only by those in contact with it, and feels in some way all that happens to them, but also by their means is affected by those that are in contact with the former, with which it itself is

---

1 This is a persistent theme in Leibniz's philosophy. In a paper as early as 1678 or 1679 he affirms it succinctly and gives his fundamental reason for supposing it to be true: "Unless there were a soul, i.e., a kind of form, a body would not be an entity, since no part of it can be assigned which would not again consist of further parts, and so nothing could be assigned in body which could be called *this something* [*hoc aliquid*] or *some one thing* [*unum quiddam*]." *Conspectus Libelli Elementorum Physicae*, in *The Labyrinth of the Continuum: Writings on the Continuum Problem, 1672-1686*, trans. and ed. Richard Arthur (New Haven, CT: Yale UP, 2001), p. 233f.

in immediate contact, it follows that this intercommunication extends to any distance whatever. (61)

Furthermore, every created monad has a body "which is particularly attached to it and of which it is the entelechy" (62). And "[t]he body belonging to a monad, which is its entelechy or its soul, constitutes together with this entelechy what may be called a *living being*, and together with the soul what may be called an *animal*. Now this body of a living being or of an animal is always an organism ..." (63). The bodies attached to monads change even radically, we learn: "all bodies are, like rivers, in a perpetual flux, and parts are entering into them and passing out of them continually. 72. Thus the soul changes its body only by degrees, little by little ..." (71-72).

The system is then *dualist*—not *substance* dualist, but dualist nonetheless. There are two distinct realms or orders of being. It should be added that there is a kind of intermediate position, defended by some interpreters of Leibniz, according to which only *living* bodies and matter are real. So, according to this interpretation, there are arms, legs, tulip petals, and so on, but no such things as rocks or rivers. (There would of course be the living organisms that swim in those rivers, but not literally any such thing as a fluid that houses them. For this view living matter is real, non-living matter merely phenomenal or ideal.) The *Monadology* does not appear to afford deciding evidence, one way or the other, as to this intermediate (sometimes understood as particularly *Aristotelian*) interpretation of Leibniz on bodies and matter. It is true that the philosopher's *examples* of bodies in the work are especially of cases of living matter—although there are, as noted earlier, the cases of the sun, and of a stick that serves as a reminder of a beating to a dog. (The stick, or its principal constituents, will once of course have been a living being.) Leibniz certainly has a good deal to say in the work about living systems found, but undetectably by the naked eye, within apparently non-living systems. He is also hugely interested in transformation or metamorphosis. The focus in *The Principles of Nature and of Grace* is, it should be said, even closer to the "Aristotelian" line of interpretation than is the *Monadology*; that is, Leibniz practically talks only of living bodies as his examples of bodies in the shorter work. However, there is a consideration that may make the "intermediate" or "Aristotelian" position less compelling as what Leibniz strictly or fully has in mind. He has told us that there are "bare" or "naked" monads, which lack sensation or memory; and, as we have seen, there is a case—from what he himself says—for the line that the really basic conception of a "perception" that Leibniz has is of *apparent-relatedness-to-something-in-a-degree-of-propinquity*. It is important to add that Leibniz insists repeatedly (particularly in his letters) that any *unity* that a body will have will be by virtue of, or a matter of a dependency upon, a constituent (simple) monad or cluster of them, and that without such monadic presence and role, the material body concerned *would be* merely phenomenal and ideal—indeed, without being. (The "*would be*" here is of course crucial: there couldn't *not* be the monadic presence; this is a *per impossibile* consideration.) At any rate, although Leibniz's primary interest is clearly in (what common sense knows as) living bodies and systems, and he is in that sense definitely a "biologistical" and Aristotelian thinker, it is considerably less clear that he thinks that rocks and rivers (for example) are merely phenomenal or ideal. They too must have constituent monads if they are real; but they don't *have* to be, it seems, on a "great chain of living" (as opposed to a "great chain of being").

In fact, just as there is an "Aristotelian" Leibniz, and a case for one, there is also a "Platonist" (or "Platonistic") Leibniz, with a case to be made for *him*. I noted above that in the *Discourse* at any rate Leibniz has repeatedly valorizing things to say about Plato (and makes negative remarks about Aristotle). Plato continues to have an occasional, and always positive, presence throughout Leibniz's later writings. For Plato a fundamental ontic distinction is drawn between things that are permanent, in their natures changeless, and immaterial, and things that do change. Both are *real* (even if, for Plato, the former are—paradoxically—*more real* than the latter). In the first category of entity are included souls or minds; in the second, bodies and every variety of physical thing (rivers, for example). Plato appears importantly to be reflecting upon his own predecessors, Parmenides and Heraclitus. We might call the two types of real entities *Beings* and *Becomings*. Given his doctrine of degrees of being, and his higher valuing of the permanent "Beings," one can understand Plato, or a philosopher much influenced by him, vacillating, or simply varying in his locutions, between saying that the "Becomings" are real and need their own ontological theoretical rendering, and saying that they are unreal, merely (at best) phenomenal. In one interesting passage, in a letter to Samuel Masson, Leibniz in fact says, of a piece of matter, that "this piece is only a fleeting thing and never remains the same more than a moment, always losing and acquiring parts. That is why Platonists said of material things that they are always becoming, and never are, nor do they exist at any time."[1] Note that Leibniz's Plato, here, will take it that material things are *real*—have a species of reality—even if they do not have being or existence at any specifiable *time*. Further, their lower-class ontic status isn't a consequence of their being items-within-the-experiences of thinking beings—even if it is also true of them that they (strictly, things *corresponding* to them) are that.[2]

Leibniz may, it is true, just be *inconsistent* between a dualist, body-realist view and an idealist one. There appear to be two primary varieties of interpretation that see Leibniz as inconsistent. For the first, Leibniz is only apparently inconsistent, for he has different views at different times. At one stage he is idealist, at another, body-realist; he has simply changed his mind about the issue. A second inconsistent Leibniz is one who has clearly

---

1    Roger Ariew and Daniel Garber, eds., *Leibniz: Philosophical Essays* (Indianapolis: Hackett, 1989), p. 227. This letter, written (in French) in July 1716, was one of Leibniz's last pieces of writing before his death on 14 November of that year. In this important letter, explicitly intended to correct what Leibniz sees as misunderstandings of his philosophical views that had appeared, he says as well that he is "far from saying that matter is a *shadow* and even a *nothing*. These expressions go too far. Matter is an aggregate, *not a substance but a substantiatum* as would be an army or a flock; and, insofar as it is considered as making up *one* thing, it is a phenomenon, very real, in fact, but a thing whose *unity* is constructed by our conception.... I do not say, as is imputed to me, that matter is a *mode*, still less that it is a mode of mind" (p. 227).

2    Leibniz asserts this same "Platonistic" view elsewhere, significantly in one of the passages from the *Theodicy* (section 382) cited in the *Monadology*: "The conclusion to be drawn from this doctrine would seem to be that the creature never exists, that it is ever newborn and ever dying, like time, movement and other transient beings. Plato believed this of material and tangible things, saying that they are in perpetual flux, *semper fluunt, nunquam sunt* (they are always flowing, they never are). But of immaterial substances he judged quite differently, regarding them alone as real: nor was he in that altogether mistaken."

formulated alternatives among which he is unable to make up his mind; he finds appeal in more than one view and goes back and forth, sometimes affirming one and sometimes another (an incompatible other).

It seems unpersuasive that there are major historical shifts in his fundamental views over the 1685-1716 span; one would expect the matter to be more sharply signalled, with new arguments given prominence—neither of which looks to be the case—had this been so.[1] Even if there are some passages that offer modest support for it, the "composite substance" option seems ruled out by too many explicit passages insisting that all genuine substances are immaterial monads. The remaining options are an idealist interpretation, an "Aristotelian" view, a non-substance dualist one (perhaps especially of "Platonist" stamp), and a Leibniz who just can't make up his mind. For all four there is a great deal of textual support. For the "Aristotelian" reading, it is indeed striking that Leibniz gives organic bodies an immense amount of attention; hardly any other kind gets that much, and it is noteworthy that they provide his primary stock of examples, that the concept and category of the organic plays an obviously significant theoretical role for him, and that he clearly wants to formulate an ontological conception that will express his own take on or variety of Aristotelian theory of form, matter, and life. He is also enormously interested in what microscopes were disclosing about the vastly more extensive presence of tiny

---

1 This may be too quick a dismissal of a "periodization" line of interpretation. Daniel Garber has above all, most recently in his *Leibniz: Body, Substance, Monad* (Oxford: Oxford UP, 2009), argued for the view that very significant changes and differences are to be seen between three phases of the metaphysical views of the mature Leibniz. Briefly, Garber sees a chiefly mind-focused stage in the 1680s and a few years beyond, then a dualist body-realist period in the late 1690s and early 1700s, and finally an emphatic mind-focused stage in the concluding decade of Leibniz's life. Garber wants strongly to insist that final-stage positions not be read into considerably earlier passages unless there is clear and explicit warrant for doing so. One may share the spirit of the latter concern, and be prepared to acknowledge different *emphases*, as also some changing technical vocabulary, in different periods, without necessarily abandoning the idea of some fundamental commonalities of system throughout Leibniz's career. (I have in fact argued above that significant elements of the system as we find it in 1714-16 can be discerned in texts from 1675 and 1678.)

life-forms than had been realized, and he wants to incorporate this new knowledge into his system. On the other hand, there are no indications that he thinks rivers themselves are alive, or that rocks are; and it would seem odd, ontologically askew, to suppose that the fish that swim in rivers are real but not the fluid in which they move, or that flowers are real but not a rock on which they grow.[1] And of course, that a philosopher doesn't give a kind of entity a great deal of *attention* doesn't as such imply that he thinks it unreal. On the whole, I suggest, the non-substance dualist line, of non-Aristotelian type, is the most satisfactory of the alternatives. But there is certainly a case to be made for the other three.[2]

---

1   In an early (1671) essay (*De Usu et Necessitate Demonstrationum Immortalitatis Animae* [*On the Use and Necessity of the Demonstrations of the Immortality of the Soul*]), Leibniz had argued explicitly that not just human beings, animals, and plants, but also *minerals* have a "kernel of substance" or "seminal centre" that remains fixed and constant even as these bodies change, sometimes radically (*Sämtliche Schriften und Briefe*, vol. II, 1, N.58 and N.59; cf. Antognazza, *Leibniz*, p. 112f). Many other passages subsequently make comparable claims about "bodies" without implying that those bodies need be organic ones. In one particularly important passage in the Preface of the *Theodicy*, Leibniz comes extremely close to saying explicitly the view intended here: "... there is organism everywhere, although all masses do not compose organic bodies. So a pond may very well be full of fish or of other organic bodies, *although it is not itself an animal or organic body, but only a mass that contains them*" (G.W. Leibniz, *Theodicy* [Cosimo, 2009], p. 68; my emphasis).
2   It must be clearly noted that some Leibnizian texts do support an idealist (hence, perhaps, also, an inconsistency?) interpretation of the metaphysics. Some of Leibniz's avowals in this direction appear particularly emphatically in some of his letters. That might seem to make them especially reliable contexts; on the other hand, Leibniz appears regularly to modulate his epistolary prose, and some of its content, in accordance with the philosophical leanings of the person to whom he is writing. At any rate, in letters of 1714 and 1715 to Nicolas Redmond, a main stimulus, Leibniz says that "material things are only phenomena, though well founded and well connected," and even more tellingly that "absolute reality rests only in the monads and their perceptions" (G.W. Leibniz, *Philosophical Papers and Letters*, ed. Leroy E. Loemker [Dordrecht: Reidel, 1969], p. 655, 659). Similarly explicitly idealist assertions appear also in the important correspondence with Burchardus de Volder, earlier, in 1704 and 1706. Selections from that correspondence may be found in a number of editions of Leibniz's writings (including Loemker). The entire correspondence will appear in a forthcoming edition to be published by Yale UP, edited and translated by Paul Lodge.

It remains to address one last important theme of the *Monadology*. For Leibniz it develops directly or naturally from the pre-established harmony, but in fact it is separable from at least the full content and intent of that theory. Perhaps more than any other part of Leibniz's philosophy, it anticipates central features of the philosophy of Immanuel Kant. The Kantian picture of the world has had wide appeal for many with its union of a thoroughgoing scientific modernism—an unqualified acceptance of a worldview and a body of achieved results, which for Kant is Newtonian and determinist—with a conception of an altogether distinct but no less real sphere of rational agency. The two for Kant cannot be united unproblematically. (For him the rational-agent sphere is postulated, not known certainly to be reality. Leibniz does not share that doubt. For Kant, the physical sphere is merely phenomenal, even if it has, for him, a real if unknowable correlate.) Leibniz states:

> 87. As we have shown ... that there is a perfect harmony between the two realms in nature, the one of efficient causes, the other of final causes, we should also notice here another harmony, namely, between the physical realm of nature and the moral realm of grace, that is, between God considered as the architect of the machine of the universe and God considered as monarch of the divine city of spirits.

It may be suggested that the focus on God in Leibniz's account of this second domain of harmony is at least partly misleading. Like Kant, Leibniz seems primarily to be thinking of the spirit monads as comprising a *community*, and it is one of moral agents. The spirits, he tells us, are "images of the Deity itself, or of the author of nature, able to know the system of the universe and to imitate something of it by architectonic samples, each spirit being like a little divinity in its own sphere" (83). Further, "the spirits are capable of entering a kind of society with God" (84), and "the assemblage of all the spirits must compose the City of God" (85). "This City of God ... is a moral world within the natural world, and is the most exalted and most divine among the works of God" (86). This is, essentially, Kant's kingdom of ends, *avant la lettre*. As for Kant, God is the *prince* of this city or kingdom, but each of its members is an end in itself, a kind of deity, a moral agent, a self.

Aiming to reach an overall assessment of Leibniz's metaphysics, we should note that Leibniz is extremely widely read, and he is deeply respectful of his predecessors, above all, the ancients (with Plato and Aristotle in paramount positions). But he means, more than anything else, while honouring them and aiming to incorporate what he sees as genuine insights of a number of contemporaries, perhaps Spinoza more than any other, to achieve a *modernist* synthesis, an original modernist philosophy. His God is chiefly a deist God, a being who has launched the world in accordance with magnificent and complex previsionary deterministic principles, and it thereafter largely runs itself. It is a world of two grand systems: a bodily one and a sphere of metaphysical *points*, only some of which comprise living organisms, and then only some of *them*—but the most interesting and important among them, i.e., conscious, reflective, rational moral agents. (Well, as we need to remember, they are "agents" who, except within the "storage space" in which they are locked, do not and cannot *act*.)

Endeavouring, finally, to step back from details of interpretation, to a still more general level of reflection on the character of Leibniz's system, we may reasonably conclude that, even if there is rational agency operating within the "locked-up" (created) monads—ourselves among them—that has nothing to do with, nor any effect upon, the real sphere of the bump and grind of the world, which is substanceless, bodily, and wholly mechanistic. The way you see the world if you see it as Leibniz did is hardly distinguishable from the way it is seen by an epiphenomenalist,[1] even if it is an epiphenomenalist world launched by an otherwise wholly inactive divine mind.[2] This is not to suggest that Leibniz was, so to speak, a "closet" mechanist or "fifth-column" saboteur of the rational-agency and theistic philosophy he claimed to endorse and promote. Rather, he wanted to please or satisfy all (at any rate, two primary) parties,

---

1 Epiphenomenalism is the naturalistic, dualist view that both mental and physical entities are real, but only the physical ones have causal efficacy.

2 For a fuller discussion of these issues, and of the case for a partly epiphenomenalist body-realist interpretation of Leibniz's system, see Peter Loptson and R.T.W. Arthur, "Leibniz's Body Realism: Two Interpretations," *The Leibniz Review* 16 (December 2006): 1-42.

and thought that he had found a way to do that. One might even see his affirmations of idealism, when they do occur, as aiming especially to reinforce the "rational agency" component of his view. Still, it is not easy to see him as having successfully or convincingly achieved his aims.

# Gottfried Wilhelm Leibniz: A Brief Chronology

| | |
|---|---|
| 1646 | Gottfried Wilhelm Leibniz is born on 1 July in Leipzig, Electorate of Saxony, to Friedrich Leubnitz or Leibnütz (1597-1652) and Catharina Schmuck (1621-64) |
| 1652 | Leibniz's father dies (15 September) |
| 1653-61 | Attends the Nikolaischule, a Latin school in Leipzig |
| 1661 | Begins studies at University of Leipzig |
| 1662 | Receives bachelor's degree in philosophy (University of Leipzig) |
| 1663 | Student (summer semester) at University of Jena |
| 1663-72 | Correspondence with Thomasius |
| 1664 | Receives master's degree in philosophy (University of Leipzig); Leibniz's mother dies (16 February) |
| 1665 | Receives bachelor's degree in law |
| 1666 | Receives doctorate in law (University of Altdorf) |
| 1668 | Employed by Johann Philipp von Schönborn, Elector and Prince-Archbishop of Mainz |
| 1670 | Writes to Hobbes (hoping, unsuccessfully, to initiate a correspondence—it appears that his letter was never delivered to Hobbes) |
| 1672-76 | In Paris |
| 1673 | First visit to London; meets Oldenburg and Boyle; elected Fellow of the Royal Society |
| 1675 | Invents the infinitesimal calculus; meets Malebranche |
| 1675-95 | Correspondence with Foucher |
| 1675-1711 | Correspondence with Malebranche |
| 1675-1716 | In the service of the Dukes of Brunswick-Luneburg (from 1692, Electors of Hanover) |
| 1676 | Second visit to London; visit to Holland: meets Swammerdamm and van Leeuwenhoek; meetings with Spinoza (in The Hague) |

| | |
|---|---|
| 1678 | Receives a copy of Spinoza's *Ethics* |
| 1679-1702 | Correspondence with Bossuet |
| 1686 | Writes *Discours de Métaphysique* |
| 1686-90 | Correspondence with Arnauld |
| 1688 | Meets Christian Knorr von Rosenroth (in Sulzbach) |
| 1688-89 | In Vienna |
| 1689-90 | In Italy (Venice, Rome, Naples, Florence, Bologna, Modena) |
| 1693-1716 | Correspondence with Bernoulli |
| 1700 | Foundation of the Berlin Society of Sciences, with Leibniz as its first president |
| 1704 | Writes *New Essays Concerning Human Understanding* |
| 1710 | *Essais de Théodicée sur la bonté de Dieu, la liberté de l'homme et l'origine du mal* (*Theodicy*) published; 2nd ed., 1712 |
| 1712 | Debates with John Toland, Berlin |
| 1714 | Writes *Principes de la nature et de la grace fondés en raison* and *Monadologie* |
| 1715-16 | Correspondence with Clarke |
| 1716 | Leibniz dies (14 November) |
| 1717 | Leibniz-Clarke correspondence published |
| 1718 | *The Principles of Nature and of Grace* published; Leibniz's 1696-98 correspondence published |
| 1720 | *Monadology* published (in a German translation) |
| 1721 | Latin translation of *Monadology* published |
| 1734-42 | Edition of Leibniz's correspondence published |
| 1745 | Leibniz-Bernoulli correspondence published; edition of Leibniz's German writings published |
| 1765 | Seven-volume edition of Leibniz's philosophical works published, including the *New Essays* |
| 1840 | First publication of the *Monadology* in the original French |
| 1846 | Publication of the Leibniz-Arnauld correspondence and of the *Discourse on Metaphysics* |

# A Note on the Texts

The translation of the *Discourse on Metaphysics* in the present volume is that of George R. Montgomery.[1] Those of *The Principles of Nature and of Grace* and the *Monadology* derive from the translations made by Robert Latta.[2] In all three cases I have made further revisions.

The text of the *Monadology* in particular poses a number of complexities. They start with the title of the work. Leibniz evidently wrote an original text and then had two copies made. In none of the three cases of the manuscript did he assign the work a title, though there appears to be reason to think he intended it to be *Principes de philosophie* (*Principles of Philosophy*). The title *Monadologie* was given to the work by Heinrich Köhler, for the German translation that he produced for the first published version of the piece in 1720. For the Latin translation of the work, by M.G. Hansch, published in *Acta eruditorum* in 1721, the title given was *Principia philosophiae seu theses in gratiam principis Eugenii conscriptae* (*Principles of philosophy or theses composed in honour of Prince Eugene*).[3] Confusingly, Leibniz himself seems to affirm in a letter, which appears to leave little doubt that he is referring to the shorter work,[4] that *The Principles of Nature and of Grace*, which he wrote earlier in 1714, was also composed with the aim of giving an account of his philosophy to Prince Eugene. Of course, the two works may have been successive attempts to achieve this goal.

In one of the earlier texts of the *Monadology*, but not the final copy, Leibniz inserted a large body of citations of passages in his *Theodicy*. These clearly involved a systematic attention to detail, and presumably a desire that this rather succinct exposition of his

---

1  George R. Montgomery, ed. and trans., *Leibniz: Discourse on Metaphysics, Correspondence with Arnauld, and Monadology* (La Salle, IL: Open Court, 1902).

2  G.W. Leibniz, *The Monadology and Other Philosophical Writings*, trans. with introduction and notes by Robert Latta (Oxford: Oxford UP, 1898).

3  I.e., Prince Eugene of Saxony. See p. 26, note 1, above.

4  *Die philosophischen Schriften*, ed. C.I. Gerhardt, Bd. I-VII (Berlin, 1875-90), vol. III, p. 624.

metaphysics offer linkages with his one published metaphysical book. The present volume offers, in Appendix D, many of the passages of the *Theodicy* that Leibniz cites. But here too there is complexity. Different editions that purport to represent the original text of the *Monadology* append some of the *Theodicy* references to distinct sections; and in some cases different passages or sections of the *Theodicy* are cited. In more than one case, putatively authoritative French editions cite sections of the *Theodicy* that do not exist; and otherwise commendable or well-executed English translations follow the French texts on which they have drawn in these errors. The most reliable published edition of the texts of the *Monadology* and of *The Principles of Nature and of Grace* appears to be Clara Strack, ed., *Leibniz sogenannte Monadologie und Principes de la nature et de la grace fondés en raison, als Manuskript gedruckt* (Berlin, 1917). This small volume provides the originals of all manuscripts, in Leibniz's orthography, with variants in the distinct copies noted. It is this edition, with the *Theodicy* citations that it provides, that is followed in the present edition. Comparisons have been made, in all three texts, with the standard Gerhardt edition of Leibniz's writings (C.I. Gerhardt, ed., *Die philosophischen Schriften von Gottfried Wilhelm Leibniz* [Berlin, 1885]). Distinct French editions of the three works,[1] as well as several English translations, have also been consulted.

---

1  Most notably, in addition to the Strack text cited above: G.W. Leibniz, *Discours de métaphysique*, suivi de *Monadologie* et autres textes, édition établie, présentée et annotée par Michel Fichant (Paris: Gallimard, 2004); Leibnitz, *La Monadologie*, édition annotée, et précédée d'une Exposition du Système de Leibnitz par Émile Boutroux (Paris: Librairie Delagrave, 1970); G.W. Leibniz, *Principes de la Nature et de la Grâce, Monadologie et autres textes 1703-1716*, présentation et notes de Christiane Frémont (Paris: G.F. Flammarion, 1996).

# DISCOURSE ON METAPHYSICS

# Discourse on Metaphysics
## [1686]

*I. Concerning the divine perfection and that God does everything in the most desirable way.*

The conception of God that is the most common and the most full of meaning is expressed well enough in the words: God is an absolutely perfect being. The implications, however, of these words fail to receive sufficient consideration. For instance, there are many different kinds of perfection, all of which God possesses, and each one of them pertains to him in the highest degree.

We must also know what perfection is. One thing that can surely be affirmed about it is that those forms or natures which are not susceptible of it to the highest degree, say the nature of numbers or of figures, do not permit of perfection. This is because the number that is the greatest of all (that is, the sum of all the numbers), and likewise the greatest of all figures, imply contradictions. The greatest knowledge, however, and omnipotence contain no impossibility. Consequently, power and knowledge do admit of perfection, and in so far as they pertain to God they have no limits.

From this it follows that God, who possesses supreme and infinite wisdom, acts in the most perfect manner not only metaphysically, but also from the moral standpoint. And with respect to ourselves it can be said that the more we are enlightened and informed about the works of God, the more we will be disposed to find them excellent and conforming entirely to what we might desire.

*II. Against those who hold that there is no goodness in the works of God, or that the principles of goodness and beauty are arbitrary.*

Therefore I am far removed from the opinion of those who maintain that there are no principles of goodness or perfection in the nature of things, or in the ideas that God has about them, and who say that the works of God are good only through the formal reason that God has made them. If this position were true, God, knowing that he is the author of things, would not have to regard them afterwards and find them good, as the Holy Scripture witnesses. Such anthropomorphic expressions are used only to let us know that excellence is recognized in regarding the works themselves, even if we do not consider their evident dependence on their author. This is confirmed by the fact that it is in reflecting upon the works that we are able to discover the worker. They must therefore bear in themselves his character. I confess that the contrary opinion seems to me extremely dangerous and closely approaches that of recent innovators who hold that the beauty of the universe and the goodness that we attribute to the works of God are only chimeras of people who think of God in human terms.[1] In saying, therefore, that things are not good according to any standard of goodness, but simply by the will of God, it seems to me that one destroys, without realizing it, all the love of God and all his glory; for why praise him for what he has done, if he would be equally praiseworthy in doing the contrary? Where will be his justice and his wisdom if he has only a certain despotic power, if arbitrary will takes the place of reasonableness, and if in accord with the definition of tyrants, justice consists in that which is pleasing to the most powerful? Besides, it seems that every act of willing supposes some reason for the willing, and this reason, of course, must precede the act. This is why, accordingly, I find so strange those expressions of certain philosophers who say that the eternal truths of metaphysics and geometry, and consequently the principles of goodness, of justice, and of perfection, are effects only of the will of God.[2] To me it seems that all these follow from his understanding, which does not depend on his will any more than does his essence.

*III. Against those who think that God might have made things better than he has.*

Nor can I approve of the opinion of certain modern writers who boldly maintain that what God has made is not perfect in the highest degree, and that he might have done better. It seems to me that the consequences of such an opinion are wholly inconsistent with the glory of God. *Uti minus malum habet rationem*

---

1 Leibniz is referring especially here to Spinoza.
2 Leibniz is referring to the so-called creation of the eternal truths, a doctrine advanced by Descartes. According to this view, the truths of mathematics, and conceptual truths, were created and endowed, by God, with the necessity that thereafter governed them.

*boni, ita minus bonum habet rationem mali.*[1] I think that one acts imperfectly if he acts with less perfection than he is capable of. To show that an architect could have done better is to find fault with his work. Furthermore, this opinion is contrary to the Holy Scriptures when they assure us of the goodness of God's work. For if comparative perfection were sufficient, then no matter how God accomplished his work, since there is an infinite number of possible imperfections, it would always be good in comparison with the less perfect; but a thing is worthy of little praise when it can be praised only in this way.

I believe that a great many passages from the divine writings and from the holy fathers will be found favouring my position, while hardly any will be found in favour of these modern thinkers' position. Their opinion is, in my judgement, unknown to the writers of antiquity and is a deduction based upon our unfamiliarity with the general harmony of the universe and with the hidden reasons for God's conduct. In our ignorance, therefore, we are tempted to decide audaciously that many things might have been done better.

These modern thinkers insist upon certain subtleties that are hardly tenable, for they imagine that nothing is so perfect that there might not have been something more perfect. This is an error. They think, indeed, that they are thus safeguarding the liberty of God. As if it were not the highest liberty to act in perfection according to the sovereign reason. For to think that God acts in anything without having any reason for his willing, even if we overlook the fact that such action seems impossible, conforms little to God's glory. For example, let us suppose that God chooses between A and B, and that he takes A without any reason for preferring it to B. I say that this action on the part of God is at least not praiseworthy, for all praise ought to be founded upon reason, which *ex hypothesi* is not present here. My opinion is that God does nothing for which he does not deserve to be glorified.

*IV. That love for God demands on our part complete satisfaction with and acquiescence in that which he has done.*

The general knowledge of this great truth that God acts always in the most perfect and most desirable manner possible is in my

---

1  "As a lesser evil is relatively good, so a lesser good is relatively evil."

opinion the basis of the love we owe to God in all things; for he who loves seeks his satisfaction in the felicity or perfection of the object loved and in the perfection of his actions. *Idem velle et idem nolle vera amicitia est.*[1] I believe that it is difficult to love God truly when, having the power to change one's disposition, one is not disposed to wish for what God desires. In fact those who are not satisfied with what God does seem to me like dissatisfied subjects whose attitude is not very different from that of rebels. I hold, therefore, that on these principles, to act in accordance with the love of God it is not sufficient to force oneself to be patient, but we must also be really satisfied with all that comes to us according to his will. I mean this acquiescence in regard to the past; as for the future, one should not be a quietist, with arms folded, open to ridicule, awaiting what God will do; according to the sophism that the ancients called λόγον ἀεργον [logon aergon], or lazy reason. It is necessary to act in accordance with the presumptive will of God as far as we can judge it, trying with all our might to contribute to the general welfare and particularly to the ornamentation and perfection of what touches us, or of what is near and, so to speak, at hand. For if the future shows that God has not wished our good intention to have its way, it does not follow that he has not wished us to act as we have; on the contrary, since he is the best of all masters, he always demands only the right intentions, and it is for him to know the hour and the proper place to let good designs succeed.

*V. What the principles of divine perfection consist of, and that the simplicity of the means counterbalances the richness of the effects.*

It is sufficient, therefore, to have this confidence in God, that he has done everything for the best and that nothing can injure those who love him. To know in particular, however, the reasons that have moved him to choose this order of the universe, to permit sin, to dispense his salutary grace in a certain manner—this passes the capacity of a finite mind, above all when such a mind has not come into the joy of the vision of God. Yet it is possible to make some general remarks about the course of providence in the government of things. Whoever acts perfectly,

---

1 Adapted from Sallust, *Catalina* 20: "Identity of likes and dislikes is the one solid foundation of friendship."

therefore, is like an excellent geometer who knows how to find the best construction for a problem; like a good architect who uses his location and the funds destined for the building most advantageously, leaving nothing that shocks or that does not display the beauty of which it is capable; like a good householder who employs his property so that there is nothing uncultivated or sterile; like a clever machinist who produces most efficiently; and like an intelligent author who encloses the most of reality in the least possible space.

Of all beings, those who are the most perfect and occupy the least possible space, that is to say those who interfere with one another the least, are the spirits whose perfections are the virtues. That is why we may not doubt that the felicity of the spirits is God's principal aim and that he puts this purpose into execution, as far as the general harmony will permit. I will return to this subject again.

When the simplicity of God's way is spoken of, particular reference is made to the means he employs, and on the other hand when the variety, richness and abundance of his way are referred to, it is the ends or effects that are the focus. Thus one ought to be proportioned to the other, just as the cost of a building should balance its expected beauty and grandeur. It is true that nothing costs God anything, just as there is no cost for a philosopher who makes hypotheses in constructing his imaginary world, because God has only to make decrees in order that a real world come into being; but in matters of wisdom the decrees or hypotheses meet the expenditure only to the extent that they are independent of one another. Reason wishes to avoid multiplicity in hypotheses or principles, just as the simplest system is preferred in astronomy.

*VI. That God does nothing that is not orderly, and that it is not even possible to conceive of events that are not regular.*

The activities or the acts of will of God are commonly divided into ordinary and extraordinary. But it is well to bear in mind that God does nothing out of order. Therefore, what passes for extraordinary is so only with regard to a particular order established among the created things, for as regards the universal order, everything conforms to it. This is so true that not only does nothing occur in this world that is absolutely irregular, but it is even impossible to conceive of such an occurrence. Because, let us suppose for example that someone jots down a quantity of points upon a sheet of paper helter skelter, as do those who exercise the ridiculous art of geomancy; now I say that it is possible to find a geometrical line whose concept shall be uniform and constant, that is, in accordance with a certain formula, and which at the same time shall pass through all of those points, and in the same order in which the hand jotted them down; also if a continuous line be traced, which is now straight, now circular, and now of any other description, it is possible to find a mental equivalent, a formula or an equation common to all the points of this line by virtue of which formula the changes in the direction of the line must occur. There is no instance of a face whose contour does not form part of a geometric line and that cannot be traced entirely by a certain mathematical motion. But when the formula is very complex, what conforms to it passes for irregular. Thus we may say that in whatever manner God might have created the world, it would always have been regular and in a certain order. God, however, has chosen the most perfect, that is to say the one that is both the simplest in hypotheses and the richest in phenomena, as might be the case with a geometric line whose construction was easy but whose properties and effects were extremely remarkable and of great significance. I use these comparisons to picture a certain imperfect resemblance to the divine wisdom and to point out what may at least raise our minds to conceive in some sort what cannot otherwise be expressed. I do not pretend at all to explain in this way the great mystery upon which depends the whole universe.

*VII. That miracles conform to the regular order although they go against the subordinate regulations; concerning what God desires or permits and concerning general and particular intentions.*

Now since nothing is done that is not orderly, we may say that miracles are quite within the order of natural operations. We use the term "natural" of these operations because they conform to certain subordinate regulations that we call the nature of things. For it can be said that this nature is only a custom of God's that he can change on the occasion of a stronger reason than the one that moved him to use these regulations. As regards general and particular intentions, according to the way in which we understand the matter, it may be said on the one hand that everything is in accordance with his most general intention, or what best conforms to the most perfect order he has chosen; on the other hand, however, it is also possible to say that he has particular intentions that are exceptions to the subordinate regulations mentioned above. Of God's laws, however, the most universal, i.e., the one that rules the whole course of the universe, is without exceptions.

It is possible to say that God desires everything that is an object of his particular intention. When we consider the objects of his general intentions, however, such as the modes of activities of created things, and especially the reasoning creatures with whom God wishes to co-operate, we must make a distinction; for if the action is good in itself, we may say that God wishes it and at times commands it, even though it does not take place; but if it is bad in itself and becomes good only by accident through the course of events, and especially after chastisement and satisfaction have corrected its malignity and rewarded the ill with interest in such a way that more perfection results in the whole train of circumstances than would have come if that ill had not occurred—if all this takes place we must say that God permits evil, and not that he desired it, although he has co-operated by means of the laws of nature that he has established. He knows how to produce the greatest good from them.

*VIII. In order to distinguish between the activities of God and the activities of created things we must explain the conception of an individual substance.*

It is quite difficult to distinguish God's actions from those of his creatures. Some think that God does everything; others imagine that he only conserves the force that he has given to created things. How far can we say either of these opinions is right?

In the first place, since activity and passivity pertain properly to individual substances (*actiones sunt suppositorum*[1]), it will be necessary to explain what such a substance is. It is indeed true that when several predicates are attributes of a single subject and this subject is not an attribute of another, we speak of it as an individual substance, but this is not enough, and such an explanation is merely nominal. We must therefore inquire what it is to be an

---

1   "Actions are of *suppositi* [substances]."

attribute in reality of a certain subject. Now it is evident that every true predication has some basis in the nature of things, and even when a proposition is not identical, that is, when the predicate is not expressly contained in the subject, it is still necessary that it be virtually contained in it, and this is what the philosophers call *in-esse*, saying thereby that the predicate is in the subject. Thus the content of the subject must always include that of the predicate in such a way that if one understands perfectly the concept of the subject, one will know that the predicate appertains to it also. This being so, we can say that this is the nature of an individual substance or of a complete being, namely, to afford a conception so complete that the concept shall be sufficient for understanding it and for deducing all the predicates of which the substance is or may become the subject. Thus the quality of king that belonged to Alexander the Great, an abstraction from the subject, is not sufficiently determined to constitute an individual, and does not contain the other qualities of the same subject, nor everything that the idea of this prince includes. God, however, seeing the individual concept, or *hæcceity*,[1] of Alexander, sees there at the same time the basis and the reason of all the predicates that can be truly uttered regarding him; for instance that he will conquer Darius and Porus, even to the point of knowing *a priori* (and not by experience) whether he died a natural death or by poison,— facts which we can learn only through history. When we carefully consider the connection of things we see also the possibility of saying that there was always in the soul of Alexander marks of all that had happened to him, evidence of all that would happen to him, and even traces of everything that occurs in the universe, although God alone could recognize them all.

*IX. That every individual substance expresses the whole universe in its own manner, and that in its full concept are included all its experiences, together with all the attendant circumstances and the whole sequence of exterior events.*

There follow from these considerations several noticeable paradoxes—among others that it is not true that two substances may be exactly alike and differ only numerically, *solo numero*, and that what St. Thomas says on this point regarding angels and intelligences

---

1 Literally, "thisness."

(*quod ibi omne individuum sit species infima*[1]) is true of all substances, provided that the specific difference is understood as geometers understand it in the case of figures; again that a substance will be able to commence only through creation and perish only through annihilation; that a substance cannot be divided into two nor can one be made out of two, and that thus the number of substances neither augments nor diminishes through natural means, although they are frequently transformed. Furthermore every substance is like an entire world and like a mirror of God, or indeed of the whole world that it portrays, each one in its own fashion; almost as the same city is variously represented according to the various situations of him who is regarding it. Thus the universe is multiplied in some way as many times as there are substances, and the glory of God is multiplied in the same way by as many wholly different representations of his works. It can indeed be said that every substance bears in some way the character of God's infinite wisdom and omnipotence, and imitates him as much as it is able to; for it expresses, although confusedly, all that happens in the universe, past, present, and future, deriving thus a certain resemblance to an infinite perception or power of knowing. And since all other substances express this particular substance and accommodate themselves to it, we can say that it exerts its power upon all the others in imitation of the omnipotence of the creator.

*X. That the belief in substantial forms has a certain basis in fact, but that these forms effect no changes in the phenomena and must not be employed for the explanation of particular events.*

It seems that the ancients, able men, who were accustomed to profound meditations and taught theology and philosophy for several centuries, and some of whom recommend themselves to us on account of their piety, had some knowledge of what we have just said, and this is why they introduced and maintained the substantial forms so much decried today. But they were not so far from the truth nor so open to ridicule as the common run of our new philosophers imagine.

I grant that the consideration of these forms is of no service in the details of physics and ought not to be employed in the expla-

---

1  "That here every individual is a lowest species" (Thomas Aquinas, *Summa Theologiae* I, q. 50, art. 4).

nation of particular phenomena. In regard to this last point, the schoolmen were at fault, as were also the physicists of times past who followed their example, thinking they had given the reason for the properties of a body in mentioning the forms and qualities without going to the trouble of examining the manner of operation; as if one should be content to say that a clock had a certain amount of clockness derived from its form, and should not inquire in what that clockness consisted. This is indeed enough for the man who buys it, provided he surrenders the care of it to someone else. The fact, however, that there was this misunderstanding and misuse of the substantial forms should not bring us to throw away something whose recognition is so necessary in metaphysics, since without these we will not be able, I hold, to know the ultimate principles nor to lift our minds to knowledge of the incorporeal natures and of the marvels of God. Yet as the geometer does not need to encumber his mind with the famous puzzle of the composition of the continuum, and as no moralist, and still less a jurist or a statesman, needs to trouble himself with the great difficulties that arise in conciliating free will with the providential activity of God (since the geometer is able to make all his demonstrations and the statesman can complete all his deliberations without entering into these discussions that are so necessary and important in philosophy and theology), so in the same way the physicist can explain his experiments, now using simpler experiments already made, now employing geometrical and mechanical demonstrations without any need of the general considerations that belong to another sphere, and if he employs the co-operation of God, or perhaps of some soul or animating force, or something else of a similar nature, he goes out of his path quite as much as that man who, when facing an important practical question, would wish to enter into profound argumentations regarding the nature of destiny and of our liberty—a fault that men quite frequently commit without realizing it when they cumber their minds with considerations regarding fate, and thus they are even sometimes turned from a good resolution or from some necessary provision.

XI. *That the opinions of the theologians and of the so-called scholastic philosophers are not to be wholly despised.*

I know that I am advancing a great paradox in pretending to resuscitate in some way the ancient philosophy, and to recall *postliminio*[1] the substantial forms almost banished from our modern thought. But perhaps I will not be condemned lightly when it is known that I have long meditated over the modern philosophy and that I have devoted much time to experiments in physics and to the demonstrations of geometry and that I, too, for a long time was persuaded of the baselessness of those "beings" that, however, I was finally obliged to take up again in spite of myself and as though by force. The many investigations that I carried on compelled me to recognize that our moderns do not do sufficient justice to Saint Thomas and to the other great men of that period, and that there is in the theories of the scholastic philosophers and theologians far more solidity than is imagined, provided that these theories are employed *à propos* and in their place. I am persuaded that if some careful and meditative mind were to take the trouble to clarify and direct their thoughts in the manner of analytic geometers, he would find a great treasure of very important truths, wholly demonstrable.

*XII. That the conception of the extension of a body is in a way imaginary and does not constitute the substance of the body.*

But to resume the thread of our discussion, I believe that he who will meditate upon the nature of substance, as I have explained it above, will find that the whole nature of bodies is not exhausted in their extension, that is to say, in their size, figure, and motion, but that we must recognize something that corresponds to soul, something that is commonly called substantial form, although these forms effect no change in the phenomena, any more than do the souls of beasts, that is if they have souls. It is even possible to demonstrate that the ideas of size, figure, and motion are not so distinctive as is imagined, and that they stand for something imaginary relative to our perceptions as do, although to a greater extent, the ideas of colour, heat, and the other similar qualities that we may doubt are actually to be found in the nature of the things outside of us. This is why these latter qualities are unable to constitute "substance" and if there is no principle of identity in bodies other than what has just been referred to, a body would not subsist for more than a moment.

The souls and the substance-forms of other bodies are entirely

---

1  "By restoration."

different from intelligent souls, which alone know their actions and not only do not perish through natural means but indeed always retain the knowledge of what they are; this makes them alone open to chastisement or recompense, and makes them citizens of the republic of the universe whose monarch is God. Hence it follows that all the other creatures should serve them, a point that we shall discuss more amply later.

*XIII. As the individual concept of each person includes once and for all everything that can ever happen to him, in it can be seen a priori the evidence or the reasons for the reality of each event, and why one happened sooner than the other. But these events, however certain, are nevertheless contingent, being based on the free choice of God and of his creatures. It is true that their choices always have their reasons, but they incline to the choices under no compulsion of necessity.*

But before going further it is necessary to meet a difficulty that may arise regarding the principles that we have set forth above. We have said that the concept of an individual substance includes once and for all everything that can ever happen to it, and that in considering this concept one will be able to see everything that can truly be said concerning the individual, just as we are able to see in the nature of a circle all the properties that can be derived from it. But does it not seem that in this way the difference between contingent and necessary truths will be destroyed, that there will be no place for human liberty, and that an absolute fatality will rule over all our actions as well as over all the rest of the events of the world? To this I reply that a distinction must be made between what is certain and what is necessary. Everyone grants that future contingencies are assured since God foresees them, but we do not say that they are necessary just because of that. But, it will be objected, if any conclusion can be deduced infallibly from some definition or concept, it is necessary; and now since we have maintained that everything that is to happen to anyone is already virtually included in his nature or concept, as all the properties are contained in the definition of a circle, the difficulty still remains. In order to meet the objection completely, I say that the connection or sequence is of two kinds: the one, absolutely necessary, whose contrary implies contradiction, occurs in the eternal verities like the truths of geometry; the other is necessary only *ex hypothesi*, and so to speak by accident, and in itself it is contingent since the contrary is not implied. This latter sequence is not founded upon ideas wholly pure and upon the pure understanding of God, but upon his free decrees and upon the processes of the universe.

Let us give an example. Since Julius Caesar will become perpetual Dictator and master of the Republic and will overthrow the liberty of Rome, this action is contained in his concept, for we have supposed that it is the nature of such a perfect concept of a subject to involve everything, so that the predicate may be included in the subject (*ut posit inesse subjecto*). We may say that it is not in virtue of this concept or idea that he is obliged to perform this action, since it pertains to him only because God knows everything. But it will be insisted in reply that his nature or form responds to this concept, and since God imposes upon him this personality, he is compelled henceforth to live up to it. I could reply by citing the similar case of the future contingencies that are not as yet real, except in the understanding and will of God, and which, because God has given them in advance this form, must correspond to it.

But I prefer to overcome a difficulty rather than to excuse it by providing the example of other difficulties, and what I am about to say will serve to clear up the one as well as the other. It is here that must be applied the distinction in the kind of relation, and I say that what happens in accordance with these decrees is assured, but that it is not therefore necessary, and if anyone did the contrary, he would do nothing impossible in itself, although it is impossible *ex hypothesi* that this should happen. For if anyone were capable of carrying out a complete demonstration by virtue of which he could prove this connection of the subject, which is Caesar, with the predicate, which is his successful enterprise, he would bring us to see in fact that the future dictatorship of Caesar had its basis in his concept or nature, so that one would see there a reason why he resolved to cross the Rubicon rather than to stop, and why he gained instead of losing the day at Pharsalus, and that it was reasonable and by consequence assured that this would occur, but one would not prove that it was necessary in itself, nor that the contrary implied a contradiction, almost in the same way in which it is reasonable and assured that God will always do what is best although what is less perfect is not thereby implied.

For it would be found that this demonstration of this predicate as belonging to Caesar is not as absolute as are those of numbers or of geometry, but that this predicate supposes a sequence of things that God has shown by his free will. This sequence is based on the first free decree of God, which was to do always what is the most perfect, and on the decree that God made following the first one, regarding human nature, which is that men should always do, although freely, what appears to be the best. Now every truth that is founded upon this kind of decree is contingent, although certain, for the decrees of God do not change the possibilities of things and, as I have already said, although God assuredly chooses the best, this does not prevent what is less perfect from being possible in itself. Although it will never happen, it is not its impossibility but its imperfection that causes him to reject it. Now nothing is necessary whose opposite is possible.

One will then be in a position to satisfy these kinds of difficulties, however great they may appear (and in fact they have not been less vexing to all other thinkers who have ever treated this matter), provided that he considers well that all contingent propositions have reasons why they are thus, rather than otherwise, or indeed (what is the same thing) that they have proof *a priori* of their truth, which render them certain and show that the connection of the subject and predicate in these propositions has its basis in the nature of the one and of the other, but he must further remember that such contingent propositions do not have the demonstrations of necessity, since their reasons are founded only on the principle of contingency or of the existence of things, that is to say, upon what is or appears to be the best among several things equally possible. Necessary truths, on the other hand, are founded upon the principle of contradiction, and upon the possibility or impossibility of the essences themselves, without regard here to the free will of God or of creatures.

*XIV. God produces different substances according to the different views that he has of the world, and by the intervention of God, the appropriate nature of each substance brings it about that what happens to one corresponds to what happens to all the others, without, however, their acting upon one another directly.*

After having seen, to a certain extent, what the nature of substances consists of, we must try to explain the dependence they have upon one another and their actions and passions. Now it is first of all very evident that created substances depend upon God who preserves them and can produce them continually by a kind of emanation just as we produce our thoughts, for when God turns, so to speak, on all sides and in all fashions, the general system of phenomena that he finds it good to produce for the sake of manifesting his glory, and when he regards all the aspects of the world in all possible manners, since there is no relation that escapes his omniscience, the result of each view of the universe as seen from a different position is a substance that expresses the universe in accordance with this view, as long as God sees fit to render his thought effective and to produce the substance, and since God's vision is always true, our perceptions are always true, and what deceives us are our judgements, which are of us.

Now we have said before, and it follows from what we have just said, that each substance is a world by itself, independent of everything else but God; therefore, all our phenomena—that is, all things that are ever able to happen to us—are only consequences of our being. Now as the phenomena maintain a certain order in accordance with our nature, or so to speak to the world that is in us (from which it follows that we can, in order to regulate our conduct, make useful observations that are justified by the outcome of the future phenomena), and as we are thus able often to judge the future by the past without deceiving ourselves, we have sufficient grounds for saying that these phenomena are true and we will not be put to the task of inquiring whether they are outside of us, and whether others perceive them also. Nevertheless, it is most true that the perceptions and expressions of all substances correspond with one another, so that each one following independently certain reasons or laws that he has noticed meets others that are doing the same, as when several have agreed to meet together in a certain place on a set day, they are able to carry out the plan if they wish. Now although all express the same phenomena, this does not bring it about that their expressions are exactly alike, but it is sufficient if they are proportional, as when several spectators think they see the same thing and are agreed about it, although each one sees or speaks according to the measure of his vision.

It is God alone (from whom all individuals emanate continually, and who sees the universe not only as they see it, but besides in a very different way from them) who is the cause of this correspondence in their phenomena and who brings it about that what is particular to one is also common to all; otherwise there would be no relation. In a way, then, we might properly say, although it seems strange, that a particular substance never acts upon another particular substance nor is acted upon by it. What happens to each one is only the consequence of its complete idea or concept, since this idea already includes all the predicates and expresses the whole universe. In fact nothing can happen to us except thoughts and perceptions, and all our thoughts and perceptions are but the consequence, contingent it is true, of our precedent thoughts and perceptions, in such a way that were I able to consider directly all that happens or appears to me at the present time, I should be able to see all that will happen to me or that will ever appear to me. This future will not fail me, and will surely appear to me even if all that is outside of me were destroyed, aside from only God and myself. Since, however, we ordinarily attribute to other things an action upon us that brings us to perceive things in a certain manner, we must consider the basis of this judgement and to inquire what truth there is in it.

*XV. The action of one finite substance upon another consists only of the increase in the degrees of the expression of the first combined with a decrease in that of the second, in so far as God has in advance fashioned them so that they shall act in accord.*

Without entering into a long discussion, it is sufficient for reconciling the language of metaphysics with that of practical life to remark that we preferably attribute to ourselves, and with reason, the phenomena that we express the most perfectly, and that we attribute to other substances those phenomena that each one expresses the best. Thus a substance that is of an infinite extension, in that it expresses all, becomes limited in proportion to its more or less perfect manner of expression. We may thus conceive of substances as interfering with and limiting one another, and hence we can say that in this sense they act upon one another, and that they, so to speak, accommodate themselves to one another. For it can happen that a single change that augments the expression of the one may diminish that of the other. Now the virtue of a particular substance is to express well the glory of God, and the better it expresses it, the less it is limited. Everything when it expresses its virtue or power, that is to say, when it acts, changes to better, and expands just to the extent that it acts. When, therefore, a change occurs by which several substances are affected (in fact every change affects them all), I think we may say that those substances that by this change pass immediately to a greater degree of perfection, or to a more perfect expression, exert power and act, while those that pass to a lesser degree disclose their weakness and suffer. I also hold that every activity of a substance that has perception implies some pleasure, and every passion some pain, except that it may very well happen that a present advantage will be eventually destroyed by a greater evil, from which it comes that one may sin in acting or exerting his power and in finding pleasure.

*XVI. The extraordinary intervention of God is included in what our particular essences express, because their expression includes everything. Such intervention, however, goes beyond the power of our natural being or of our distinct expression, because these are finite and follow certain subordinate regulations.*

There remains for us at present only to explain how it is possible that God has influence at times upon men or upon other substances by an extraordinary or miraculous intervention, since it seems that nothing extraordinary or supernatural can happen to them, since all the events that occur to them are only the consequences of their natures. We must recall what was said above in regard to the miracles in the universe. These always conform to the universal law of the general order, although they may contravene the subordinate regulations, and since every person or substance is like a little world that expresses the great world, we can say that this extraordinary action of God upon this substance is nevertheless miraculous, although it is included in the general order of the universe in that it is expressed by the individual essence or concept of this substance. This is why, if we understand in our natures all that they express, nothing is supernatural in them, because they reach out to everything, an effect always expressing its cause, and God being the veritable cause of the substances. But as what our natures express the most perfectly pertains to them in a particular manner, that being their special power, and since they are limited, as I have just explained, there are many things that surpass the powers of our natures and even of all limited natures. As a consequence, to speak more clearly, I say that the miracles and the extraordinary interventions of God have the peculiarity of not being foreseeable by any created mind, however enlightened it may be. This is because the distinct comprehension of the fundamental order surpasses them all, while on the other hand, what is called natural depends upon less fundamental regulations that the creatures are able to understand. In order then that my words may be as irreprehensible as the meaning I am trying to convey, it will be well to associate certain words with certain significations. We may call the concept that includes everything we express and that expresses our union with God himself, nothing going beyond it, our essence. But what is limited in us may be designated as our nature or our power, and in accordance with this terminology whatever goes beyond the natures of all created substances is supernatural.

*XVII. An example of a subordinate regulation in the law of nature, which demonstrates that God always preserves the same amount of force but not the same quantity of motion—against the Cartesians and many others.*

I have frequently spoken of subordinate regulations, or of the laws of nature, and it seems that it would be good to give an example. Our new philosophers are unanimous in employing that famous law that God always preserves the same amount of motion in the universe. In fact it is a very plausible law, and in times past I held it as indubitable. But since then I have learned what its fault consists of. Monsieur Descartes and many other clever mathematicians have thought that the quantity of motion, that is to say the velocity multiplied by the bulk of the moving body, is exactly equivalent to the moving force, or, to speak in mathematical terms, the force varies as the velocity multiplied by the bulk. Now it is reasonable that the same force is always preserved in the universe. So also, looking to phenomena, it will be readily seen that a mechanical perpetual motion is impossible, because the force in such a machine, being always diminished a little by friction and so ultimately destined to be entirely spent, would necessarily have to recoup its losses, and consequently would keep on increasing of itself without any new impulse from without; and we see furthermore that the force of a body is diminished only in proportion as it gives up force, either to a contiguous body or to its own parts, in so far as they have a separate movement.

The mathematicians to whom I have referred think that what can be said of force can be said of the quantity of motion. In order, however, to show the difference I make two suppositions: in the first place, that a body falling from a certain height acquires a force enabling it to remount to the same height, provided that its direction is turned that way, or provided that there are no hindrances. For instance, a pendulum will rise exactly to the height from which it has fallen, provided the resistance of the air and of certain other small particles do not diminish a little its acquired force.

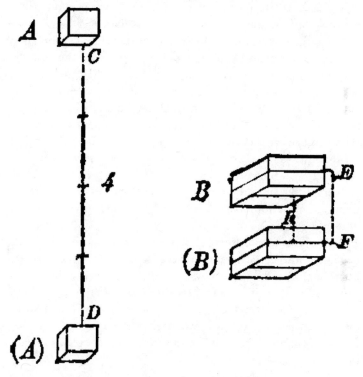

I suppose in the second place that it will take as much force to lift a body (A) weighing one pound to the height CD, four feet, as to raise a body B weighing four pounds to the height EF, one foot. These two suppositions are granted by our new philosophers.

It is therefore clear that the body A falling from the height CD acquires exactly as much force as the body B falling from the height EF, for the body (B) at F, having by the first supposition sufficient force to return to E, has therefore the force to carry a body of four pounds to the distance of one foot, EF. And likewise the body (A) at D, having the force to return to C, has also the force required to carry a body weighing one pound, its own weight, back to C, a distance of four feet. Now by the second supposition the force of these two bodies is equal.

Let us now see if the quantity of motion is the same in each case. It is here that we will be surprised to find a very great difference, for Galileo has proved that the velocity acquired by the fall CD is double the velocity acquired by the fall EF, although the height is four times as great. Multiplying, therefore, the body A, whose bulk is 1, by its velocity, which is 2, the product or the quantity of movement will be 2, and on the other hand, if we multiply the body B, whose bulk is 4, by its velocity, which is 1, the product or quantity of motion will be 4. Hence the quantity of the motion of the body (A) at the point D is half the quantity of the motion of the body (B) at the point F, yet their forces are equal, and there is therefore a great difference between the quantity of motion and the force. This is what we set out to show.

We can see therefore how the force ought to be estimated by the quantity of the effect that it is able to produce, for example by the height to which a body of certain weight can be raised. This is a very different thing from the velocity that can be imparted to it, and in order to impart to it double the velocity we must have double the force.

Nothing is simpler than this proof, and Monsieur Descartes has fallen into error here, only because he trusted too much to his thoughts even when they had not been ripened by reflection. But it astonishes me that his disciples have not noticed this error, and I am afraid that they are beginning to imitate little by little certain Peripatetics[1] whom they ridicule, and that they are accustoming themselves to consult the books of their master, rather than reason or nature.

*XVIII. The distinction between force and the quantity of motion is, among other reasons, important for showing that we must have recourse to metaphysical considerations in addition to discussions of extension if we wish to explain the phenomena of matter.*

This consideration of the force, distinguished from the quantity of motion, is important, not only in physics and mechanics for

---

1 Aristotelians.

finding the real laws of nature and the principles of motion, and even for correcting many practical errors that have crept into the writings of certain able mathematicians, but also in metaphysics for better understanding the principles. Because motion, if we regard only its exact and formal meaning, that is, change of place, is not something entirely real, and when several bodies change their places reciprocally, it is not possible to determine, by considering the bodies alone, where to attribute movement or repose, as I could demonstrate geometrically, if I wished to stop for it now.

But the force or the proximate cause of these changes is something more real, and there are sufficient grounds for attributing it to one body rather than to another, and it is only through this latter investigation that we can determine the one to which the movement must appertain. Now this force is something different from size, form or motion, and it can be seen from this consideration that the whole meaning of a body is not contained solely in its extension and its modifications, as our moderns persuade themselves. We are therefore obliged to restore certain beings or forms that they have banished. It appears more and more clear that although all the particular phenomena of nature can be explained mathematically or mechanically by those who understand them, yet nevertheless, the general principles of corporeal nature and even of mechanics are metaphysical rather than geometric, and belong to certain indivisible forms or natures as the causes of the appearances, rather than to corporeal mass or extension. This reflection is able to reconcile the mechanical philosophy of the moderns with the circumspection of those intelligent and well-meaning persons who, with a certain justice, fear that we are becoming too far removed from immaterial beings and that we are thus prejudicing piety.

## XIX. *The utility of final causes in Physics.*

As I do not wish to judge people in ill part I bring no accusation against our new philosophers who pretend to banish final causes from physics, but I must nevertheless avow that the consequences of such a banishment appear to me dangerous, especially when joined to the position that I refuted at the beginning of this treatise. That position seemed to go the length of discarding final causes entirely as though God proposed no end and no good in his activity, or as if good were not to be the object of his will. I hold on the contrary that it is just in this that the principle of all existences and of the laws of nature must be sought; hence God always proposes the best and most perfect.

I am quite willing to grant that we are liable to err when we wish to determine the purposes or councils of God, but this is the case only when we try to limit them to some particular design, thinking that he has had in view only a single thing, while in fact he regards everything at once. As for instance, if we think that God has made the world only for us, it is a great blunder, although it may be quite true that he has made it entirely for us, and that there is nothing in the universe that does not touch us and that does not accommodate itself to the regard that he has for us according to the principle laid down above. Therefore when we see some good effect or some perfection that happens or that follows from the works of God we are able to say assuredly that God has purposed it, for he does nothing by chance and is not like us who sometimes fail to do well. Therefore, far from being able to fall into error in this respect—as do the extreme statesmen who postulate too much foresight in the designs of princes, or as do commentators who seek too much erudition in their authors—it will be impossible to attribute too much reflection to God's infinite wisdom, and there is no matter in which error is less to be feared, provided we confine ourselves to affirmations and provided we avoid negative statements that limit the designs of God.

All those who see the admirable structure of animals find themselves led to recognize the wisdom of the author of things, and I advise those who have any sentiment of piety—and indeed of true philosophy—to distance themselves from the expressions of certain pretentious minds, who instead of saying that eyes were made for seeing, say that we see because we find ourselves having eyes. When one seriously holds such opinions, which hand everything over to material necessity or to a kind of chance (although either alternative ought to appear ridiculous to those who understand what we have explained above), it is difficult to recognize an intelligent author of nature. The effect should correspond to its cause, and indeed it is best known through the recognition of its cause, so that it is reasonable to introduce a sovereign intelligence ordering things, and in place of making use of the wisdom of this sovereign being, to employ only the properties of matter to explain phenomena. As if in order to account for the capture of an important place by a prince, the historian should say it was because the particles of powder in the cannon having been touched by a spark of fire expanded with a rapidity capable of pushing a hard solid body against the walls of the place, while the little particles that composed the brass of the cannon were so well interlaced that they did not separate under this impact—as if he should account for it in this way instead of making us see how the foresight of the conqueror brought him to choose the time and the proper means, and how his ability surmounted all obstacles.

*XX. A noteworthy disquisition in Plato's* Phaedo *against the philosophers who were too materialistic.*

This reminds me of a fine disquisition by Socrates in Plato's *Phaedo*, which agrees perfectly with my opinion on this subject and seems to have been uttered expressly for our too materialistic philosophers. This agreement has led me to a desire to translate it, although it is a little long. Perhaps this example will give some of us an incentive to share in many of the other beautiful and well-balanced thoughts that are found in the writings of this famous author.[1] [...]

*XXI. If the mechanical laws depended upon geometry alone without metaphysical influences, the phenomena would be very different from what they are.*

Now since the wisdom of God has always been recognized in the detail of the mechanical structures of certain particular bodies, it should also be shown in the general economy of the world and in the constitution of the laws of nature. This is so true that even in the laws of motion in general, the plans of this wisdom have been noticed. For if bodies were only extended masses, and motion were only a change of place, and if everything ought to be and could be deduced by geometric necessity from these two definitions alone, it would follow, as I have shown elsewhere, that the smallest body on contact with a very large one at rest

---

1 Leibniz apparently intended to supply a translation of the relevant section of the *Phaedo* here, for there is a gap in his manuscript at the end of the section.

would impart to it its own velocity, yet without losing any of the velocity that it had. A quantity of other rules wholly contrary to the formation of a system would also have to be admitted. But the decree of the divine wisdom in preserving always the same force and the same total direction has provided for a system.

I find indeed that many of the effects of nature can be accounted for in a twofold way, that is to say by a consideration of efficient causes, and again independently by a consideration of final causes. An example of the latter is God's decree always to achieve his effect by the easiest and most determined way. I have shown this elsewhere in accounting for the catoptric and dioptric laws, and I will speak more at length about it in what follows.

*XXII. Reconciliation of the two methods of explanation, the one using final causes, and the other efficient causes, thus satisfying both those who explain nature mechanically and those who have recourse to incorporeal natures.*

It is worth making the preceding remark in order to reconcile those who hope to explain mechanically the formation of the first tissue of an animal and all the interrelation of the parts, with those who account for the same structure by referring to final causes. Both explanations are good; both are useful not only for admiring the work of a great artificer, but also for discovering useful facts in physics and medicine. And writers who take these diverse routes should not speak ill of each other.

For I see that those who attempt to explain beauty by the divine anatomy ridicule those who imagine that the apparently fortuitous flow of certain liquids has been able to produce such a beautiful variety and that they regard them as overbold and irreverent. These others on the contrary treat the former as simple and superstitious, and compare them to those ancients who regarded the physicists as impious when they maintained that it was not Jupiter who thundered but some material found in the clouds. The best plan would be to join the two ways of thinking. To use a practical comparison, we recognize and praise the ability of a workman not only when we show what designs he had in making the parts of his machine, but also when we explain the instruments which he employed in making each part, above all if these instruments are simple and ingeniously contrived. God is also a workman able enough to produce a machine a thousand times more ingenious than our body, by employing only certain quite simple liquids purposely composed so that ordinary laws of nature alone are required to develop them to produce such a marvellous effect. But it is also true that this development would not take place if God were not the author of nature.

Yet I find that the method of efficient causes, which goes much deeper and is in a measure more immediate and *a priori*, is also more difficult when we come to details, and I think that our philosophers are still very frequently far removed from making the most of this method. The method of final causes, however, is easier and can be frequently employed to find out important and useful truths that we should have to seek for a long time if we were confined to that other more physical method, of which anatomy is able to furnish many examples. It seems to me that Snellius,[1] who was the first discoverer of the laws of refraction, would have waited a long time before finding them if he had wished to seek out first how light was formed. But he apparently followed the method that the ancients employed for catoprics, that is, the method of final causes. Because, while seeking the easiest way in which to conduct a ray of light from one given point to another by reflection from a given plane (supposing that that was the design of nature), they discovered the equality of the angles of incidence and reflection, as can be seen from a little treatise by Heliodorus of Larissa[2] and also elsewhere. This principle Mons. Snellius, I believe, and afterwards independently of him, M. Fermat,[3] applied most ingeniously to refraction. For since the rays while in the same media always maintain the same proportion of sines, which in turn correspond to the resistance of the media, it appears that they follow the easiest way, or at least the way that is the most specific for passing from a given point in one medium to a given point in another medium. The demonstration of this same theorem given by M. Descartes, using efficient causes, is much less satisfactory. At least we have grounds to think that he would never have found the principle by that means if he had not learned in Holland of Snellius' discovery.

---

1 Willebrord Snellius [Snel van Royen] (1580-1626), Dutch astronomer and mathematician.
2 Greek mathematician who lived, evidently, in the third century CE.
3 Pierre de Fermat (ca. 1601-65), French mathematician.

*XXIII. Returning to immaterial substances we explain how God acts upon the understanding of spirits and ask whether one always keeps the idea of what one thinks about.*

I have thought it appropriate to insist a little upon final causes, upon incorporeal natures, and upon an intelligent cause with respect to bodies so as to show the use of these conceptions in physics and in mathematics. This is for two reasons: first to purge from mechanical philosophy the impiety that is imputed to it; second, to elevate to nobler lines of thought the thinking of our philosophers who incline to materialistic considerations alone. Now, however, it will be good to return from corporeal substances to the consideration of immaterial natures and particularly of spirits, and to speak of the methods that God uses to enlighten them and to act upon them. Yet we must not forget that there are here at the same time certain laws of nature about which I can speak more amply elsewhere. It will be enough for now to touch upon ideas and to inquire if we see everything in God and how God is our light.

First of all we should remark that the wrong use of ideas occasions many errors. For when one reasons in regard to anything, one imagines that one has an idea of it, and this is the foundation upon which certain philosophers, ancient and modern, have constructed a demonstration of God that is extremely imperfect. It must be, they say, that I have an idea of God, or of a perfect being, since I think of him and we cannot think without having ideas; now the idea of this being includes all perfections and since existence is one of these perfections, it follows that he exists. But I reply, inasmuch as we often think of impossible chimeras, for example of the highest degree of swiftness, of the greatest number, of the meeting of the conchoid with its base or determinant, such reasoning is not sufficient. It is therefore in this sense that we can say that there are true and false ideas about whether the thing in question is possible or not. And it is when one is assured of the possibility of a thing that one can boast of having an idea of it. Therefore, the argument above proves that God exists, if he is possible. This is in fact an excellent privilege of the divine nature, to need only a possibility or an essence in order to actually exist, and it is just this that is called self-sufficient being, *ens a se.*

*XXIV. What clear and obscure, distinct and confused, adequate and inadequate, and intuitive and assumed knowledge is, and the definition of nominal, real, causal, and essential.*

In order to understand better the nature of ideas, it is necessary to touch somewhat upon the various kinds of knowledge. When I am able to recognize a thing among others, without being able to say what its differences or characteristics consist of, the knowledge is confused. Sometimes indeed we may know clearly, that is without being in the slightest doubt, that a poem or a picture is well or badly done because there is in it *an "I know not what"*[1] that satisfies or shocks us. Such knowledge is not yet distinct. Such is the knowledge of an assayer who discerns the true gold from the false by means of certain proofs or marks that make up the definition of gold.

But distinct knowledge has degrees, because ordinarily the conceptions that enter into the definition will themselves be in need of definition, and are known only confusedly. When at length everything that enters into a definition or into distinct knowledge is known distinctly, even back to the primitive conception, I call that knowledge adequate. When my mind understands at once and distinctly all the primitive ingredients of a conception, then we have intuitive knowledge. This is extremely rare, as most human knowledge is only confused or indeed assumed.

It is good also to distinguish nominal from real definition. I call a definition nominal when there is doubt whether an exact conception of it is possible, as for instance when I say that an endless screw is a line in three dimensional space whose parts are congruent or fall one upon another. Now although this is one of the reciprocal properties of an endless screw, he who did not know by other means what an endless screw was could doubt if such a line were possible, because the other lines whose ends are congruent (there are only two: the circumference of a circle and the straight line) are plane figures, that is to say they can be described *in plano.*[2] This instance enables us to see that any reciprocal property can serve as a nominal definition, but when the property brings us to see the possibility of a thing it makes the definition real, and as

---

1 Leibniz's French ("je ne sais quoi") is almost as familiar, untranslated, in English.
2 "On a plane."

long as one has only a nominal definition one cannot be sure of the consequences that one draws, because if it conceals a contradiction or an impossibility one would be able to draw the opposite conclusions. That is why truths do not depend upon names and are not arbitrary, as some of our new philosophers think.

There is also a considerable difference among real definitions, for when the possibility proves itself only by experience, as in the definition of quicksilver, whose possibility we know because such a body, which is both an extremely heavy fluid and quite volatile, actually exists, the definition is merely real and nothing more. If, however, the proof of the possibility is *a priori*, the definition is not only real but also causal, as for instance when it contains the possible generation of a thing. Finally, when the definition, without assuming anything that requires a proof *a priori* of its possibility, carries the analysis clear to the primitive conception, the definition is perfect or essential.

*XXV. In what cases knowledge is added to mere contemplation of the idea.*

Now it is manifest that we have no idea of a conception when it is impossible. And in case the knowledge, where we have the idea of it, is only assumed, we do not visualize it because such a conception is known only in like manner as conceptions internally impossible. And if it be in fact possible, it is not by this kind of knowledge that we learn its possibility. For instance, when I am thinking of a thousand or of a chiliagon,[1] I frequently do it without contemplating the idea. Even if I say a thousand is ten times a hundred, I frequently do not trouble to think what ten and a hundred are, because I assume that I know, and I do not consider it necessary to stop just at present to conceive of them. Therefore it may well happen, as it in fact does happen often enough, that I am mistaken in regard to a conception that I assume I understand, although it is an impossible truth or at least is incompatible with others with which I join it, and whether I am mistaken or not, this way of assuming our knowledge remains the same. It is, then, only when our knowledge is clear in regard to confused conceptions, and when it is intuitive in regard to those that are distinct, that we see its entire idea.

---

1  A thousand-sided plane geometric figure.

In order to see clearly what an idea is, we must guard ourselves against a misunderstanding. Many regard the idea as the form or the differentiation of our thinking, and according to this opinion we have the idea in our mind, in so far as we are thinking of it, and each separate time when we think of it anew we have another idea although similar to the preceding one. Some, however, take the idea as the immediate object of thought, or as a permanent form that remains even when we are no longer contemplating it. As a matter of fact our soul has the power of representing to itself any form or nature whenever the occasion comes for thinking about it, and I think that this activity of our soul is, so far as it expresses some nature, form or essence, properly the idea of the thing. This is in us, and is always in us, whether we are thinking of it or not. (Our soul expresses God and the universe and all essences as well as all existences.) This position is in accord with my principles that naturally nothing enters into our minds from outside.

It is a bad habit we have of thinking as though our minds received certain messages, as it were, or as if they had doors or windows. We have in our minds all those forms for all periods of time because the mind at every moment expresses all its future thoughts and already thinks confusedly of everything that it will ever think distinctly. Nothing can be taught us of which we have not already in our minds the idea. This idea is, as it were, the material out of which the thought will form itself.

This is what Plato has excellently brought out in his doctrine of reminiscence, a doctrine that contains a great deal of truth, provided that it is properly understood and purged of the error of pre-existence, and provided that one does not conceive of the soul as having already known and thought at some other time what it learns and thinks now. Plato has also confirmed his position by a beautiful experiment. He introduces [in the *Meno*] a small boy, whom he leads by short steps to extremely difficult truths of geometry bearing on incommensurables, all this without teaching the boy anything, merely drawing out replies by a well-arranged series of questions. This shows that the soul virtually knows those things and needs only to be reminded to recognize the truths.[1] Consequently it possesses at least the idea upon which those truths depend. We may even say that it already possesses those truths, if we consider them as the relations of the ideas.

*XXVII. In what respect our souls can be compared to blank tablets and how conceptions are derived from the senses.*

Aristotle preferred to compare our souls to blank tablets prepared for writing, and he maintained that nothing is in the understanding that does not come through the senses. This position is in accord with the popular conceptions, as Aristotle's approach usually is. Plato thinks more profoundly. Such tenets or practical commonplaces are nevertheless allowable in ordinary use somewhat in the same way as those who accept the Copernican theory still continue to speak of the rising and setting of the sun. I find indeed that these usages can be given a real meaning containing no error, quite in the same way as I have already pointed out that we may truly say particular substances act upon one another. In this same sense we may say that knowledge is received from without through the medium of the senses because certain exterior things contain or express more particularly the causes that determine us to certain thoughts; because in the ordinary uses of life we attribute to the soul only what belongs to it most manifestly and particularly, and there is no advantage in going further. When, however, we are dealing with the exactness of metaphysical truths, it is important to recognize the powers and independence of the soul that extend infinitely further than is commonly supposed.

In order, therefore, to avoid misunderstandings it would be good to choose separate terms for the two. The expressions that are in the soul whether one is conceiving of them or not may be called ideas, while those that one conceives of or constructs may be called conceptions, *conceptus*. But whatever terms are used, it is always false to say that all our conceptions come from the so-called external senses, because those conceptions that I have of myself and of my thoughts, and consequently of being, of substance, of action, of identity, and of many others, come from an inner experience.

---

1  "Notre âme ... n'a besoin que d'*animadversion* pour connaître les verités ..."

*XXVIII. The only immediate object of our perceptions that exists outside of us is God, and in him alone is our light.*

In the strictly metaphysical sense no external cause acts upon us except God alone, and he is in immediate relation with us only by virtue of our continual dependence upon him. Whence it follows that there is absolutely no other external object that comes into contact with our souls and directly excites perceptions in us. We have in our souls ideas of everything, only because of the continual action of God upon us, that is to say, because every effect expresses its cause and therefore the essences of our souls are certain expressions, imitations or images of the divine essence, divine thought and divine will, including all the ideas that are contained there. We may say, therefore, that God is for us the only immediate external object, and that we see things through him. For example, when we see the sun or the stars, it is God who gives to us and preserves in us the ideas, and whenever our senses are affected according to his own laws in a certain manner, it is he who, by his continual concurrence, determines our thinking. God is the sun and the light of souls, *lumen illuminans omnem hominem venientem in hunc mundum,*[1] although this is not the current conception. I think I have already remarked that during the scholastic period many believed God to be the light of the soul, *intellectus agens animae rationalis,*[2] following in this the Holy Scriptures and the fathers, who were always more Platonic than Aristotelian in their mode of thinking. The Averroists[3] misused this conception, but others, among whom were several mystic theologians, and William of Saint Amour[4] also, I think, understood this conception in a manner that assured the dignity of God and was able to raise the soul to a knowledge of its welfare.

*XXIX. Yet we think directly by means of our own ideas and not through God's.*

Nevertheless I cannot approve of the position of certain able philosophers who seem to hold that our ideas themselves are in God

---

1   "The light that lights every man that comes into this world" (John 1:9).
2   "The active intellect of the rational soul."
3   Followers of Averroes (1126-98), or Ibn Rushd, whose Arabic commentaries on Aristotle were translated into influential Latin texts in the thirteenth century.
4   William of Saint Amour (ca. 1200-72), scholastic philosopher.

and not at all in us.[1] I think that in taking this position they have sufficiently considered neither the nature of substance, which we have just explained, nor the complete purview and independence of the soul which includes all that happens to it, and expresses God, and with him all possible and actual beings in the same way that an effect expresses its cause. It is indeed inconceivable that the soul should think using the ideas of something else. The soul when it thinks of anything must be affected dynamically in a certain manner, and it must have in itself in advance not only the passive capacity of being thus affected, a capacity already wholly determined, but also an active power by virtue of which it has always had in its nature the marks of the future production of this thought, and the disposition to produce it at its proper time. All of this shows that the soul already includes the idea that is comprised in any particular thought.

*XXX. How God inclines our souls without necessitating them; that there are no grounds for complaint; that we must not ask why Judas sinned because this free act is contained in his concept, the only question being why Judas the sinner is admitted to existence, preferably to other possible persons; concerning the original imperfection or limitation before the fall and concerning the different degrees of grace.*

Regarding the action of God upon the human will there are many quite different considerations that it would take too long to investigate here. Nevertheless the following is what can be said in general. In co-operating with ordinary actions God only follows the laws which he has established, that is to say, he continually preserves and produces our being so that the ideas come to us spontaneously or with freedom in the order carried by the concept of our individual substance. In this concept they can be foreseen for all eternity. Furthermore, by virtue of the decree that God has made that the will shall always seek the apparent good in certain particular respects (in regard to which this apparent good always has in it something of reality expressing or imitating God's will), he, without at all necessitating our choice, determines it by what appears most desirable. For absolutely

---

1  Leibniz chiefly means Nicolas Malebranche (1638-1715), another of the major rationalist philosophers of the early modern period, with whom he had extensive interactions.

speaking, our will, as contrasted with necessity, is in a state of indifference, being able to act otherwise, or wholly to suspend its action, either alternative being and remaining possible.

It therefore falls to the soul to be on guard against appearances, by means of a firm will, to reflect and to refuse to act or decide in certain circumstances, except after mature deliberation. It is, however, true and has been assured from all eternity that certain souls will not employ their power upon certain occasions. But who could do more than God has done, and can such a soul complain of anything except itself? All these complaints after the deed are unjust, in the same way that they would have been unjust before the deed. Would this soul a little before committing the sin have had the right to complain of God as though he had determined the sin? Since the determinations of God in these matters cannot be foreseen, how would the soul know that it was preordained to sin unless it had already committed the sin? It is merely a question of wishing to or not wishing to, and God could not have set an easier or juster condition. Therefore all judges, without asking the reasons that have disposed a man to have an evil will, consider only how far this will is wrong. But, you object, perhaps it has been ordained from all eternity that I will sin. Find your own answer; perhaps it has not been. Now then, without asking for something that you are unable to know and that can give you no light, act according to your duty and your knowledge.

But, someone will object, how is it then that this man will assuredly do this sin? The reply is easy: it is that otherwise he would not be a man. For God foresees from all time that there will be a certain Judas, and in the concept or idea of him that God has is contained this future free act. The only question, therefore, that remains is why this certain Judas, the betrayer who is possible only because of the idea of God, actually exists. To this question, however, we can expect no answer here on earth except to say in general that it is because God has found it good that he should exist, despite the sin that he foresaw. This evil will be more than overbalanced. God will derive a greater good from it, and it will finally turn out that this series of events in which is included the existence of this sinner is the most perfect among all the possible series of events. An explanation in every case of the admirable economy of this choice cannot be given while we are sojourners on earth. It is enough to know the excellence without understanding it. It is here that we must recognize *altitudinem divitiarum*, the unfathomable depth of the divine wisdom, without hesitating at a detail that involves an infinite number of considerations.

It is clear, however, that God is not the cause of ill. For not only after the loss of innocence by men has original sin possessed the soul, but even before that there was an original limitation or imperfection in the very nature of all creatures, which rendered them open to sin and able to fall. There is, therefore, no more difficulty in the supralapsarian view[1] than there is in the other views of sin. To this also, it seems to me, can be reduced the opinion of Saint Augustine and of other authors: that the root of evil is in the privation, that is to say, in the lack or limitation of creatures that God graciously remedies by whatever degree of perfection it pleases him to give. This grace of God, whether ordinary or extraordinary, has its degrees and its measures. Grace is always efficacious in itself to produce a certain proportionate effect, and furthermore it is always sufficient not only to keep someone from sin but even to effect his salvation, provided that he co-operates with what is in him. Grace does not always, however, have sufficient power to overcome the inclination, for, if it did, it would no longer be limited in any way, and this superiority to limitations is reserved to that unique grace that is absolutely efficacious. This grace is always victorious, whether through its own self or through the congruity of circumstances.

*XXXI. Concerning the motives of election; concerning faith foreseen and the absolute decree and that it all reduces to the question why God has chosen and resolved to admit to existence just such a possible person, whose concept includes just such a sequence of free acts and of free gifts of grace. This at once puts an end to all difficulties.*

Finally, the grace of God is wholly unprejudiced and creatures have no claim upon it. Just as it is not sufficient in accounting for God's choice in his dispensations of grace to refer to his absolute or conditional prevision of men's future actions, so it is also wrong

---

1  Supralapsarianism is the view (often specially associated with Calvinism) that God's decrees or decisions about human destinies following death were made before the fall ("lapsus") of Adam and Eve.

to imagine his decrees as absolute with no reasonable motive. As concerns foreseen faith and good works, it is very true that God has elected none but those whose faith and charity he foresees, *quos se fide donaturum praescivit.* The same question, however, arises again as to why God gives to some rather than to others the grace of faith or of good works. Concerning God's ability to foresee not only faith and good deeds, but also their content and predisposition, or what a man for his part contributes to them (since there are as truly diversities on the part of men as on the part of grace, and although he needs to be aroused to good and needs to become converted, a man still acts in accordance with his temperament)—concerning his ability to foresee, there are many who say that God, knowing what a particular man will do without grace (that is, without his extraordinary assistance, or knowing at least what will be the human contribution), resolves to give grace to those whose natural dispositions are the best, or at any rate are the least imperfect and evil. But if this were the case then the natural dispositions, in so far as they were good, would be like gifts of grace, since God would have given advantages to some over others; and therefore, since he would well know that the natural advantages that he had given would serve as motives for his grace or for his extraordinary assistance, would not everything be reduced to his mercy?

I think, therefore, that since we do not know how much and in what way God regards natural dispositions in the dispensations of his grace, it would be safest and most exact to say, in accordance with our principles and as I have already remarked, that there must be among possible beings the person Peter or John, whose concept or idea contains all that particular sequence of ordinary and extraordinary manifestations of grace together with the rest of the accompanying events and circumstances, and that it has pleased God to choose him among an infinite number of persons equally possible for actual existence. When we have said this there seems nothing left to ask, and all difficulties vanish.

For in regard to that great and ultimate question why it has pleased God to choose him among so great a number of possible persons, it is surely unreasonable to demand more than the general reasons that we have given. The reasons in detail surpass our ken. Therefore, instead of postulating an absolute decree, which being without reason would be unreasonable, and instead of postulating reasons that do not succeed in solving the difficulties and in turn themselves need reasons, it will be best to say with St. Paul that there are for God's choice certain great reasons of wisdom and congruity that he follows, which, however, are unknown to mortals and are founded upon the general order, whose goal is the greatest perfection of the world. This is what is meant when the motives of God's glory and of the manifestation of his justice are spoken of, as well as when men speak of his mercy, and his perfection in general: that immense vastness of wealth, in short, with which the soul of the same St. Paul was to be thrilled.

*XXXII. Usefulness of these principles in matters of piety and of religion.*

In addition, it seems that the thoughts that we have just explained, and particularly the great principle of the perfection of God's operations and the concept of substance, which includes all its changes with all its accompanying circumstances, far from injuring, serve rather to confirm religion, serve to dissipate great difficulties, to inflame souls with a divine love and to raise the mind to a knowledge of incorporeal substances much more than the present-day hypotheses. For it appears clearly that all other substance depend upon God just as our thoughts emanate from our own substance; that God is all in all and that he is intimately united to all created things, in proportion however to their perfection; that it is he alone who determines them from without by his influence, and if to act is to determine directly, it may be said in metaphysical language that God alone acts upon me and he alone causes me to do good or ill, other substances contributing only because of his determinations; because God, who takes all things into consideration, distributes his bounties and compels created beings to accommodate themselves to one another. Thus God alone constitutes the relation or communication between substances. It is through him that the phenomena of the one meet and accord with the phenomena of the others, so that there may be a reality in our perceptions. In common parlance, however, an action is attributed to particular causes in the sense that I have explained above because it is not necessary to make continual mention of the universal cause when speaking of particular cases.

It can be seen also that every substance has a perfect spontaneity (which becomes liberty with intelligent substances).

Everything that happens to it is a consequence of its idea or its being, and nothing determines it except God only. It is for this reason that a person of exalted mind and revered saintliness may say that the soul ought often to think as if there were only God and itself in the world.

Nothing can make us hold to immortality more firmly than this independence and vastness of the soul that protect it completely against exterior things, since it alone constitutes our universe and together with God is sufficient for itself. It is as impossible for it to perish except through annihilation as it is impossible for the universe to destroy itself, the universe whose animate and perpetual expression it is. Furthermore, the changes in this extended mass that is called our body cannot possibly affect the soul, nor can the dissipation of the body destroy what is indivisible.

*XXXIII. Explanation of the relation between the soul and the body, a matter that has been regarded as inexplicable or else as miraculous; concerning the origin of confused perceptions.*

We can also see the explanation of that great mystery "the union of the soul and the body," that is to say, how it comes about that the passions and actions of the one are accompanied by the actions and passions, or else the appropriate phenomena, of the other. For it is not possible to conceive how one can have an influence upon the other, and it is unreasonable to have recourse at once to the extraordinary intervention of the universal cause in an ordinary and particular case. The following, however, is the true explanation. We have said that everything that happens to a soul or to any substance is a consequence of its concept; hence the idea itself or the essence of the soul brings it about that all of its appearances or perceptions should be born out of its nature and precisely in such a way that they correspond of themselves to what happens in the universe at large, but more particularly and more perfectly to what happens in the body associated with it, because it is in a particular way and only for a certain time according to the relation of other bodies to its own body that the soul expresses the state of the universe. This last fact enables us to see how our body belongs to us, without, however, being attached to our essence. I believe that those who are careful thinkers will decide favourably for our principles because of this single reason, viz., that they are able to see what the relation between the soul and the body consists of, a parallelism that appears inexplicable in any other way.

We can also see that the perceptions of our senses, even when they are clear, must necessarily contain certain confused elements, for as all the bodies in the universe are in sympathy, ours receives the impressions of all the others, and while our senses respond to everything, our soul cannot pay attention to every particular. That is why our confused sensations are the result of a variety of perceptions. This variety is infinite. It is almost like the confused murmuring that is heard by those who approach the shore of a sea. It comes from the continual beatings of innumerable waves. If now, out of many perceptions that do not at all fit together to make one, no particular perception surpasses the others, and if they make impressions that are about equally strong or equally capable of holding the attention of the soul, they can be perceived only confusedly.

*XXXIV. Concerning the difference between spirits and other substances, souls or substantial forms; that the immortality that men desire includes memory.*

Supposing that the bodies that constitute an *unum per se*,[1] as human bodies, are substances, and have substantial forms, and supposing that animals have souls, we are obliged to grant that these souls and these substantial forms cannot entirely perish, any more than can the atoms or the ultimate elements of matter, according to the position of other philosophers; for no substance perishes, although it may become very different. Such substances also express the whole universe, although more imperfectly than do spirits. The principal difference, however, is that they do not know that they are, nor what they are. Consequently, not being able to reason, they are unable to discover necessary and universal truths. It is also because they do not reflect regarding themselves that they have no moral qualities, whence it follows that they undergo a thousand transformations—as we see a caterpillar change into a butterfly; the result from a moral or practical standpoint is the same as if we said that they perished in each case, and we can indeed say it from the physical standpoint

---

1 "One, or unity, in themselves."

in the same way that we say bodies perish in their dissolution. But the intelligent soul, knowing that it exists, having the ability to say that word "I" so full of meaning, not only continues and exists, metaphysically far more certainly than do the others, but it remains the same from the moral standpoint, and constitutes the same personality, for it is its memory or knowledge of this ego that renders it open to punishment and reward. Also the immortality that is required in morals and in religion does not consist merely in this perpetual existence, which pertains to all substances, for if in addition there were no remembrance of what one had been, immortality would not be at all desirable. Suppose that some individual could suddenly become King of China on condition, however, of forgetting what he had been, as though being born again, would it not amount to the same practically, or as far as the effects could be perceived, as if the individual were annihilated, and a king of China were the same instant created in his place? The individual would have no reason to desire this.

*XXXV. The excellence of spirits; that God considers them preferable to other creatures; that the spirits express God rather than the world, while other simple substances express the world rather than God.*

In order, however, to prove by natural reasons that God will preserve forever not only our substance, but also our personality, that is to say the recollection and knowledge of what we are (although the distinct knowledge is sometimes suspended during sleep and in swoons), it is necessary to join to metaphysics moral considerations. God must be considered not only as the principle and the cause of all substances and of all existing things, but also as the chief of all persons or intelligent substances, as the absolute monarch of the most perfect city or republic, such as is constituted by all the spirits together in the universe, God being the most complete of all spirits at the same time that he is greatest of all beings. For assuredly the spirits are the most perfect of substances and best express the divinity. Since all the nature, purpose, virtue, and function of substance is, as has been sufficiently explained, to express God and the universe, there is no room for doubting that those substances that express them in full knowledge of what they are doing, and that are able to understand the great truths about God and the universe, do express God and the universe incomparably better than do those natures that are either brutish and incapable of recognizing truths, or are wholly destitute of sensation and knowledge. The difference between intelligent substances and those that are not intelligent is quite as great as between a mirror and one who sees.

As God is himself the greatest and wisest of spirits it is easy to understand that the spirits with which he can, so to speak, enter into conversation and even into social relations by communicating to them in particular ways his feelings and his will so that they are able to know and love their benefactor, must be much nearer to him than the rest of created things, which may be regarded as the instruments of spirits. In the same way we see that all wise persons consider far more the condition of a man than of anything else, however precious it may be; and it seems that the greatest satisfaction which a soul, satisfied in other respects, can have is to see itself loved by others. However, with respect to God there is this difference that his glory and our worship can add nothing to his satisfaction, the recognition of creatures being nothing but a consequence of his sovereign and perfect felicity and being far from contributing to it or from causing it even in part. Nevertheless, what is reasonable in finite spirits is found eminently in him, and as we praise a king who prefers to preserve the life of a man before that of the most precious and rare of his animals, we should not doubt that the most enlightened and most just of all monarchs has the same preference.

*XXXVI. God is the monarch of the most perfect republic composed of all the spirits, and the happiness of this city of God is his principal purpose.*

Spirits are of all substances the most capable of perfection, and their perfections are different in that they interfere with one another the least, or rather that they aid one another the most, for only the most virtuous can be the most perfect friends. Hence it follows that God who in all things has the greatest perfection will have the greatest care for spirits and will give not only to all of them in general, but even to each one in particular the highest perfection that the universal harmony will permit.

We can even say that it is because he is a spirit that God is the originator of existences, for if he had lacked the power of will to choose what is best, there would have been no reason why one possible being should exist rather than any other. Therefore

God's being a spirit himself dominates all the consideration that he may have toward created things. Spirits alone are made in his image, being as it were of his blood or as children in the family, since they alone are able to serve him of free will, and to act consciously imitating the divine nature. A single spirit is worth a whole world, because it not only expresses the whole world, but it also knows it and governs itself as does God. In this way we may say that though every substance expresses the whole universe, the other substances express the world rather than God, while spirits express God rather than the world. This nature of spirits, so noble that it enables them to approach divinity as much as is possible for created things, has as a result that God derives infinitely more glory from them than from the other beings, or rather the other beings furnish to spirits the material for glorifying him.

This moral quality of God that constitutes him Lord and Monarch of spirits influences him so to speak personally and in a unique way. It is through this that he humanizes himself, that he is willing to suffer anthropologies,[1] and that he enters into social relations with us; and this consideration is so dear to him that the happy and prosperous condition of his empire, which consists in the greatest possible felicity of its inhabitants, becomes supreme among his laws. Happiness is to persons what perfection is to beings. And if the dominant principle in the existence of the physical world is the decree to give it the greatest possible perfection, the primary purpose in the moral world or in the city of God that constitutes the noblest part of the universe ought to be to extend the greatest happiness possible.

We must not therefore doubt that God has so ordained everything that spirits not only shall live forever, because this is

---

1  "... souffrir des anthropologies ..."; it is unclear whether Leibniz means here to be making a reference (a very oblique one, if it is) to the Incarnation, in Christian theology—God becoming man, in Christ; or something else. It may be that, just as Leibniz holds that there aren't *literally* miracles, so too it cannot literally be that God becomes a human substance, or monad; rather that something occurs that *corresponds* to the Incarnation of theology, but whose literal or fully accurate metaphysical description would need to be put otherwise. Leibniz does at any rate appear to want to stress that what is involved is a kind of *suffering* on God's part, and the deity's placing himself on a kind of level with human beings.

unavoidable, but that they shall also preserve forever their moral quality, so that his city may never lose a person, quite in the same way that the world never loses a substance. Consequently they will always be conscious of their being, otherwise they would be open to neither reward nor punishment, a condition that is the essence of a republic, and above all of the most perfect republic where nothing can be neglected.

In short, God being at the same time the most just and the most good-natured of monarchs, and requiring only a good will on the part of men, provided that it be sincere and intentional, his subjects cannot desire a better condition. To render them perfectly happy, he desires only that they love him.

*XXXVII. Jesus Christ has revealed to men the mystery and the admirable laws of the kingdom of heaven, and the greatness of the supreme happiness that God has prepared for those who love him.*

The ancient philosophers knew very little of these important truths. Jesus Christ alone has expressed them divinely well, and in a way so clear and simple that the dullest minds have understood them. His gospel has entirely changed the face of human affairs. It has brought us to know the kingdom of heaven, or that perfect republic of spirits that deserves to be called the city of God. He it is who has discovered to us its wonderful laws. He alone has made us see how much God loves us and with what care everything that concerns us has been provided for; how God, inasmuch as he cares for the sparrows, will not neglect reasoning beings, who are infinitely more dear to him; how all the hairs of our heads are numbered; how heaven and earth may pass away but the word of God and what belongs to the means of our salvation will not pass away; how God has more regard for the least one among intelligent souls than for the whole machinery of the world; how we ought not to fear those who are able to destroy the body but are unable to destroy the soul, since God alone can render the soul happy or unhappy; and how the souls of the righteous are protected by his hand against all the upheavals of the universe, since God alone is able to act upon them; how none of our acts are forgotten; how everything is to be accounted for; even careless words and even a spoonful of water that is well used; in fact how everything must result in the greatest welfare of the good, for then shall the righteous become like suns and neither our sense nor our minds have ever tasted of anything approaching the joys that God has laid up for those who love him.

# THE PRINCIPLES OF NATURE AND
# OF GRACE, BASED ON REASON

# The Principles of Nature and of Grace, Based on Reason
## [1714]

1. *Substance* is a being capable of action. It is simple or composite. *Simple substance* is that which has no parts. *Composite* substance is the collection of simple substances or *monads*. *Monas* is a Greek word that signifies unity, or that which is one.

Composites, or bodies, are multitudes; and simple substances, lives, souls, spirits are unities. And there must be simple substances everywhere, because without simple substances there would be no composites; and consequently all nature is full of life.

2. Monads, having no parts, cannot be formed or decomposed. They cannot begin or end naturally; and consequently they last as long as the universe, which will be changed but will not be destroyed. They cannot have shapes; otherwise they would have parts. And consequently a monad, in itself and at a given moment, cannot be distinguished from another except by its internal qualities and actions, which can be nothing else than its *perceptions* (that is, representations of the composite, or of what is external, in the simple), and its *appetitions* (that is, its tendencies to pass from one perception to another), which are the principles of change. For the simplicity of substance does not prevent multiplicity of the modifications, which are to be found together in this same simple substance, and must consist in the variety of relations to things that are external.

It is just as in a *centre* or point, entirely simple as it is, there is an infinity of angles formed by the lines that meet at the point.

3. All nature is a *plenum*. There are everywhere simple substances, separated in effect from one another by activities of their own that continually change their relations; and each important simple substance, or monad, which forms the centre of a composite substance (as, for example, of an animal) and the principle of its unity, is surrounded by a *mass* composed of an infinity of other monads, which constitute the body proper of this central monad; and in accordance with the affections of its body the monad represents, as in a kind of *centre*, the things that are outside of itself. And this *body* is *organic*, though it forms a sort of automaton or natural machine, which is a machine not only in

its entirety, but also in its smallest perceptible parts. And as, because the world is a *plenum*, everything is connected and each body acts upon every other body, more or less, according to their distance, and by reaction is itself affected thereby, it follows that each monad is a living mirror, or endowed with internal activity, representative according to its point of view of the universe, and as regulated as the universe itself. And the perceptions in the monad spring from one another, by the laws of desires [*appétits*] or of the *final causes of good and evil*, which consist in observable, regular or irregular, perceptions, just as the changes of bodies and external phenomena spring one from another, by the laws of *efficient causes*, that is, of motions. Thus there is a perfect *harmony* between the perceptions of the monad and the motions of bodies, pre-established at the beginning between the system of efficient and that of final causes. And in this consists the accord and physical union of the soul and the body, although neither one can change the laws of the other.

4. Each monad, with a particular body, makes a living substance. Thus there is not only life everywhere, accompanied with members or organs, but also an infinity of degrees among monads, some dominating more or less over others. But when the monad has organs so adjusted that by their means prominence and distinctness appear in the impressions that they receive, and consequently in the perceptions that represent these (as, for example, when by means of the shape of the humours of the eyes, the rays of light are concentrated and act with more force), this may lead to *feeling* [*sentiment*], that is, to a perception accompanied by *memory*, namely, by a certain reverberation lasting a long time, so as to make itself heard upon occasion. And such a living being is called an *animal*, as its monad is called a soul. And when this soul is elevated to *reason*, it is something more sublime and is reckoned among spirits, as will soon be explained.

It is true that animals are sometimes in the condition of simple living beings, and their souls in the condition of simple monads, namely, when their perceptions are not sufficiently distinct to be remembered, as happens in a deep dreamless sleep, or in a swoon. But perceptions that have become entirely confused must be re-developed in animals, for reasons that I shall shortly [§12] enumerate. Thus it is good to make distinction between the *perception*, which is the inner state of the monad representing external things, and *apperception*, which is the *consciousness* or the reflective knowledge of this inner state; the latter not being given to all souls, nor at all times to the same soul. And it is for want of this distinction that the Cartesians have failed, taking no account of the perceptions of which we are not conscious, as people take no account of imperceptible bodies. This is also what made the same Cartesians believe that only spirits are monads, that there is no soul of brutes, and still less other *principles of life*. And as they shocked too much the common opinion of men by refusing feeling to brutes, they have, on the other hand, accommodated themselves too much to the prejudices of the multitude, by confounding a *long swoon*, caused by a great confusion of perceptions, with *death strictly speaking*, where all perception would cease. This has confirmed the ill-founded belief in the destruction of some souls, and the bad opinion of some so-called strong minds, who have contended against the immortality of our soul.

5. There is a connection in the perceptions of animals that bears some resemblance to reason; but it is founded only in the memory of *facts* or effects, and not at all in the knowledge of *causes*. Thus a dog shuns the stick with which it has been beaten, because memory represents to it the pain that the stick had caused it. And men, in so far as they are empirics, that is to say, in three-fourths of their actions, act simply as the brutes do. For example, we expect that there will be daylight tomorrow because we have always had the experience; only an astronomer foresees it by reason, and even this prediction will finally fail when the cause of day, which is not eternal, shall cease. But *true reasoning* depends upon necessary or eternal truths, such as those of logic, of numbers, of geometry, which establish an indubitable connection of ideas and unfailing inferences. The animals in whom these inferences are not noticed, are called *brutes*; but those that know these necessary truths are properly called *rational animals*, and their souls are called *spirits*. These souls are capable of performing acts of reflection, and of considering what is called the *ego, substance, soul, spirit*, in a word, immaterial things and truths. And it is this that renders us capable of the sciences and of demonstrative knowledge.

6. Modern research has taught us, and reason confirms it, that the living beings whose organs are known to us, that is to say,

plants and animals, do not come from putrefaction or from chaos, as the ancients believed, but from *pre-formed* seeds, and consequently by the transformation of pre-existing living beings. There are animalcules in the seeds of larger animals, which by means of conception assume a new outward form, which they make their own, and by means of which they can nourish themselves and increase their size, in order to pass to a larger theatre and to accomplish the propagation of the large animal. It is true that the souls of spermatic human animals are not rational, and do not become so until conception destines [*determine*] these animals to human nature. And as in general animals are not born entirely in conception or *generation*, neither do they perish entirely in what we call *death*; for it is reasonable that what does not begin naturally should not end either in the order of nature. Therefore, quitting their mask or their rags, they merely return to a more minute theatre, where they can, nevertheless, be just as sensitive and just as well ordered as in the larger. And what we have just said of the large animals takes place also in the generation and death of spermatic animals themselves, that is to say, they are growths of other smaller spermatic animals, in comparison with which they may pass for large; for everything extends *ad infinitum* in nature.

Thus not only souls, but also animals, are ingenerable and imperishable: they are only developed, enveloped, reclothed, unclothed, transformed: souls never quit the whole of their body and do not pass from one body into another that is entirely new to them.

There is therefore no *metempsychosis*, but there is *metamorphosis*; animals change, take and leave only parts: the same thing that happens little by little and by small invisible particles, but continually, in nutrition; and suddenly, visibly, but rarely, in conception or in death, which cause a gain or loss all at one time.

7. Thus far we have spoken as simple *physicists*: now we must advance to *metaphysics*, making use of the *great principle*, little employed in general, which teaches that *nothing happens without a sufficient reason*; that is to say, that nothing happens without its being possible for him who should sufficiently understand things, to give a reason sufficient to determine why it is so and not otherwise. This principle laid down, the first question which should rightly be asked, will be, *Why is there something rather than*

*nothing?* For nothing is simpler and easier than something. Further, suppose that things must exist, we must be able to give a reason *why they must exist thus* and not otherwise.

8. Now this sufficient reason for the existence of the universe cannot be found *in the series of contingent things*, that is, of bodies and of their representations in souls; for matter being indifferent in itself to motion and to rest, and to this or another motion, we cannot find the reason of motion in it, and still less of a certain motion. And although the present motion that is in matter comes from the preceding motion, and that from still another preceding, in this way we make no progress, go as far as we may; for the same question always remains. Thus it must be that the sufficient reason, which has no need of another reason, be outside this series of contingent things and be found in a substance that is its cause, or that is a necessary being, carrying the reason of its existence within itself; otherwise we would still not have a sufficient reason in which we could rest. And this final reason of things is called *God*.

9. This primitive simple substance must contain in itself eminently the perfections contained in the derivative substances that are its effects; thus it will have perfect power, knowledge and will: that is, it will have supreme omnipotence, omniscience, and goodness. And as *justice*, taken very generally, is nothing but goodness in conformity with wisdom, there must also be supreme justice in God. The reason that has led to the existence of things through him makes them also depend upon him for their continued existence and working: and they continually receive from him whatever makes them have any perfection; but any imperfection that remains in them comes from the essential and original limitation of the creature.

10. It follows from the supreme perfection of God that in creating the universe he has chosen the best possible plan, in which there is the greatest variety along with the greatest order; the best arranged ground, place, time; the most results produced in the simplest ways; the most power, knowledge, happiness, and goodness in the creatures that the universe could permit. For since all the possible things in the understanding of God claim existence in proportion to their perfections, the result of all these

claims must be the most perfect actual world that is possible. And without this it would not be possible to give a reason why things have turned out so rather than otherwise.

11. The supreme wisdom of God led him to choose the *laws of motion* best adjusted and most suited to abstract or metaphysical reasons. There is preserved the same quantity of total and absolute force, or of action; the same quantity of relative force or of reaction; lastly the same quantity of directive force. Furthermore, action is always equal to reaction, and the whole effect is always equivalent to its full cause. And it is not surprising that we could not, by the mere consideration of the *efficient causes* or of matter, account for those laws of motion that have been discovered in our time, and a part of which has been discovered by myself. For I have found that it was necessary to have recourse to *final causes*, and that these laws do not depend upon the *principle of necessity*, like logical, arithmetical, and geometrical truths, but upon the *principle of fitness*, that is, upon the choice of wisdom. And this is one of the most effective and evident proofs of the existence of God, to those who can examine these matters thoroughly.

12. It follows, further, from the perfection of the supreme author, that not only is the order of the entire universe the most perfect possible, but also that each living mirror representing the universe in accordance with its point of view, that is to say, each *monad*, each substantial centre, must have its perceptions and its desires as well regulated as is compatible with all the rest. From this it follows, still farther, that *souls*, that is, the most dominant monads, or rather, animals themselves, cannot fail to awaken from the state of stupor in which death or some other accident may put them.

13. For all is regulated in things, once and for all, with as much order and mutual connection as is possible, supreme wisdom and goodness not being able to act except with perfect harmony. The present is pregnant with the future, the future might be read in the past, the distant is expressed in the near. One could become acquainted with the beauty of the universe in each soul, if one could unfold all that is enfolded in it, which only develop perceptibly in time. But as each distinct perception of the soul includes innumerable confused perceptions, which embrace the

whole universe, the soul itself knows the things of which it has perception only so far as it has distinct and clear perceptions of them; and it has perfection in proportion to its distinct perceptions.

Each soul knows the infinite, knows all, but confusedly; as in walking on the seashore and hearing the great noise that it makes, I hear the particular sounds of each wave, of which the total sound is composed, but without distinguishing them. Our confused perceptions are the result of the impressions that the whole universe makes upon us. It is the same with each monad. God alone has a distinct knowledge of all, for he is the source of all. It has been well said that he is like a centre everywhere, but his circumference is nowhere, since everything is immediately present to him without any distance from this centre.

14. As regards the rational soul, or *spirit*, there is something in it more than in the monads, or even in simple souls. It is not only a mirror of the universe of creatures, but also an image of the divinity. The *spirit* not only has a perception of the works of God, but is even capable of producing something that resembles them, although in miniature. For, to say nothing of the marvels of dreams, in which we invent without trouble (but also involuntarily) things that, when awake, we should have to think a long time in order to hit upon, our soul is architectonic also in its voluntary actions, and, discovering the sciences according to which God has regulated things (*pondere, mensura, numero,*[1] *etc.*), it imitates, in its department and in its little world, where it is permitted to exercise itself, what God does in the large world.

15. This is why all spirits, whether of men or of genii, entering by virtue of reason and of eternal truths into a sort of society with God, are members of the City of God, that is to say, of the most perfect state, formed and governed by the greatest and best of monarchs, where there is no crime without punishment, no good actions without proportionate recompense, and, finally, as much virtue and happiness as is possible; and this is not by a derangement of nature, as if what God prepares for souls disturbed the laws of bodies, but by the very order of natural things, in virtue

---

1  "By weight, measure, number ..."; Leibniz is quoting from Wisdom 11:21 (Vulgate).

of the harmony pre-established for all time between the *realms of nature and of grace*, between God as architect and God as monarch; so that *nature* itself leads to grace, and *grace*, in making use of nature, perfects it.

16. Thus although reason cannot teach us the details, reserved to revelation, of the great future, we can be assured by this same reason that things are made in a manner surpassing our desires. God also being the most perfect and most happy, and consequently, the most lovable of substances, and *truly pure love* consisting in the state that finds pleasure in the perfections and happiness of the loved object, this love ought to give us the greatest pleasure of which we are capable, when God is its object.

17. And it is easy to love him as we ought, if we know him as I have just described. For although God is not visible to our external senses, he does not cease to be very lovable and to give very great pleasure. We see how much pleasure honours give men, although they do not at all consist in the qualities of the external senses.

Martyrs and fanatics (although the emotion of the latter is ill-regulated) show what pleasure of the spirit can accomplish; and, what is more, even sensuous pleasures are really intellectual pleasures that are confusedly known.

Music charms us, although its beauty consists only in the harmonies of numbers and in the counting—of which we are not conscious, and which the soul nevertheless does make—of the beats or vibrations of sounding bodies, which meet at certain intervals. The pleasures that sight finds in proportions are of the same nature; and those caused by the other senses amount to much the same thing, although we may not be able to explain it so distinctly.

18. It may even be said that from the present time on, the *love of God* makes us enjoy a foretaste of future felicity. And although it is disinterested, it itself constitutes our greatest good and interest even if we should not seek these therein and should consider only the pleasure that it gives, without regard to the utility it produces; for it gives us perfect confidence in the goodness of our author and master, producing a true tranquillity of mind, not as with the Stoics who force themselves to patience, but by

a present contentment, assuring to us also a future happiness. And besides the present pleasure, nothing can be more useful for the future; for the love of God fulfills also our hopes, and leads us in the road of supreme happiness, because by virtue of the perfect order established in the universe, everything is done in the best possible way, as much for the general good as for the greatest individual good of those who are convinced of this and are content with the divine government; this conviction cannot be wanting to those who know how to love the source of all good. It is true that supreme felicity, by whatever *beatific vision* or knowledge of God it be accompanied, can never be full; because, since God is infinite, he cannot be wholly known.

Therefore our happiness will never, and ought not, consist in full joy, where there would be nothing further to desire, rendering our mind stupid, but in a perpetual progress to new pleasures and to new perfections.

# THE MONADOLOGY

# The Monadology
## [1714]

1. The *monad* of which we shall here speak is merely a simple substance, which enters into composites: *simple*, that is to say, without parts.[1]

2. And there must be simple substances, since there are composites; for a composite is nothing but a collection or *aggregatum* of simple substances.

3. Now where there are no parts, there can be neither extension nor figure nor divisibility. These monads are the veritable atoms of nature, and, in one word, the elements of all things.

4. Their dissolution also is not at all to be feared, and there is no conceivable way in which a simple substance can perish naturally.[2]

5. For the same reason there is no conceivable way in which a simple substance can come into being by natural means, since it cannot be formed by composition.

6. Thus it may be said that the monads can only begin or end all at once; that is to say, they can only begin by creation and end by annihilation, whereas that which is composite begins or ends by parts.

7. There is also no way of explaining how a monad can be altered in quality or internally changed by any other creature, for nothing can be transposed within it, nor can there be conceived in it any internal movement that could be excited, directed, augmented or diminished within it, as can be done in composites, where there is change among the parts. The monads have no windows through which anything could come in or go out. The accidents[3] cannot detach themselves or go about outside of substances, as

---

1  *Théodicée*, §10. [All footnote references to this earlier work, *Theodicy* (1710), are Leibniz's. See Appendix D.]

2  §89.

3  I.e., properties, characteristics.

did formerly the sensible species of the schoolmen. Thus neither substance nor accident can enter a monad from outside.

8. Nevertheless, the monads must have some qualities; otherwise they would not even be entities. And if simple substances did not differ at all in their qualities there would be no way of perceiving any change in things, since what is in the compound can come only from the simple ingredients, and the monads, if they had no qualities, would be indistinguishable from one another, since also they do not differ in quantity. Consequently, a plenum being supposed, each place would always receive, in any motion, only the equivalent of what it had had before, and one state of things would be indistinguishable from another.

9. It is necessary, indeed, that each monad be different from every other. For there are never in nature two beings that are exactly alike and in which it is not possible to find an internal difference, or one founded upon an intrinsic quality (*dénomination*).

10. I take it also for granted that all created beings, consequently the created monads as well, are subject to change, and even that this change is continuous in each.

11. It follows from what has just been said that the natural changes of the monads proceed from an *internal principle*, since an external cause could not influence their inner being.[1]

12. But, besides the principle of change, there must be an individuating *detail of changes*, which forms, so to speak, the specification and variety of the simple substances.

13. This detail must involve a multitude in the unity or in that which is simple. For since every natural change takes place by degrees, something changes and something remains; and consequently, there must be in the simple substance a plurality of affections and of relations, although it has no parts.

14. The passing state, which involves and represents a multiplicity in the unity or in the simple substance, is nothing but what is

---

1   §§396 and 400.

called *perception*, which must be distinguished from apperception or consciousness, as will appear in what follows. Here it is that the Cartesians especially failed, having taken no account of the perceptions of which we are not conscious. This also made them believe that only spirits are monads, and that there are neither animal souls nor other entelechies.[1] They, with most people, have failed to distinguish between a prolonged state of unconsciousness (*étourdissement*) and death strictly speaking, and have therefore agreed with the old scholastic prejudice of entirely separate souls, and have even confirmed ill-balanced minds in the belief in the mortality of the soul.

15. The action of the internal principle that causes the change or passage from one perception to another may be called *appetition*; it is true that desire cannot always completely attain to the whole perception to which it tends, but it always attains something of it and reaches new perceptions.

16. We experience in ourselves a multiplicity in a simple substance, when we find that the most trifling thought of which we are conscious involves a variety in the object. Thus all those who admit that the soul is a simple substance ought to admit this multiplicity in the monad, and M. Bayle ought not to have found any difficulty in it, as he has done in his Dictionary, article *Rorarius*.[2]

17. It must be confessed, moreover, that *perception* and what depends on it *are inexplicable by mechanical causes,* that is, by figures and motions. And, supposing that there were a machine so constructed as to think, feel, and have perception, we could conceive of it as enlarged and yet preserving the same proportions, so that we might enter it as into a mill. And this granted, we should only find on visiting it pieces that push against one another, but never anything by which to explain a perception. This must be sought, therefore, in the simple substance and not in the composite or in the machine. Furthermore, nothing but this (namely, perceptions and their changes) can be found in the simple substance. It is also in this alone that all the *internal activities* of simple substances can consist.[3]

---

1 See Introduction, p. 35, note 1.
2 See Appendix C.
3 Preface, p. 37 [Gerhardt edition].

18. The name of *entelechies* might be given to all simple substances or created monads, for they have within themselves a certain perfection (ἔχουσι τὸ ἐντελές) [echousi to enteles]; there is a certain sufficiency (αὐτάρκεια) [autarkeia] that makes them the sources of their own actions, and so to speak, incorporeal automata.[1]

19. If we choose to give the name *soul* to everything that has *perceptions* and *desires* in the general sense that I have just explained, all simple substances or created monads may be called souls, but as feeling is something more than a simple perception, I am willing that the general name of monads or entelechies shall suffice for those simple substances that have only perceptions, and that those substances only shall be called *souls* whose perception is more distinct and is accompanied by memory.

20. For we experience in ourselves a state in which we remember nothing and have no distinguishable perception, as when we fall into a swoon or when we are overpowered by a profound and dreamless sleep. In this state the soul does not differ sensibly from a simple monad; but as this state is not continuous and as the soul comes out of it, the soul is something more than a mere monad.[2]

21. And it does not at all follow that in such a state the simple substance is without any perception. This is indeed impossible, for the reasons mentioned above; for it cannot perish, nor can it subsist without some affection, which is nothing else than its perception; but when there is a great number of minute perceptions, in which nothing is distinct, we are stunned; as when we turn continually in the same direction many times in succession, from which arises a dizziness that may make us swoon, and that does not let us distinguish anything. And death may produce for a time this condition in animals.

22. And as every present state of a simple substance is naturally a consequence of its preceding state, so its present is pregnant with its future.[3]

---

1  §87.
2  §64.
3  §360.

23. Therefore, since on being awakened from a stupor we are *aware* of our perceptions, we must have had them immediately before, although we were unconscious of them; for one perception can come in a natural way only from another perception, as a motion can come in a natural way only from a motion.[1]

24. From this we see that if there were nothing distinct, nothing, so to speak, in relief and of a higher flavour in our perceptions, we would always be in a dazed state. This is the condition of simply bare monads.

25. We also see that nature has given to animals heightened perceptions, by the pains she has taken to furnish them with organs that collect many rays of light or many undulations of air, in order to render these more efficacious by uniting them. There is something of the same kind in odour, in taste, in touch, and perhaps in a multitude of other senses that are unknown to us. And I shall presently explain how what takes place in the soul represents what occurs in the organs.

26. Memory furnished the soul with a sort of *consecutiveness* that imitates reason but that ought to be distinguished from it. We observe that animals, having the perception of something that strikes them and of which they have had a similar perception before, expect, through the representation in their memory, what was associated with it in the preceding perception, and experience feelings similar to those that they had had at that time. For instance, if we show dogs a stick, they remember the pain it has caused them and whine and run.[2]

27. And the strong imagination that impresses and moves them arises from either the magnitude or the multitude of preceding perceptions. For often a strong impression produces all at once the effect of a long-continued *habit*, or of many oft-repeated moderate perceptions.

28. Men act like brutes, in so far as the association of their perceptions results from the principle of memory alone, resembling

---

1  §§401 to 403.
2  Prelim., §65.

the empirical physicians who practise without theory; and we are simple empirics in three-fourths of our actions. For example, when we expect that there will be daylight tomorrow, we are acting as empirics, because that has up to this time always taken place. It is only the astronomer who judges of this by reason.

29. But the knowledge of necessary and eternal truths is what distinguishes us from mere animals and furnishes us with *reason* and the sciences, raising us to a knowledge of ourselves and of God. This is what we call the rational soul or *spirit* in us.

30. It is also by the knowledge of necessary truths, and by their abstractions, that we rise to *acts of reflection*, which make us think of that which calls itself "*I*," and observe that this or that is within *us*: and it is thus that, in thinking of ourselves, we think of being, of substance, simple or composite, of the immaterial and of God himself, conceiving that what is limited in us is in him without limits. And these reflective acts furnish the principal objects of our reasonings.[1]

31. Our reasonings are founded on *two great principles, that of contradiction*, in virtue of which we judge to be *false* what involves contradiction, and *true*, what is opposed or contradictory to the false.[2]

32. And [the other great principle is] *that of sufficient reason*, in virtue of which we hold that no fact can be real or existent, no statement true, unless there be a sufficient reason why it is so and not otherwise, although most often these reasons cannot be known to us.[3]

33. There are also two kinds of *truth*, those of *reasoning* and those of *fact*. Truths of reasoning are necessary and their opposite is impossible, and those of *fact* are contingent and their opposite is possible. When a truth is necessary its reason can be found by analysis, resolving it into more simple ideas and truths until we reach those that are primitive.[4]

---

1  Pref., p. 27 [Gerhardt edition].
2  §§44, 169.
3  §§44, 196.
4  §§170, 174, 189, 280-82, 367; Abridgement, Objection 3.

34. It is thus that mathematicians by analysis reduce speculative *theorems* and practical *canons* to *definitions*, *axioms*, and *postulates*.

35. And there are finally simple ideas, definitions of which cannot be given; there are also axioms and postulates, in a word, *primary principles*, which cannot be proved, and indeed need no proof; and these are *identical propositions*, whose opposite involves an express contradiction.

36. But there must also be a *sufficient reason* for *contingent truths*, or those of *fact*—that is, for the sequence of things diffused through the universe of created objects—where the resolution into particular reasons might run into a detail without limits, on account of the immense variety of the things in nature and the division of bodies *ad infinitum*. There is an infinity of figures and of movements, present and past, which enter into the efficient cause of my present writing, and there is an infinity of slight inclinations and dispositions, past and present, of my soul, which enter into the final cause.[1]

37. And as all this *detail* only involves other contingents, anterior or more detailed, each one of which needs a like analysis for its explanation, we make no advance: and the sufficient or final reason must be outside of the sequence or *series* of this detail of contingencies, however infinite it may be.

38. And thus it is that the final reason of things must be found in a necessary substance, in which the variety of particular changes exists only eminently, as in its source; and this is what we call God.[2]

39. Now this substance, being a sufficient reason of all this detail, which also is linked together throughout, *there is but one God, and this God is sufficient.*

40. We may also conclude that this supreme substance is unique, universal, and necessary; there is nothing outside of itself that is independent of it, and its existence is a simple consequence of its

---

1 §§36, 37, 44, 45, 49, 52, 121, 122, 337, 340, 344.
2 §7.

being possible. Accordingly, it must be incapable of limitations and must contain as much of reality as is possible.

41. From this it follows that God is absolutely perfect; for *perfection* is nothing but amount of positive reality, in the strict sense, setting aside the limits or bounds in things which have them. And where there are no limits, that is, in God, perfection is absolutely infinite.[1]

42. It follows also that the creatures derive their perfections from the influence of God, but that their imperfections arise from their own nature, which is incapable of existing without limits. For it is in this that they differ from God.[2]

43. It is also true that in God there is the source not only of existences but also of essences, so far as they are real, or of what is real in the possible. For the understanding of God is the region of eternal truths, or of the ideas on which they depend, and without him there would be nothing real in the possibilities of things, and not only would there be nothing existing, but nothing would even be possible.[3]

44. However, if there is a reality in essences or possibilities or indeed in the eternal truths, this reality must be founded in something existing and actual, and consequently in the existence of the necessary being, in whom essence involves existence, or with whom it is sufficient to be possible in order to be actual.[4]

45. Hence God alone (or the necessary being) has this prerogative, that he must exist if he is possible. And since nothing can hinder the possibility of that which possesses no limitations, no nega-

---

1   §22; Preface, p. 27.
2   §§20, 27-31, 153, 167, 377 seqq. [In the first copy, revised by Leibniz, the following is added: "This *original imperfection* of creatures is noticeable in the *natural inertia* of bodies. §§30, 380; Abridgement, Objection 5."]
3   §20.
4   §§184, 189, 335. [Leibniz, in the ontological argument here summarized, makes use of what is now called the 'S5' modal principle—$\Diamond\Box\alpha\to\Box\alpha$ (in this instance: 'if it is possible that a necessary being exists, then that necessary being does exist').]

tion, and, consequently, no contradiction, this alone is sufficient to establish the existence of God *a priori*. We have also proved it by the reality of the eternal truths. But we have a little while ago [§§36-39] proved it also *a posteriori*, since contingent beings exist, which can only have their final or sufficient reason in a necessary being who has the reason of his existence in himself.

46. Yet we must not imagine, as some do, that the eternal truths, being dependent upon God, are arbitrary and depend upon his will, as Descartes seems to have held, and afterwards M. Poiret.[1] This is true only of contingent truths, the principle of which is *fitness* or the choice of the *best*, whereas necessary truths depend solely on his understanding and are its internal object.[2]

47. Thus God is the only primitive unit or the only original simple substance, of which all the created or derivative monads are the products, born, so to speak, every moment by continual fulgurations from the Divinity, limited by the receptivity of the creature, of whose essence it is to have limits.[3]

48. In God there is *Power*, which is the source of all; also *Knowledge*, which contains the detail of ideas; and finally *Will*, which effects changes or products according to the principle of the best. These correspond to what in created monads forms the subject or basis, the perceptive faculty, and the appetitive faculty. But in God these attributes are absolutely infinite or perfect; and in the created monads or in the *entelechies* (or *perfectihabiis*, as Hermolaus Barbarus[4] translated the word), they are only imitations proportioned to the perfection of the monads.[5]

49. The creature is said to *act* externally in so far as it has perfection, and to be *acted on* by another in so far as it is imperfect. Thus *action* is attributed to the monad in so far as it has distinct perceptions, and *passivity* in so far as it has confused perceptions.[6]

---

1 [Pierre Poiret (1646-1719).]
2 §§180, 184, 185, 335, 351, 380.
3 §§382-91, 398, 395.
4 [Hermolaus Barbarus (1454-93), Italian Aristotelian scholar.]
5 §§7, 149, 150, 87.
6 §§32, 66, 386.

50. And one creature is more perfect than another, in that there is found in it what serves to account *a priori* for what takes place in the other, and it is in this way that it is said to act upon the other.

51. But in simple substances the influence of one monad upon another is purely *ideal*, and it can have its effect only through the intervention of God, inasmuch as in the ideas of God a monad may demand with reason that God in regulating the others from the commencement of things, have regard to it. For since a created monad can have no physical influence upon the inner being of another, it is only in this way that one can be dependent upon another.[1]

52. And hence it is that the actions and passive reactions of creatures are mutual. For God, in comparing two simple substances, finds in each one reasons that compel him to adjust the other to it, and consequently what in certain respects is active is according to another point of view passive: *active* in so far as what one sees distinctly in it serves to give reason for what takes place in another; and *passive* in so far as the reason for what takes place in it, is found in what is distinctly known in another.[2]

53. Now, as there is an infinite number of possible universes in the ideas of God, and as only one of them can be actual, there must be a sufficient reason for the choice of God, which leads him to select one rather than another.[3]

54. And this reason can only be found in the *fitness*, or in the degrees of perfection, that these worlds possess, since each possible thing has the right to aspire to existence according to the measure of perfection that it possesses.[4]

55. And this is the cause of the existence of the best, which wisdom makes known to God, which his goodness makes him choose, and which his power makes him produce.[5]

---

1  §§9, 54, 65, 66, 201; Abridgement, Objection 3.
2  §66.
3  §§8, 10, 44, 173, 196 seqq., 225, 414-16.
4  §§74, 167, 350, 201, 130, 345, seqq., 352, 354. [In the first copy revised by Leibniz the following is found added here: "Thus there is nothing absolutely arbitrary."]
5  §§8, 78, 80, 84, 119, 204, 206, 208; Abridgement, Objections 1 and 8.

56. Now this *connection*, or this adaptation, of all created things to each and of each to all, brings it about that each simple substance has relations that express all the others, and that, consequently, it is a perpetual living mirror of the universe.[1]

57. And as the same city looked at from different sides appears entirely different, and is as if multiplied *perspectively*; so also it happens that, as a result of the infinite multitude of simple substances, there are as it were so many universes, which are nevertheless only aspects of a single one, according to the different *points of view* of each monad.[2]

58. And this is the way to obtain as great a variety as possible, but with the greatest possible order; that is, it is the way to obtain as much perfection as possible.[3]

59. Moreover, this hypothesis (which I dare to call demonstrated) is the only one that brings into relief the grandeur of God. M. Bayle recognized this, when in his Dictionary (Art. *Rorarius*) he raised objections to it; in which indeed he was disposed to think that I attributed too much to God and more than is possible. But he can state no reason why this universal harmony, which brings it about that each substance expresses exactly all the others through the relations that it has to them, is impossible.

60. Besides, we can see, in what I have just said, the *a priori* reasons why things could not be otherwise than they are. Because God, in regulating all, has had regard to each part, and particularly to each monad, whose nature being representative, nothing can limit it to representing only a part of things; although it may be true that this representation is but confused as regards the detail of the whole universe, and can be distinct only in the case of a small part of things, that is to say, in the case of those that are nearest or greatest in relation to each of the monads; otherwise each monad would be a divinity. It is not as regards the object but only as regards the modification of the knowledge of the object, that monads are limited. They all tend confusedly

---

1 §§130, 360.
2 §147.
3 §§120, 124, 241 seqq., 214, 243, 275.

toward the infinite, toward the whole; but they are limited and differentiated by the degrees of their distinct perceptions.

61. And composites are analogous in this respect with the things that are simple. For since the world is a *plenum*, rendering all matter connected, and since in a plenum every motion has some effect on distant bodies in proportion to their distance, so that each body is affected not only by those in contact with it, and feels in some way all that happens to them, but also by their means is affected by those that are in contact with the former, with which it itself is in immediate contact, it follows that this intercommunication extends to any distance whatever. And consequently every body feels the effect of all that takes place in the universe, so that he who sees all might read in each what is happening everywhere, and even what has happened or shall happen, observing in the present what is far off in time as well as in space: σύμπνοια πάντα [sumpnoia panta],[1] as Hippocrates said. But a soul can read in itself only what is distinctly represented in it. It cannot all at once unroll everything that is enfolded in it, for these things reach into the infinite.

62. Thus, although each created monad represents the entire universe, it represents more distinctly the body that is particularly attached to it and of which it is the entelechy; and as this body expresses the whole universe through the connection of all matter in the plenum, the soul also represents the whole universe in representing this body, which belongs to it in a particular way.[2]

63. The body belonging to a monad, which is its entelechy or soul, constitutes together with this entelechy what may be called a *living being*, and together with the soul what may be called an *animal*. Now this body of a living being or of an animal is always an organism, for since every monad is in its way a mirror of the universe, and since the universe is regulated in a perfect order, there must also be an order in the representative, that is, in the perceptions of the soul, and hence in the body, through which the universe is represented in the soul.[3]

---

1   ["All things conspire."]
2   §400.
3   §403.

64. Thus each organic body of a living being is a kind of divine machine or natural automaton, which infinitely surpasses all artificial automata. Because a machine that is made by man's art is not a machine in each one of its parts; for example, the teeth of a brass wheel have parts of fragments which to us are no longer artificial and have nothing in themselves to show the special use to which the wheel was intended in the machine. But nature's machines, that is, living bodies, are machines even in their smallest parts *ad infinitum*. Herein lies the difference between nature and art, that is, between the divine art and ours.[1]

65. And the author of nature has been able to employ this divine and infinitely marvellous artifice, not only because each portion of matter is infinitely divisible, as the ancients recognized, but also each part is actually subdivided *ad infinitum*, each part into further parts, of which each has some motion of its own: otherwise it would be impossible for each portion of matter to express the whole universe.[2]

66. From this we see that there is a world of creatures of living beings, of animals, of entelechies, of souls, in the smallest particle of matter.

67. Each portion of matter may be conceived of as a garden full of plants, and as a pond full of fishes. But each branch of the plant, each member of the animal, each drop of its humors is also such a garden or such a pond.

68. And although the earth and air that lie between the plants of the garden, or the water between the fish of the pond, are neither plant nor fish, they still contain more of them, but for the most part so tiny as to be imperceptible to us.

69. Therefore there is nothing fallow, nothing sterile, nothing dead in the universe, no chaos, no confusion except in appearance; somewhat as a pond would appear from a distance, in which we might see the confused movement and swarming,

---

1 §§134, 146, 194, 403.
2 Prelim., §70; Théod., §195.

so to speak, of the fishes in the pond, without discerning the fish themselves.[1]

70. We see thus that each living body has a ruling entelechy, which in the animal is the soul; but the members of this living body are full of other living beings, plants, animals, each of which has also its entelechy or governing soul.

71. But it must not be imagined, as has been done by some people who have misunderstood my thought, that each soul has a mass or portion of matter belonging to it or attached to it forever, and that consequently it possesses other inferior living beings, destined to its service forever. For all bodies are, like rivers, in a perpetual flux, and parts are entering into them and passing out of them continually.

72. Thus the soul changes its body only by degrees, little by little, so that it is never deprived of all its organs at once. There is often a metamorphosis in animals, but never metempsychosis or transmigration of souls. There are also no entirely *separate* souls, nor *genii* without bodies. God alone is wholly without body.[2]

73. For this reason also, it happens that there is, strictly speaking, neither absolute birth nor complete death, consisting in the separation of the soul from the body. What we call *birth* is development or growth, as what we call *death* is envelopment and diminution.

74. Philosophers have been greatly puzzled about the origin of forms, entelechies, or souls; but today, when we know by exact investigations upon plants, insects, and animals that the organic bodies of nature are never products of chaos or putrefaction, but always come from seeds, in which there was undoubtedly some *pre-formation*, it has been thought that not only the organic body was already there before conception, but also a soul in this body, and, in a word, the animal itself; and that by means of conception this animal has merely been prepared for a great transformation, in order to become an animal of another kind. Something

---

1  Preface, pp. 40, 41.
2  Théod., §§90, 124.

similar is seen outside of birth, as when worms become flies, and caterpillars become butterflies.[1]

75. The *animals*, some of which are raised by conception to the grade of larger animals, may be called *spermatic*; but those among them, which remain in their own kind, that is, the most part, are born, multiply, and are destroyed like the large animals, and it is only a small number of chosen ones that pass to a larger theatre.

76. But this is only half the truth. I have, therefore, held that if the animal never commences by natural means, neither does it end by natural means; and that not only will there be no birth, but also no utter destruction or death, strictly speaking. And these reasonings, made *a posteriori* and drawn from experience, harmonize perfectly with my principles deduced *a priori*, as above [cf. 3, 4, 5].[2]

77. Thus it may be said that not only the soul (mirror of an indestructible universe) is indestructible, but also the animal itself, although its mechanism often perishes in part and takes on or puts off organic coatings.

78. These principles have given me a way of explaining naturally the union or rather the conformity of the soul and the organic body. The soul follows its own peculiar laws and the body also follows its own laws, and they agree with each other in virtue of the *pre-established harmony* prevailing among all substances, since they are all representations of one and the same universe.[3]

79. Souls act according to the laws of final causes through appetitions, ends, and means. Bodies act in accordance with the laws of efficient causes or of motion. And the two realms, that of efficient causes and that of final causes, are in harmony with one another.

---

1  §§86, 88, Preface p. 5 seq. (Gerhardt, p. 40), 90, 187, 188, 403, 397; Preface, p. 40, seq.
2  §90.
3  Preface, p. 36; Théod., §§340, 352, 353, 358.

80. Descartes recognized that souls cannot impart any force to bodies, because there is always the same quantity of force in matter. Nevertheless he believed that the soul could change the direction of bodies. But this was because, in his day, the law of nature that affirms also the conservation of the same total direction in matter, was not known. If he had known this, he would have lighted upon my system of pre-established harmony.[1]

81. According to this system, bodies act as if (to suppose the impossible) there were no souls, and souls act as if there were no bodies, and both act as if each influenced the other.

82. As to *spirits* or rational souls, although I find that the same thing that I have stated (namely, that the animal and the soul begin with the world and end no more than the world) holds good at bottom with regard to all living beings and animals, yet there is this peculiarity in rational animals, that their spermatic animalcules, as long as they remain such, have only ordinary or sensitive souls; but as soon as those that are, so to speak, elected, attain by actual conception to human nature, their sensitive souls are elevated to the rank of reason and to the prerogative of spirits.[2]

83. Among other differences that exist between ordinary souls and minds (*esprits*), some of which I have already mentioned, there is also, this, that souls in general are the living mirrors or images of the universe of creatures, but minds or spirits are in addition images of the Deity itself, or of the author of nature, able to know the system of the universe and to imitate something of it by architectonic samples, each mind being like a little divinity in its own sphere.[3]

84. Hence it is that the spirits are capable of entering into a kind of society with God, and that he is, in relation to them, not only what an inventor is to his machine (as God is in relation to the other creatures), but also what a prince is to his subjects, and indeed a father to his children.

---

1 Pref. (Gerhardt, p. 44); Théod., §§22, 59, 60, 61, 63, 66, 345, 346, seqq., 354, 355.
2 §§91, 397.
3 §147.

85. Whence it is easy to conclude that the assemblage of all the spirits (*esprits*) must compose the City of God, that is, the most perfect state that is possible, under the most perfect of monarchs.[1]

86. This City of God, this truly universal monarchy, is a moral world within the natural world, and is the most exalted and most divine among the works of God; it is in this that the glory of God truly consists, for he would have none if his greatness and goodness were not known and admired by spirits. It is, too, in relation to this divine city that he properly has goodness; whereas his wisdom and power are everywhere manifest.

87. As we have shown above that there is a perfect harmony between the two realms in nature, the one of efficient causes, the other of final causes, we should also notice here another harmony, namely, between the physical realm of nature and the moral realm of grace, that is, between God considered as the architect of the machine of the universe and God considered as monarch of the divine city of spirits.[2]

88. This harmony makes things progress toward grace by natural means. This globe, for example, must be destroyed and repaired by natural means, at such times as the government of spirits may demand it, for the punishment of some and the reward of others.[3]

89. It may be said, further, that God as architect satisfies in every respect God as legislator, and that therefore sins, by the order of nature and perforce even of the mechanical structure of things, must carry their punishment with them; and that in the same way, good actions will obtain their rewards by mechanical ways through their relation to bodies, although this cannot and ought not always happen immediately.

90. Finally, under this perfect government, there will be no good action unrewarded, no bad action unpunished; and everything

---

1 §146; Abridgement, Objection 2.
2 §§62, 74, 118, 248, 112, 130, 247.
3 §§18 seqq., 110, 244, 245, 340.

must result in the well-being of the good, that is, of those who are not disaffected in this great State, who, after having done their duty, trust in providence, and who love and imitate, as is fitting, the author of all good, finding pleasure in the contemplation of his perfections, according to the nature of truly *pure love*, which takes pleasure in the happiness of the beloved. This is what causes wise and virtuous persons to work for all that seems in harmony with the divine will, presumptive or antecedent, and nevertheless to content themselves with what God in reality brings to pass by his secret, consequent, and decisive will, recognizing that if we could sufficiently understand the order of the universe, we should find that it surpasses all the wishes of the wisest, and that it is impossible to render it better than it is, not only for all in general, but also for ourselves in particular, if we are attached, as we should be, to the author of all, not only as to the architect and efficient cause of our being, but also as to our master and final cause, who ought to be the whole aim of our will, and who, alone, can make our happiness.[1]

---

1  §§134 fin., 278; Preface, pp. 27, 28.

# Appendix A: From Anne, Viscountess *Conway*, Principles of the Most Ancient and Modern Philosophy *(ca. 1675; published in a Latin translation 1690)*

[Anne Conway (1631-79) was an aristocratic Englishwoman, married to Viscount Conway. An invalid most of her adult life, she suffered from debilitating headaches and lived in seclusion at Ragley Hall, Warwickshire. Of prodigious natural ability and philosophical interests, she developed her own philosophical views, partly under the stimulus provided by the writings and conversation of the Cambridge Platonist Henry More (1614-87) and the Dutch cabbalist philosopher Francis Mercury van Helmont (1618-98), with both of whose work Leibniz was well acquainted. Following her death, a notebook she left containing her metaphysical system was translated (from English) and published in a Latin edition in Amsterdam in 1690. (That text was in turn re-translated into English in 1692.) Clearly independently developed, Conway's system bears striking similarities to Leibniz's. Her work was brought to Leibniz's attention by van Helmont, and he read and praised her views highly. In a letter to Thomas Burnett (of 1697), Leibniz says: "My views in philosophy approach somewhat those of the late Countess [sic] of Conway, and occupy a mid-place between Plato and Democritus, since I believe that everything happens mechanically as Democritus and Descartes want, against the view of M. More and those like-minded; and that nevertheless everything happens at the same time vitally and following final causes, everything being full of life and of perceptions, against the opinion of the Democriteans."[1] Leibniz makes further laudatory comment on Conway in the *New Essays Concerning Human Understanding.* The passage presented below is chapter III of Conway's treatise, followed by brief excerpts from chapter VII. They show affinity to Leibniz's work, including Conway's use of the

---

1   G.W. Leibniz, *Die philosophischen Schriften*, ed. C.I. Gerhardt, 7
    vols. (Berlin: Weidmann, 1875-90), vol. 3, p. 205.

term *monad*. Leibniz's use of the term post-dates his reading of Conway's *Principles*, and he might possibly have adopted it from her work. Other possible sources include More, Giordano Bruno (1548-1600), and Leibniz's teacher Jakob Thomasius (1622-84); or it may have been Leibniz's own invention. The text used is that of the English translation of 1692,[1] lightly modernized, both orthographically and grammatically.]

## CHAP. III.

*§.1.* GOD is the most free Agent, and yet of all the most necessary. *§.2.* Indifferency of Will, which the School-men imagined to be in God, is a mere Fiction. *§.3.* God created the World, not for any external necessity, but out of the internal impulse of his Divine Goodness and Wisdom. *§.4.* Creatures were created Infinite, and there are Worlds Infinite. *§.5.* The least Creature that we can conceive hath within it Infinite Creatures. *§.6.* Yet that doth not make Creatures equal with God. *§.7.* A refutation of those imaginary Spaces, which the Schools did imagine to exist without the Creatures. *§.8.* Successive Motion hath no place in God. *§.9.* An Answer to the Objection. *§.10.* All Creatures are united after a certain manner.

§.1. MOREOVER, if the aforementioned attributes of God be duly considered, and especially these two—to wit, his wisdom and goodness—that indifference of will, which the school-men and philosophers falsely so called, have imagined to be in God, will be utterly refuted and wholly turned out of doors. This also they have improperly called free-will, for although the will of God be most free, so that whatsoever he does on behalf of his creatures, he does freely without any external violence, compulsion, or any cause coming from them: whatever he does, he does of his own accord. Yet that indifference of acting, or not acting, can by no means be said to be in God, because this would be an imperfection and would make God like corruptible creatures; for this indifference of will is the foundation of all change and

---

1   The Latin text of 1690, and that of the 1692 English translation, are published in Anne Conway, *The Principles of the Most Ancient and Modern Philosophy*, ed. Peter Loptson (The Hague: Martinus Nijhoff, 1st ed., 1982; Delmar, NY: Scholars' Facsimiles and Reprints, 2nd ed., 1998).

corruptibility in creatures, so that there would be no evil in creatures if they were not changeable. Therefore, if the same should be supposed to be in God, he must be supposed to be changeable, and so would be like corruptible man, who often does a thing out of his mere pleasure, not out of a true and solid reason or the guidance of wisdom. In this he is like those cruel tyrants who are in the world, who act many things out of their mere will or pleasure, relying on their power, so that they can render no other reason for what they do than the fact that it is their mere pleasure; whereas any good man who acts, or is about to act, can render a suitable reason for it, because he knows and understands that true goodness and wisdom has required him to do it. Therefore he wills that it be effected, because it is just, so that if he did not do it he would neglect his duty.

§.2. FOR true justice or goodness has in itself no latitude or indifference.... From this it is clear that this indifference of will has no place in God, because it is an imperfection; although God is the most free agent, yet he is also above all the most necessary agent so that it is impossible that he should not do, whatever he does in or for his creatures. Seeing his infinite wisdom, goodness, and justice is a law unto him, which he cannot transgress.... HENCE therefore it evidently follows, that it was not indifferent to God, whether he would give being to his creatures or not; but he made them out of a certain internal impulse of his divine wisdom and goodness, and so he created the world or creatures as soon as he could; for this is the nature of a necessary agent, to do whatsoever it can. Therefore seeing he could create the world or creatures in infinite times, before 6,000 years, or before 60,000 years, or 600,000, etc., it follows he has done it; for God can entirely do that which implies no contradiction; but this does not imply a contradiction, if the worlds or creatures be said to have been or existed in infinite times, before this moment, even as they are infinite times after this moment: if there be no contradiction in the latter, there is also no contradiction in the former.

[...]

§.4. THESE attributes duly considered, it follows that creatures were created in infinite numbers, or that there is an infinity of worlds or creatures made of God: for seeing God is infinitely powerful, there can be no number of creatures so great, that he cannot always make more; and because, as is already proved, he does whatever he can do, certainly his will, goodness, and bounty are as large and extensive as his power. From this it clearly follows that creatures are infinite, and created in infinite manners; so that they cannot be limited or bounded with any number or measure. For example, let us suppose the whole universality of creatures to be a circle, whose semi-diameter contains so many diameters of the earth as there are grains of dust or sand in the whole globe of the earth; and if the same should be divided into atoms, so small that 100,000 of them could be contained in one grain of poppy-seed: now who can deny that anything other than the infinite power of God could have made this number greater, and yet still greater, even to an infinite multiplication? Since it is easier for this infinite power to multiply the real beings of creatures than for a skilful arithmetician to make any number greater and greater, which can never be so great, but that it may be (by addition or multiplication) increased *ad infinitum*, and furthermore, since it is already demonstrated that God is a necessary agent, and does whatsoever he can do, it must be that he does multiply, and yet still continues to multiply and augment the essences of creatures, *ad infinitum*....

§.5. ALSO by the like reason it is proved that not only the whole body or system of creatures considered together is infinite, or contains in itself a kind of infinity, but also that every creature, even the least that we can discern with our eyes or conceive in our minds, has within it such an infinity of parts, or rather entire creatures, that they cannot be numbered. And it cannot be denied that God can place one creature within another, so he can place two as well as one, and four as well as two, so also eight as well as four, so that he could multiply them without end, always placing the less within the greater. And since no creature can be so small that there cannot be always a smaller one, no creature is so great that there cannot be always a greater: now it follows that in the smallest creature there may exist or be comprehended infinite creatures, which may be all of them bodies, and after a fashion, in regard of themselves, impenetrable of one another. As to those creatures that are spirits and can penetrate each other, in every created spirit there may be some infinity of spirits, all of which may be of equal extension with the aforesaid spirit as they are one with another; for in this case those spirits are more subtle and ethereal, which penetrate the gross and more corporeal, from which there can be no lack of room, that one must be constrained to give place to another. Of the nature of bodies and spirits, more shall be said in its proper place, this being sufficient to demonstrate that in every creature, whether it be a spirit or a body, there is an infinity of creatures, each of which contains an infinity, and again each of these, and so *ad infinitum*.

§.6. ALL these do greatly extol and set forth the great power and goodness of God, such that his eternity is clearly seen by the works of his hands, indeed in every creature that he has made. Nor can it be objected, we make creatures equal with God; for as one infinite may be greater than another, so God is still infinitely greater than all his creatures, and without any comparison. And thus indeed the invisible things of God are clearly seen, as they are understood by, or in those things, that are made; for by how much the greater and more magnificent the works are, by so much the more is the greatness of the workman seen. Therefore those who teach that the whole number of creatures is finite, and consists of so many individuals as may be numbered; and that the whole body of the universe takes up just so many acres or miles, or diameters of the earth, according to longitude, latitude, and profundity, consider so great majesty with too low and unseemly a conception. And so that god that they fancy to themselves is not the true God, but an idol of their own imagination, whom they confine to so narrow an habitation, as a few little bees shut up within the limits of a hive, containing the measure of a few inches: for what else is that world, which they suppose, in respect of that truly great and universal world above described?

§.7. BUT if they say, they do not shut up God within this finite universe, but do imagine him to exist in infinite imaginary spaces, both outside and inside of it. To this may be answered, if those spaces are merely imaginary, certainly then they are nothing but foolish fictions of the brain; but if they are real beings, what can they be but creatures of God? Besides, either God works in those spaces, or he does not: if he does not, then God is not there; for wherever he is, there he works; since this is his nature, that he must so act, as it is the nature of fire to burn, or of the sun to shine: for so God perpetually works; and his work is to create, or give being to creatures, according to that eternal idea or wisdom that is in him....

§.8. BUT this continual action or operation of God, as it is in him, or proceeds from him, or has respect unto him, is only one continual act or command of his will, and has neither time nor succession in it, nor first, nor last, but is together and always present with God. Thus nothing of him is either past or to come, because he has not parts: but so far as he appears or terminates in creatures, he has time and succession of parts....

§.9. ... and here it is to be noted, when I say the least particle of body, or matter so called, may be always divided into smaller parts, ad infinitum, so that no actual division can be made in any matter that is not always farther divisible, or capable to be divided into smaller parts, and that without end. Yet I would not hereby determine what the absolute power of God will or can do, as some do vainly and grossly dispute, but only hint at what the power of God probably may do, or will do, so far as he operates in and with his creatures: in as much as in all productions and generations, as well as in all resolutions and divisions, in the nature of bodies, or the creature, he never divides and never can divide any body into such small parts that each of these is not always capable of a further division; for the body of no creature can ever be reduced into its least parts, indeed, into such that it cannot be reduced back again, either by the most subtle operation of any creature, or created power. And this answer may suffice for our present purpose: for God makes no division in any body or matter, except in so far as he co-operates with the creatures, and therefore he never reduces creatures into their smallest parts, because then all motion and operation in creatures would cease (for it is the nature of all motion to wear and divide a thing into subtiler parts). To do this would be contrary to the wisdom and goodness of God; for if all motion and operation should cease in any particular creature, that creature would be altogether unprofitable and useless in the creation, and so would be no better than if it were a mere *non ens*, or nothing. But as was said before, God cannot do what is contrary to his wisdom and goodness, or any of his attributes ... mathematical division of things is never made *in minima*, but things may be physically divided into their smallest parts, as when concrete matter is so far divided that it departs into physical *monades*, as it was in the first state of its materiality....

§.10. MOREOVER the consideration of this infinite divisibility of everything into ever smaller parts is no unnecessary or unprofitable theory, but a thing of very great importance: thereby may be understood the reasons and causes of things, and how all creatures from the highest to the lowest are inseparably united with one another by means of subtler parts interceding or coming in between, which are the emanations of one creature into another, by which also they act upon one another at the greatest distance. This is the foundation of all sympathy and antipathy that happens in creatures: and if these things be well understood by anyone, he may easily see into the most secret and hidden causes of things, which ignorant men call occult qualities.

## CHAP. VII.

... here is to be observed, that though the spirit of man is commonly spoken in the singular, as though it were but one thing, the said spirit is a certain composition of more, indeed innumerable spirits, just as the body is a composition of more bodies and has a certain order and government in all its parts, much more so is the spirit a great army of spirits, wherein there are distinct offices under one governing spirit.

[...]

... every creature that has life, sense, or motion ought to be a number, or a multiplicity—indeed, a number without number, or infinite in respect of any created intellect. But if that is the case, ought not the central or governing spirit to be but one only atom; for otherwise how can it be called a centre, and the chief spirit, having dominion over the rest? I answer in the negative: for this centre itself, or the chief and governing spirit, is manifold, for the reasons before alleged; but it is called a centre because all the other spirits converge upon it, and lines from all parts of the circumference again depart out or proceed from it; and indeed the unity of the spirits that compose or make up this centre, or governing spirit, is firmer and more tenacious than that of all the other spirits, which are, as it were, the angels or ministering spirits of their prince or captain. Indeed, in man this unity is so great that nothing can dissolve it (although the unity of the greatest plenty of ministering spirits, which belong not to the composition of this centre, may be dissolved). Hence it comes to pass that the soul of every man shall remain an entire everlasting soul, or be of endless duration, that it may receive the proper fruit of its labour, and that the universal law of justice (which is written on everything) requires, which is a most strong and indissoluble band, to preserve this unity. For what is more congruous with this infinite justice and wisdom than this, that they who have joined together and consented to work either good or evil shall together receive their due reward and punishment, which cannot be if they should be dissipated or separated one from another; and the same reason proves that the central spirits of all other creatures remain indissoluble, and that although new central spirits are continually formed in the production of things, no central spirit is dissolved, but further promoted, or at least diminished according to its present dignity or indignity, capacity or incapacity.

# Appendix B: From Antonie van Leeuwenhoek's 1699 Letter to Antonio Magliabechi

[Antonie van Leeuwenhoek (1632-1723) was the founder of microbiology. A Dutch microscopist, he spent most of his very long life in Delft, in the Netherlands. He developed more advanced microscopes than had existed previously, and with them he discovered and described a great variety of micro-organisms, especially in water and other liquids. (The term he uses for every variety—of the immense variety—of micro-organisms that he observed, studied, and depicted, is "little animals" or "animalcules.") Beginning in 1674, he communicated these findings to the Royal Society in London, chiefly by means of a series of letters containing reports of his work. They were written in Dutch and sent at the earlier stage of his work to Henry Oldenburg (ca. 1615-77), the German-born first secretary of the Royal Society (from 1663 to 1677). Oldenburg translated lengthy portions of several of the letters into English, a number of these being read to the fellows of the Society and published in the *Philosophical Transactions of the Royal Society*. (Summaries of Leeuwenhoek's findings were also translated into French, and published in the *Journal des savants*, in 1678.) In addition to these texts, a joint Dutch and Latin edition of Leeuwenhoek's letters and reports was published. Leibniz came into the orbit of the Royal Society during this same period, likewise through Henry Oldenburg, and became acquainted with Leeuwenhoek and his work. In fact, Leibniz delivered, to Leeuwenhoek, Oldenburg's confirmation of receipt of one of the particularly important early letters, on the occasion of his famous visit to Spinoza in The Hague in October 1676. Subsequently Leibniz was to have an extensive correspondence with Leeuwenhoek. Several passages in Leibniz's writings, very abundantly including a number of sections of the *Monadology*, show vividly the significance of Leeuwenhoek's discoveries of tiny organisms, imperceptible by the naked eye, and themselves of variable sizes and natural properties, for Leibniz's metaphysical vision and system. The monads are not of course themselves micro-organisms, but the latter provided a kind of real-world modelling of realities concealed within appearances, and the prompting of a conception of a universe teeming with life. The letter from which an excerpt appears here was written to a Florentine scholar, Antonio Magliabechi,[1] in 1699, several decades after Leeuwenhoek's research had begun. It was published in an edition of some of Leeuwenhoek's work, translated by Samuel Hoole, in 1807.[2]]

*A description of some species of minute Insects, found in fresh water, in a Letter to Signor Anthonio Magliabechi, at Florence.*

In reliance on your accustomed friendship, I have been induced to impart to you my observations and reflections respecting some very minute animalcules, hitherto very little noticed, which are found in the waters of this country.

Being employed in searching after certain animalcules, which I expected to find in those ditches or canals which divide our fields, I saw various species of creatures, but none of those which I was then in search of. Among these I observed certain animalcules, within whose bodies I saw so quick a motion as to exceed belief; they were about the size of a large grain of sand, and their bodies being transparent, that internal motion could plainly be seen. Among other things, I saw in the body of one of these animalcules a bright and round corpuscle, placed near the head, and in which a very wonderful swift motion was to be seen, consisting of an alternate extension and contraction. This particle I concluded to be the heart, and that the rapid motion of the parts round about it, which I observed in this animalcule, and the motion that I had seen in the others, proceeded from the action of the heart.

Upon observing in one of these animalcules eight or nine greenish particles, I began to think that those were unborn young ones; to ascertain this I put one of the animalcules into a little water, being the quantity of five or six drops, so that I

---

1 Antonio Magliabechi (1633-1714) was a noted scholar, and librarian to the Grand Duke of Tuscany.
2 In Samuel Hoole, *The Select Works of Antony van Leeuwenhoek*, containing his *Microscopical Discoveries in many of the works of nature*, translated from the Dutch and Latin editions published by the author (London: The Philanthropic Society, 1807), vol. II, part III, pp. 82ff.

might thereby see the young when newly issued from the parent and swimming in the water: but the next day, finding the animal dead, I opened its body while lying in the water, and then I not only very plainly saw most of the unborn young ones, but I could also discern the organs or limbs provided for their use in swimming.

This animalcule was of such a pretty shape that I often viewed it with great admiration: indeed, I was so much pleased with its formation, that I thought larger animals viewed with the naked eye would, in comparison with this, appear rudely made. The death of this creature seemed to me to be caused by want of food, because I had seen it frequently void its excrements, whence I concluded that it required a large supply of nutriment in proportion to its size.

After this I discovered another species of animalcule, almost of the same size with the former ones, but of entirely different make. This animalcule had a long forked tail, and each of the forked parts again divided into four parts, which last parts were provided with various organs.

But observing one of these animalcules (though of the same species) to appear as if the hind part of its body was formed in a very different manner, I put two of them into a small portion of water, in order to examine them by a microscope of greater magnifying power. By the help of this, I perceived that those parts near the tail, and which appeared like two bunches of grapes, were in fact the animal's eggs, so placed together that there were about three or four eggs in breadth, and nine or ten in length, joined to each other, but of a round shape, at each extremity, and the whole bearing the appearance of a bunch of grapes.

# Appendix C: From Pierre Bayle, Historical and Critical Dictionary (1695-1702)

[Pierre Bayle (1647-1706), an almost exact contemporary of Leibniz, was an originally Calvinist-Protestant, then Catholic, then again Calvinist—and perhaps (scholarly views differ) ultimately non-Christian—philosopher who achieved extraordinary prominence in the 1690s, and beyond, as the author of a huge work of reference, the *Historical and Critical Dictionary*. Originally published in two volumes, it had expanded to almost eight million words by the time of Bayle's death; the fifth edition, of 1740, consists of ten volumes. Amazingly widely read and influential, the *Dictionary* had special significance as the source of and stimulus to religious and other forms of skepticism in the eighteenth century. Originally from France, Bayle eventually settled in the Netherlands, in Rotterdam, where he spent the latter part of his life. A part of one of the *Dictionary*'s articles is reprinted here. The article—"Rorarius"[1]—contains an extensive critical discussion of aspects of Leibniz's philosophy, to which Leibniz responded at length, sometimes with great animation, in the *Monadology* and in other works. The *Dictionary* has a complex structure. It consists of articles on topics and personages—ancient, contemporary, real, mythological—with accompanying sets of notes and comments (the whole written by Bayle). It is usually in the latter that the philosophical heart of the work is to be found. Bayle sometimes adds footnotes to his footnotes, which makes for a complex if not daunting read. (In the passage excerpted below, for example, 'H' and 'L' designate footnotes in Bayle's text, and 'd' indicates a footnote that Bayle has provided, within 'H'.) The translation—the first English translation of the work—appeared in 1710. The translator, Pierre des Maizeaux (1673-1745), was primary translator of subsequent editions of the *Dictionary* as well. (The full ten-volume edition of 1734-41

---

1  Hieronymus Rorarius (1485-1556), papal emissary at the court of Ferdinand of Hungary.

also involved the contributions of Thomas Birch, John Peter Bernard, and John Lockman. The "Rorarius" article was only slightly modified by des Maizeaux in the later edition. The earlier text represents the English version that would have been available and current during Leibniz's lifetime.) It has been lightly modernized.]

... The author, who has best confuted the opinion of *Descartes* concerning the souls of beasts, would have done us a singular favour, if he could have cleared ... the common opinion from the great difficulties that attend it. Mr. Leibniz, one of the greatest wits of *Europe*, being sensible of these difficulties, has given us some hints, which (*H*) deserve to be considered. I shall mention part of what he says upon this subject, were it only to propose my doubts....

(*H*) *Has given us some hints, which deserve to be considered.*]
(d)[1] He approves the opinion of some moderns, who think that animals are organized in the seed; and besides he believes ... that matter alone cannot constitute a true unity, and that therefore every animal is united to a form, which is a simple and indivisible being. Moreover he supposes ... that this form never leaves its subject; from whence it results that properly speaking, there is no death nor generation in nature. He ... excepts the soul of man from all this; he lays it aside, &c. This hypothesis ... frees us from some difficulties. There's no longer any need to answer the pressing objections raised against the schoolmen. The soul of a beast, say their adversaries, is a substance distinct from the body; it must therefore be produced by creation, and destroyed by annihilation: heat ... must therefore have the power to create souls, and to ... annihilate them, than which nothing can be more absurd. The answers of the Aristotelians to this objection do not deserve to be mentioned ...

(d) [Bayle's footnote:] See M. Leibniz's article inserted in the *Journal des Savans* of the 27 June 1695 ... [The article to which

---

1  This is Bayle's footnote symbol. See the corresponding text in footnote (d) below. The footnote continues until the (L) that appears below.

Bayle refers is the essay entitled "Système nouveau de la nature et de la communication des substances, aussi bien que de l'union qu'il y a entre l'Ame et le corps" ("New System of Nature and of the Communication of Substances, as well as of the Union of Soul and Body"). Bayle's several subsequent citations from the work are omitted.]

Mr. *Leibniz*'s hypothesis ... induces us to believe, (1) that God in the beginning of the world created the forms of all bodies, and consequently all the souls of beasts: (2) that those souls have subsisted ever since, being inseparably united to the first organized bodies in which God placed them. The transmigration of souls becomes needless in this hypothesis, without which there would be a necessity to admit of it. I shall set down part of Mr. *Leibniz*'s Discourse, that my readers may see whether I have taken his sense right. "... Here the *transformations* of *Swammerdam*, *Malpighius*, and *Leeuwenhoeck*,[1] some of the most excellent observators of our time, came to my assistance, and made me more easily believe that animals, or any other organized beings, do not begin to exist when we think they do, and that their seeming generation is only an unfolding, and a kind of augmentation. I have observed that the author of the *Recherche de la vérité* [Malebranche], Mr. *Régis*, Mr. *Hartsoeker*,[2] and some other able men are not far from this opinion. But the greatest question remains still, viz. what becomes of those souls or forms after the death of the animal, or the destruction of the organized being? This is the most perplexing thing; because it does not seem reasonable that souls should remain needlessly in a chaos or confused matter. This made me think at last that the only way left is to say that not only the souls, but also the animals themselves, and their organized machines are preserved, though the destruction of the gross particles has reduced them to a smallness that is as imperceptible as it was before they were born. And indeed

1   Jan Swammerdam (1637-80), Dutch biologist and microscopist; Marcello Malpighi (1628-94), Italian physician and physiologist; for Antonie van Leeuwenhoek, see Appendix B.
2   For Nicolas Malebranche, see p. 90, note 1; Pierre-Sylvain Régis (1632-1707), French Cartesian philosopher, and critic of Spinoza; Nicolaas Hartsoeker (1656-1725), Dutch mathematician and physicist.

nobody can exactly fix the true time of death, which may pass a long time for a mere suspension of visible actions, and at the bottom is never anything else in mere animals: as it appears from the *resuscitations* of flies drowned, and then buried under pulverized chalk, and many such like, which sufficiently show that there would be many other *resuscitations*, traced up higher, if men were able to put again the machine in order.... It is therefore natural that the animals having been always alive and organized (as some persons of great penetration begin to acknowledge) should always continue so. And since there is no birth, nor a quite new generation of animals, it follows that there will be no final extinction of them, nor an entire death taken in a strict metaphysical sense; and consequently that instead of the transmigration of souls, there is only a transformation of the same animal, according as its organs are differently folded, and more or less open and unfolded."[1]

[...]

There are some things in *M. Leibniz*'s hypothesis, that are liable to some difficulties, though they show the great extent of his genius. He will have it, for instance, that the soul of a dog acts independently upon outward bodies; ... "*that it stands upon its own bottom, by a perfect* spontaneity *with respect to itself, and yet with a perfect* conformity *to outward things ... that its internal perceptions arise from its original constitution, that is to say, representative (capable of expressing beings out of itself, with respect to its organs) which was bestowed upon it from the time of its creation, and makes its individual character.*" From whence it results, that it would feel hunger and thirst at such an hour, though there were not any one body in the universe, and though *nothing should exist but God and that soul*. He explains ... his thought by the example of two *pendulums* that should perfectly agree: That is, he supposes that according to the particular laws, which put the soul upon action, it must feel hunger at such an hour; and that according to the particular laws, which direct the motion of matter, the body that is united to that soul must be modified at that same hour, as it is modified when the soul is hungry. I'll forbear preferring

---

1 This is also taken from Leibniz's piece of 27 June 1695.

this system to that of occasional causes, till the learned author has perfected it. I cannot apprehend the connexion of internal and spontaneous actions, which would have this effect, that the soul of a dog would feel pain immediately after having felt joy, though it were alone in the universe. I understand why a dog passes immediately from pleasure to pain, when being very hungry, and eating a piece of bread, he is suddenly struck with a cudgel; but I cannot apprehend that his soul should be so framed, that at the very moment he is beaten, he would feel pain, though he were not beaten, and though he should continue to eat bread without any trouble or hindrance. Nor do I see how the *spontaneity* of that soul should be consistent with the sense of pain, and in general with all unpleasing perceptions. Besides, the reason why this learned man does not like the Cartesian system seems to me to be a false supposition; for it cannot be said that the system of occasional causes brings in God acting by a miracle ..., *Deum ex machina*, in the mutual dependency of the body and soul: for since God does only intervene according to general laws, he cannot be said to act in an extraordinary manner. Does the internal and active virtue communicated to the forms of bodies, according to *Mr. Leibniz*, know the train of actions which it is to produce? By no means; for we know by experience that we are ignorant whether we shall have such and such perceptions in an hour's time. It were therefore necessary that the forms should be directed by some external principle in the production of their actions. But this would be *Deus ex machina* as well as in the system of occasional causes.... To conclude, as he supposes with great reason that all souls are simple and indivisible, one cannot apprehend how they can be compared with a *pendulum*, that is, how by their original constitution they can diversify their operations, by using the spontaneous activity bestowed upon them by their creator. One may clearly conceive that a simple being will always act in a uniform manner, if no external cause hinders it. If it was composed of several pieces as a machine, it would act different ways, because the peculiar activity of each piece might change every moment the activity of others: but how will you find in a simple substance the cause of a change of operation?

(L).[1] *Of the Observations which I design to make upon* M. Leibniz's *Reflections.*]

I declare first of all that I am very glad I have proposed some small difficulties against the system of that great philosopher, since they have occasioned some answers, whereby that subject has been made clearer to me, and I have more distinctly discovered the wonderful part of it. I look now upon that system as an important conquest, which enlarges the bounds of philosophy. We had only two hypotheses, that of the schools, and that of the *Cartesians*: the one was a *way of influence* of the body upon the soul, and of the soul upon the body; the other was a *way of assistance*, or occasional causality. But here is a new acquisition, a new hypothesis, which may be called ... *a way of pre-established harmony*. We are beholden for it to Mr. *Leibniz*, and it is impossible to conceive of anything that gives us a nobler idea of the power and wisdom of the author of all things. This, together with the advantage of removing all notions of a miraculous conduct, would move me to prefer this new system to that of the *Cartesians*, if I could conceive a possibility in the way of *pre-established harmony*....

... Let us apply his system concerning the union of the soul with the body to the person of *Julius Caesar.*

II. We must say according to this system that the body of *Julius Caesar* did so exercise its moving faculty, that from its birth to its death, it went through continual changes, which did most exactly answer the perpetual changes of a certain soul that it did not know, and that made no impression upon it. We must say that the rule, according to which that faculty of *Caesar*'s body exerted itself, was such that he would have gone to the Senate upon such a day, and at such an hour; that he would have spoke there such and such words, &c. though God had been willing to annihilate his soul the next day after it was created. We must say that this moving faculty did punctually change and modify itself according to the volubility of the thoughts of that ambitious

---

1   This is a footnote to a part of Bayle's entry that has not been included in this selection. It comprises the remainder of the material in this appendix.

spirit; and that it was affected precisely in a certain manner, rather than in another, because the soul of *Caesar* passed from a certain thought to another. Can a blind power modify itself so exactly by virtue of an impression, communicated thirty or forty years before, and which was never renewed since, and which is left to itself, without ever knowing what it is to do?

# Appendix D: From G.W. Leibniz, Theodicy *(1710)*

[Leibniz's *Theodicy* was the only book-length publication of his to appear during his lifetime. (He had written an earlier book, *The New Essays on Human Understanding*, which was to be published long after his death, in 1765.) *Essais de Théodicée sur la Bonté de Dieu, la Liberté de l'Homme et l'Origine du Mal* to give the work its full title—was to widely extend and augment the fame and reputation of its author. The *Theodicy* is one of the many important sources for the investigation of the philosophy of Leibniz; but it has a special additional role for the purposes of the present volume. When Leibniz wrote the *Monadology*, while in Vienna in 1714, he thought fit to include in it references following very many of its numbered sections to sections of the *Theodicy*, which he evidently thought buttressed or significantly reinforced the brief and sometimes cryptic utterances of the later work. The reader will find below a number of the sections of the *Theodicy* cited in the *Monadology*, particularly including passages that help elucidate some of the central claims and ideas of the *Monadology*, and of Leibniz's metaphysical system more broadly. The translation is by E.M. Huggard,[1] lightly modernized in some passages.]

## PREFACE

[...]

It is clear that Jesus Christ, completing what Moses had begun, wished that the Divinity should be the object not only of our fear and veneration but also of our love and devotion. Thus he made men happy by anticipation and gave them here on Earth a foretaste of future felicity. For there is nothing so agreeable as loving

---

1 G.W. Leibniz, *Theodicy: Essays on the Goodness of God, the Freedom of Man, and the Origin of Evil*. Edited by Austin Farrer and translated by Eveleen M. Huggard. Originally published by Routledge & Keegan Paul, 1951. Reproduced by permission of Taylor & Francis Books UK.

what is worthy of love. Love is that mental state that makes us take pleasure in the perfections of the object of our love, and there is nothing more perfect than God, nor any greater delight than in him. To love him it suffices to contemplate his perfections, a thing easy indeed, because we find the ideas of these within ourselves. The perfections of God are those of our souls, but he possesses them in boundless measure; he is an Ocean, of which only drops have been granted to us; there is in us some power, some knowledge, some goodness, but in God they are all in their entirety. Order, proportions, harmony delight us; painting and music are samples of these: God is all order; he always keeps truth of proportions, he makes universal harmony; all beauty is an effusion of his rays.

It follows manifestly that true piety and even true felicity consist in the love of God, but a love so enlightened that its fervour is attended by insight. This kind of love begets the pleasure in good actions that gives relief to virtue, and, relating all to God as to the centre, transports the human to the divine. For in doing one's duty, in obeying reason, one carries out the orders of Supreme Reason. One directs all one's intentions to the common good, which is none other than the glory of God. Thus one finds that there is no greater individual interest than to espouse that of the community, and one gains satisfaction for oneself by taking pleasure in the acquisition of true benefits for men. Whether one succeeds in this or not, one is content with what comes to pass, being once resigned to the will of God and knowing that what he wills is best. But before he declares his will by the event, one endeavours to find it out by doing what appears most in accord with his commands. When we are in this state of mind, we are not disheartened by ill success; we regret only our faults; and the ungrateful ways of men cause no relaxation in the exercise of our kindly disposition. Our charity is humble and full of moderation; it presumes not to domineer; attentive alike to our own faults and to the talents of others, we are inclined to criticize our own actions and to excuse and vindicate those of others. We must work out our own perfection and do wrong to no man. There is no piety where there is not charity; and without being kindly and beneficent one cannot show sincere religion.

But the difficulty is great, above all, in relation to God's dispositions for the salvation of men. There are few saved or chosen; therefore the choice of many is not God's decreed will. And since it is admitted that those whom he has chosen deserve it no more than the rest, and are not even fundamentally less evil, the goodness that they have coming only from the gift of God, the difficulty is increased. Where is, then, his justice (people will say), or at the least, where is his goodness? Partiality, or respect of persons, goes against justice, and he who without cause sets bounds to his goodness cannot have it in sufficient measure. It is true that those who are not chosen are lost by their own fault: they lack good will or living faith; but it rested with God alone to grant it to them. We know that besides inward grace there are usually outward circumstances that distinguish men, and that training, conversation, and example often correct or corrupt natural disposition....

I hope to remove all these difficulties. I will point out that absolute necessity, which is called also logical and metaphysical and sometimes geometrical, and which would alone be formidable in this connexion, does not exist in free actions, and that thus freedom is exempt not only from constraint but also from real necessity. I will show that God himself, although he always chooses the best, does not act by an absolute necessity, and that the laws of nature laid down by God, founded upon the fitness of things, keep the mean between geometrical truths, absolutely necessary, and arbitrary decrees, which M. Bayle and other modern philosophers have not sufficiently understood. Further I will show that there is an indifference in freedom, because there is no absolute necessity for one course or the other; yet there is never an indifference of perfect equipoise. And I will demonstrate that there is in free actions a perfect spontaneity beyond all that has been conceived before. Finally I will make it plain that the hypothetical and the moral necessity that subsist in free actions are open to no objection, and that the "Lazy Reason"[1] is a pure sophism.

Likewise concerning the origin of evil in its relation to God, I offer a vindication of his perfections that shall extol no less his holiness, his justice, and his goodness than his greatness, his power, and his independence. I show how it is possible for everything

---

1 This was a piece of fallacious reasoning identified by this name in antiquity. It takes the form of inferring that because it was predetermined that some event would occur as a consequence of an action that some agent would perform, then that agent need not bother to perform his or her action; the consequence will have been predetermined to happen anyway.

to depend upon God, for him to co-operate in all the actions of creatures, even, if you will, to create these creatures continually, and nevertheless not to be the author of sin. Here also it is demonstrated how the privative nature of evil should be understood. Much more than that, I explain how evil has a source other than the will of God, and that one is right therefore to say of moral evil that God wills it not, but simply permits it. Most important of all, however, I show that it has been possible for God to permit sin and misery, and even to co-operate in and promote it, without detriment to his holiness and his supreme goodness: although, generally speaking, he could have avoided all these evils.

I had published a new system, which seemed well adapted to explain the union of the soul and the body: it met with considerable applause even from those who were not in agreement with it, and certain competent persons testified that they had already been of my opinion, without having reached so distinct an explanation, before they saw what I had written on the matter. M. Bayle examined it in his *Historical and Critical Dictionary*, article "Rorarius."[1] He thought that my expositions were worthy of further development; he drew attention to their usefulness in various connexions, and he laid stress upon what might still cause difficulty. I could only reply in a suitable way to expressions so civil and to reflexions so instructive as his....

... I endeavoured to make clear that in reality mechanism is sufficient to produce the organic bodies of animals, without any need of other plastic natures, provided there be added the *preformation* already completely organic in the seeds of the bodies that come into existence, contained in those of the bodies from which they spring, right back to the primary seeds. This could proceed only from the Author of things, infinitely powerful and infinitely wise, who, creating all in the beginning in due order, had *pre-established* there all order and artifice that was to be. There is no chaos in the inward nature of things, and there is organism everywhere in a matter whose disposition proceeds from God. More and more of it would come to light if we pressed closer our examination of the anatomy of bodies; and we should continue to observe it even if we could go on to infinity, like Nature, and make subdivision as continuous in our knowledge as Nature has made it in fact.

In order to explain this marvel of the formation of animals, I

---

1 See Appendix C.

made use of a Pre-established Harmony, that is to say, of the same means I had used to explain another marvel, namely the correspondence of soul with body, in which I proved the uniformity and the fecundity of the principles I had employed.... Moreover, as God orders all things at once beforehand, the accuracy of the path of this vessel would be no more strange than that of a fuse passing along a cord in fireworks, since the whole disposition of things preserves a perfect harmony between them by means of their influence upon one another....

For having made new discoveries on the nature of active force and the laws of motion, I have shown that they have no geometrical necessity, as Spinoza appears to have believed they had. Neither, as I have made plain, are they purely arbitrary, even though this is the opinion of M. Bayle and of some modern philosophers: but they are dependent upon the fitness of things, as I have already pointed out above, or upon what I call the "principle of the best." Moreover one recognizes therein, as in every other thing, the marks of the first substance, whose productions bear the stamp of a supreme wisdom and make the most perfect of harmonies. I have shown also that this harmony connects both the future with the past and the present with the absent. The first kind of connexion unites times, and the other places. This second connexion is displayed in the union of the soul with the body, and in general in the communication of true substances with one another and with material phenomena. But the first takes place in the preformation of organic bodies, or rather of all bodies, since there is organism everywhere, although all masses do not compose organic bodies. So a pond may very well be full of fish or of other organic bodies, although it is not itself an animal or organic body, but only a mass that contains them....

It will perhaps be good to add the observation, before finishing this preface, that in denying the physical influence of the soul upon the body or of the body upon the soul, that is, an influence causing the one to disturb the laws of the other, I by no means deny the union of the one with the other that forms a suppositum; but this union is something metaphysical, which changes nothing in the phenomena.... And for this reason one may say also in a metaphysical sense that the soul acts upon the body and the body upon the soul. Moreover, it is true that the soul is the entelechy or the active principle, whereas the corporeal alone or the mere material contains only the passive. Consequently the principle of action is in the soul, as I have explained more than once in the *Leipzig Journal*.

[...]

## PRELIMINARY DISSERTATION ON THE CONFORMITY OF FAITH WITH REASON

[...]

65. The *external* senses, properly speaking, do not deceive us. It is our inner sense that often makes us go too fast. That occurs also in brute beasts, as when a dog barks at his reflexion in the mirror: for beasts have *consecutions* of perception that resemble reasoning, and that occur also in the inner sense of men, when their actions have only an empirical quality. But beasts do nothing that compels us to believe that they have what deserves to be properly called a *reasoning* sense, as I have shown elsewhere. Now when the understanding uses and follows the false decision of the inner sense (as when the famous Galileo thought that Saturn had two handles) it is deceived by the judgement it makes upon the effect of appearances, and it infers from them more than they imply. For the appearances of the senses do not promise us absolutely the truth of things, any more than dreams do. It is we who deceive ourselves by the use we make of them, that is, by our consecutions. Indeed we allow ourselves to be deluded by probable arguments, and we are inclined to think that phenomena such as we have found linked together often are always so....

[...]

## ESSAYS ON THE JUSTICE OF GOD AND THE FREEDOM OF MAN IN THE ORIGIN OF EVIL

### PART ONE

[...]

7. *God is the first reason of things*: for such things as are bounded, as all that we see and experience are contingent and have nothing in them to render their existence necessary, it being plain

that time, space, and matter, united and uniform in themselves and indifferent to everything, might have received entirely other motions and shapes, and in another order. Therefore one must seek the reason for the existence of the world, which is the whole assemblage of *contingent* things, and seek it in the substance that carries with it the reason for its existence, and that in consequence is *necessary* and eternal. Moreover, this cause must be intelligent: for this existing world being contingent and an infinity of other worlds being equally possible, and holding, so to say, equal claim to existence with it, the cause of the world must have had regard or reference to all these possible worlds in order to fix upon one of them. This regard or relation of an existent substance to simple possibilities can be nothing other than the *understanding* that has the ideas of them, while to fix upon one of them can be nothing other than the act of the *will* that chooses. It is the *power* of this substance that renders its will efficacious. Power relates to *being*, wisdom or understanding to *truth*, and will to *good*. And this intelligent cause ought to be infinite in all ways, and absolutely perfect in *power*, in *wisdom*, and in *goodness*, since it relates to all that is possible. Furthermore, since all is connected together, there is no ground for admitting more than *one*. Its understanding is the source of *essences*, and its will is the origin of *existences*. There in few words is the proof of one God with his perfections, and through him of the origin of things.

8. Now this supreme wisdom, united to a goodness that is no less infinite, can only have chosen the best. For as a lesser evil is a kind of good, even so a lesser good is a kind of evil if it stands in the way of a greater good; and there would be something to correct in the actions of God if it were possible to do better. As in mathematics, when there is no maximum nor minimum, in short nothing distinguished, everything is done equally, or when that is not possible nothing at all is done: so it may be said likewise in respect of perfect wisdom, which is no less orderly than mathematics, that if there were not the best (*optimum*) among all possible worlds, God would not have produced any. I call "world" the whole succession and the whole agglomeration of all existent things, lest it be said that several worlds could have existed in different times and different places. For they must be reckoned all together as one world or, if you will, as one universe. And even if one filled all times and all places, it would still remain true

that one might have filled them in innumerable ways, and that there would be an infinitude of possible worlds among which God must have chosen the best, since he does nothing without acting in accordance with supreme reason.

9. Some adversary not being able to answer this argument will perchance answer the conclusion with a counter-argument, saying that the world could have been without sin and without sufferings; but I deny that then it would have been *better*. For it must be known that all things are *connected* in each one of the possible worlds: the universe, whatever it may be, is all of one piece, like an ocean: the smallest movement extends its effect there to any distance whatsoever, even though this effect becomes less perceptible in proportion to the distance. In this God has ordered all things beforehand once and for all, having foreseen prayers, good and bad actions, and all the rest; and each thing *as an idea* has contributed, before its existence, to the resolution that has been made upon the existence of all things; so that nothing can be changed in the universe (any more than in a number) save its essence or, if you will, save its *numerical individuality*. Thus, if the smallest evil that comes to pass in the world were missing in it, it would no longer be this world; which, with nothing omitted and all allowance made, was found the best by the Creator who chose it.

... What will become of the consideration of our globe and its inhabitants? Will it not be something incomparably less than a physical point, since our earth is as a point in comparison with the distance of some fixed stars? Thus since the proportion of the part of the universe that we know is almost lost in nothingness compared with what is unknown and yet have cause to assume, and since all the evils that may be raised in objection before us are in this near nothingness, it may be that all evils are almost nothingness in comparison with the good things that are in the universe.

20. But it is necessary also to meet the more speculative and metaphysical difficulties that have been mentioned and that concern the cause of evil. The question is asked first of all, where does evil come from? *Si Deus est, unde malum? Si non est, unde bonum?*[1]

---

1  "If God exists, where does evil come from? If he does not exist, where does good come from?" (Boethius, *The Consolation of Philosophy*, Book 1, Prose 4 [Boethius cites Epicurus for the view expressed; the quotation itself appears earlier in Lactantius, *De ira Dei* 13.21]).

22. But someone will say to me: why do you speak to us of "permitting"? Is it not God that does the evil and that wills it? Here it will be necessary to explain what "permission" is, so that it may be seen how this term is not employed without reason. But before that, one must explain the nature of will, which has its own degrees. Taking it in the general sense, one may say that *will* consists in the inclination to do something in proportion to the good it contains. This will is called *antecedent* when it is detached, and considers each good separately in the capacity of a good. In this sense it may be said that God tends to all good, as good, *ad perfectionem simpliciter simplicem*,[1] to speak like the schoolmen, and by an antecedent will. He is earnestly disposed to sanctify and to save all men, to exclude sin, and to prevent damnation. It may even be said that this will is efficacious *of itself (per se)*, that is, in such sort that the effect would ensue if there were not some stronger reason to prevent it: for this will does not pass into final exercise (*ad summum conatum*[2]), or it would never fail to produce its full effect, God being the master of all things. Success both entire and infallible belongs only to the *consequent will*, as it is called. This alone is complete; and in regard to it this rule obtains, that one never fails to do what one wills, when one has the power. Now this consequent will, final and decisive, results from the conflict of all the antecedent wills, of those that tend towards good, even as of those that repel evil; and from the concurrence of all these particular wills comes the total will. So in mechanics compound movement results from all the tendencies that concur in one and the same moving body, and satisfies each one equally, in so far as it is possible to do all at one time. It is as if the moving body took equal account of these tendencies, as I once showed in one of the Paris Journals (7 September 1693), when giving the general law of the compositions of movement. In this sense also it may be said that the antecedent will is efficacious in a sense and even effective with success.

27. It is indeed beyond question that we must refrain from preventing the sin of others when we cannot prevent their sin without sinning ourselves. But someone will perhaps bring up the objection that it is God himself who acts and who effects all

---

1  "For simple perfection in the simple sense."
2  "With the greatest effort."

that is real in the sin of the creature. This objection leads us to consider the *physical co-operation* of God with the creature, after we have examined the *moral co-operation*, which was the more perplexing.... But one cannot say in relation to God what "to conserve" is, without reverting to the general opinion. Also it must be taken into account that the action of God in conserving should have some reference to what is conserved, according to what it is and to the state in which it is; thus his action cannot be general or indeterminate. These generalities are abstractions not to be found in the truth of individual things, and the conservation of a man standing is different from the conservation of a man seated. This would not be so if conservation consisted only in the act of preventing and warding off some foreign cause that could destroy what one wishes to conserve, as often happens when men conserve something. But apart from the fact that we are obliged ourselves sometimes to maintain what we conserve, we must bear in mind that conservation by God consists in the perpetual immediate influence that the dependence of creatures demands. This dependence attaches not only to the substance but also to the action, and one can perhaps not explain it better than by saying, with theologians and philosophers in general, that it is a continued creation.

28. The objection will be made that God therefore now creates man as a sinner, he who in the beginning created him innocent. But here it must be said, with regard to the moral aspect, that God being supremely wise cannot fail to observe certain laws, and to act according to the rules, both physical and moral, that wisdom has made him choose. And the same reason that has made him create man innocent, but liable to fall, makes him re-create man when he falls; for God's knowledge causes the future to be for him as the present, and prevents him from rescinding the resolutions made.

... Let us now compare the force that the current exercises on boats, and communicates to them, with the action of God, who produces and conserves whatever is positive in creatures, and gives them perfection, being, and force: let us compare, I say, the inertia of matter with the natural imperfection of creatures, and the slowness of the laden boat with the defects to be found in the qualities and the action of the creature; and we shall find that there is nothing so just as this comparison. The current is the cause of the boat's movement, but not of its retardation; God is the cause of perfection in the nature and the actions of the creature, but the limitation of the receptivity of the creature is the cause of the defects there are in its action. Thus the Platonists, St. Augustine, and the schoolmen were right to say that God is the cause of the material element of evil that lies in the positive, and not of the formal element, which lies in privation. Even so one may say that the current is the cause of the material element of the retardation, but not of the formal: that is, it is the cause of the boat's speed without being the cause of the limits to this speed. And God is no more the cause of sin than the river's current is the cause of the retardation of the boat. Force also in relation to matter is as the spirit in relation to the flesh; the spirit is willing and the flesh is weak, and spirits act ... *quantum non noxia corpora tardant*.[1]

31. There is, then, a wholly similar relation between such and such an action of God, and such and such a passion or reception of the creature, which in the ordinary course of things is perfected only in proportion to its "receptivity," such is the term used. And when it is said that the creature depends upon God in so far as it exists and in so far as it acts, and even that conservation is a continual creation, this is true in that God gives ever to the creature and produces continually all that in it is positive, good, and perfect, every perfect gift coming from the Father of lights. The imperfections, on the other hand, and the defects in operations spring from the original limitation that the creature could not but receive with the first beginning of its being, through the ideal reasons that restrict it. For God could not give the creature all without making of it a God; therefore there must be different degrees in the perfection of things, and limitations also of every kind.

36. But let us pass to the difficulties. Philosophers agree today that the truth of contingent futurities is determinate, that is to say that contingent futurities are future, or that they will be, that they will happen: for it is as sure that the future will be, as it is

---

1 "Insofar as harmful bodies do not slow them down" (Virgil, *Aeneid* 6, 731).

sure that the past has been. It was true already a hundred years ago that I should write today, as it will be true after a hundred years that I have written. Thus the contingent is not, because it is future, any the less contingent; and *determination*, which would be called certainty if it were known, is not incompatible with contingency. Often the certain and the determinate are taken as one thing, because a determinate truth is capable of being known: thus it may be said that determination is an objective certainty.

37. This determination comes from the very nature of truth, and cannot injure freedom: but there are other determinations taken from elsewhere, and in the first place from the foreknowledge of God, which many have held to be contrary to freedom. They say that what is foreseen cannot fail to exist, and they say so truly; but it follows not that what is foreseen is necessary, for *necessary truth* is the one of which the contrary is impossible or implies contradiction. Now this truth that states that I shall write tomorrow is not of that nature; it is not necessary. Yet supposing that God foresees it, it is necessary that it come to pass; that is, the consequence is necessary, namely, that it exist, since it has been foreseen; for God is infallible. This is what is termed a *hypothetical necessity*. But our concern is not this necessity: it is an *absolute necessity* that is required, to be able to say that an action is necessary, that it is not contingent, that it is not the effect of a free choice. Besides it is very easily seen that foreknowledge in itself adds nothing to the determination of the truth of contingent futurities, save that this determination is known: and this does not augment the determination or the "futurition" (as it is termed) of these events, the one on which we agreed at the outset.

44. Nevertheless, objective certainty or determination does not bring about the necessity of the determinate truth. All philosophers acknowledge this, asserting that the truth of contingent futurities is determinate, and that nevertheless they remain contingent. The thing indeed would imply no contradiction in itself if the effect did not follow; and therein lies contingency. To better understand this point, we must take into account that there are two great principles of our arguments. The one is the principle of *contradiction*, stating that of two contradictory

propositions one is true, the other false; the other principle is that of the *determinant reason*: it states that nothing ever comes to pass without there being a cause or at least a reason determining it, that is, something to give an *a priori* reason why it is existent rather than non-existent, and in this way rather than in any other. This great principle holds for all events, and a contrary instance will never be supplied: and although more often than not we are insufficiently acquainted with these determinant reasons, we perceive nevertheless that there are such. Were it not for this great principle we could never prove the existence of God, and we would lose an infinitude of very just and very profitable arguments of which it is the foundation; moreover, it suffers no exception, for otherwise its force would be weakened. Besides, nothing is so weak as those systems where all is unsteady and full of exceptions. That fault cannot be laid to the charge of the system I approve, where everything happens in accordance with general rules that at most are mutually restrictive.

45. We must therefore not imagine with some schoolmen, whose ideas tend towards the chimerical, that free contingent futurities have the privilege of exemption from this general rule of the nature of things. There is always a prevailing reason that prompts the will to its choice, and for the maintenance of freedom for the will it suffices that this reason should incline without necessitating. That is also the opinion of all the ancients, of Plato, of Aristotle, of St. Augustine. The will is never prompted to action save by the representation of the good, which prevails over the opposite representations. This is admitted even in relation to God, the good angels, and the souls in bliss: and it is acknowledged that they are none the less free in consequence of that. God fails not to choose the best, but he is not constrained to do so: indeed, there is no necessity in the object of God's choice, for another sequence of things is equally possible. For that very reason the choice is free and independent of necessity, because it is made between several possibles, and the will is determined only by the preponderating goodness of the object. This is therefore not a defect where God and the saints are concerned: on the contrary, it would be a great defect, or rather a manifest absurdity, were it otherwise, even in men here on Earth, and if they were capable of acting without any inclining reason. Of such absurdity no example will ever be found; and even supposing one takes a

certain course out of caprice, to demonstrate one's freedom, the pleasure or advantage one thinks to find in this conceit is one of the reasons tending towards it.

52. All is therefore certain and determined beforehand in man, as everywhere else, and the human soul is a kind of *spiritual automaton*, although contingent actions in general and free action in particular are not on that account necessary with an absolute necessity, which would be truly incompatible with contingency. Thus neither futurition in itself, certain as it is, nor the infallible prevision of God, nor the predetermination either of causes or of God's decrees destroys this contingency and this freedom. That is acknowledged in respect of futurition and prevision, as has already been set forth. Since, moreover, God's decree consists solely in the resolution he forms, after having compared all possible worlds, to choose the one that is the best, and bring it into existence together with all that this world contains, by means of the all-powerful word *Fiat*, it is plain to see that this decree changes nothing in the constitution of things: God leaves them just as they were in the state of mere possibility, that is, changing nothing either in their essence or nature, or even in their accidents, which are represented perfectly already in the idea of this possible world. Thus what is contingent and free remains no less so under the decrees of God than under his prevision.

53. But could God himself (it will be said) then change nothing in the world? Assuredly he could not now change it, without derogation to his wisdom, since he has foreseen the existence of this world and of what it contains, and since, likewise, he has formed this resolution to bring it into existence: for he cannot be mistaken nor repent, and he did not need to form an imperfect resolution applying to one part and not the whole. Thus, all being ordered from the beginning, it is only because of this hypothetical necessity, recognized by everyone, that after God's prevision or after his resolution nothing can be changed: and yet the events in themselves remain contingent. For (setting aside this supposition of the futurition of the thing and of the prevision or of the resolution of God, a supposition that already lays it down as a fact that the thing will happen, and in accordance with which one must say, "Unumquodque, quando est, oportet esse,

aut unumquodque, siquidem erit, oportet futurum esse"[1]), the event has nothing in it to render it necessary and to suggest that no other thing might have happened in its stead. And as for the connexion between causes and effects, it only inclined, without necessitating, the free agency, as I have just explained; thus it does not produce even a hypothetical necessity, save in conjunction with something from outside, to wit, this very maxim, that the prevailing inclination always triumphs.

54. It will be said also that, if all is ordered, God cannot then perform miracles. But one must bear in mind that the miracles that happen in the world were also enfolded and represented as possible in this same world considered in the state of mere possibility; and God, who has since performed them, when he chose this world had even then decreed to perform them. Again the objection will be made that vows and prayers, merits and demerits, good and bad actions avail nothing, since nothing can be changed. This objection causes the most perplexity to people in general, and yet it is purely a sophism. These prayers, these vows, these good or bad actions that occur today were already before God when he formed the resolution to order things. Those things that happen in this existing world were represented, with their effects and their consequences, in the idea of this same world, while it was still possible only; they were represented therein, attracting God's grace whether natural or supernatural, requiring punishments or rewards, just as it has happened actually in this world since God chose it. The prayer or the good action was even then an *ideal cause* or *condition*, that is, an inclining reason able to contribute to the grace of God, or to the reward, as it now does in reality. Since, moreover, all is wisely connected together in the world, it is clear that God, foreseeing what would happen freely, ordered all other things on that basis beforehand, or (what is the same) he chose that possible world in which everything was ordered in this fashion.

59. I have just shown how the action of the will depends upon its causes; that there is nothing so appropriate to human nature as this dependence of our actions; and that otherwise one would slip into

---

1 "When any particular thing exists, it must exist, or if any particular thing is going to exist, it must be going to exist."

a preposterous and unendurable fatality, namely into the *Fatum Mahometanum*,[1] which is the worst of all because it overthrows foresight and good counsel. It is well to show, notwithstanding, how this dependence of voluntary actions does not fundamentally preclude the existence within us of a wonderful *spontaneity*, which in a certain sense makes the soul in its resolves independent of the physical influence of all other creatures. This spontaneity, previously little recognized, which exalts our command over our actions to the highest pitch, is a consequence of the system of Pre-established Harmony, of which I must give some explanation here. The scholastic philosophers believed that there was a reciprocal physical influence between body and soul: but since it has been recognized that thought and dimensional mass have no mutual connexion, and that they are creatures differing *toto genere*,[2] many moderns have acknowledged that there is no *physical communication* between soul and body, despite the *metaphysical communication* always subsisting, which causes soul and body to comprise one and the same *suppositum*, or what is called a person. This physical communication, if there were such, would cause the soul to change the degree of speed and the directional line of some motions that are in the body, and *vice versa* the body to change the sequence of the thoughts that are in the soul. But this effect cannot be inferred from any notion conceived in the body and in the soul; though nothing is better known to us than the soul, since it is inmost to us, that is to say inmost to itself.

62. Being on other considerations already convinced of the principle of Harmony in general, I was in consequence convinced likewise of the *preformation* and the Pre-established Harmony of all things amongst themselves, of that between nature and grace, between the decrees of God and our actions foreseen, between all parts of matter, and even between the future and the past, the whole in conformity with the sovereign wisdom of God, whose works are the most harmonious it is possible to conceive. Thus I could not fail to arrive at the system that declares that God created the soul in the beginning in such a fashion that it must produce and represent to itself successively what takes place within the body, and the body also in such a fashion that it must

---

1  "Mohammedan [i.e, Muslim] fate."
2  "In every respect."

do of itself what the soul ordains. Consequently the laws that connect the thoughts of the soul in the order of final causes and in accordance with the evolution of perceptions must produce pictures that meet and harmonize with the impressions of bodies on our organs; and likewise the laws of movements in the body, which follow one another in the order of efficient causes, meet and so harmonize with the thoughts of the soul that the body is induced to act at the time when the soul wills it.

64. Moreover, since all that passes in the soul depends, according to this system, only upon the soul, and its subsequent state is derived only from it and from its present state, how can one give it a greater *independence*? It is true that there still remains some imperfection in the constitution of the soul. All that happens to the soul depends upon it, but depends not always upon its will; that would be too much. Nor are such happenings even recognized always by its understanding or perceived with distinctness. For there is in the soul not only an order of distinct perceptions, forming its dominion, but also a series of confused perceptions or passions, forming its bondage: and there is no need for astonishment at that; the soul would be a Divinity if it had none but distinct perceptions. It has nevertheless some power over these confused perceptions also, even if in an indirect manner. For although it cannot change its passions immediately, it can work from afar towards that end with enough success, and endow itself with new passions and even habits. It even has a like power over the more distinct perceptions, being able to endow itself indirectly with opinions and intentions, and to hinder itself from having this one or that, and stay or hasten its judgement. For we can seek means beforehand to arrest ourselves, when occasion arises, on the sliding step of a rash judgement; we can find some incident to justify postponement of our resolution even at the moment when the matter appears ready to be judged. Although our opinion and our act of willing are not directly objects of our will (as I have already observed), one sometimes takes measures nevertheless to will and even to believe in due time, what one does not will, or believe, now. So great is the profundity of the spirit of man.

65. And now, to bring to a conclusion this question of *spontaneity*, it must be said that, on a rigorous definition, the soul has within it the principle of all its actions, and even of all its

passions, and that the same is true in all the simple substances scattered throughout Nature, although there is freedom only in those that are intelligent. In the popular sense notwithstanding, speaking in accordance with appearances, we must say that the soul depends in some way upon the body and upon the impressions of the senses: much as we speak with Ptolemy and Tycho in everyday converse, and think with Copernicus, when it is a question of the rising and the setting of the sun.[1]

66. One may however give a true and philosophic sense to this *mutual dependence* that we suppose between the soul and the body. It is that the one of these two substances depends upon the other ideally, in so far as the reason for what is done in the one can be furnished by what is in the other. This had already happened when God ordered beforehand the harmony that there would be between them. Even so would that automaton, which should fulfil the servant's function, depend upon me *ideally*, in virtue of the knowledge of him who, foreseeing my future orders, would have rendered it capable of serving me at the right moment all through the next day. The knowledge of my future intentions would have actuated this great craftsman, who would accordingly have fashioned the automaton: my influence would be objective, and his physical. For in so far as the soul has perfection and distinct thoughts, God has accommodated the body to the soul, and has arranged beforehand that the body is impelled to execute its orders....

... and I see not why there should be less objection to making the atoms of Epicurus or of Gassendi endure, than to affirming the subsistence of all truly simple and indivisible substances, which are the sole and true atoms of Nature. And Pythagoras

---

1 Ptolemy (Claudius Ptolemaeus) (fl. 127-145) was a Greek astronomer and geographer, whose writings had immense impact on the astronomical and terrestrial-geographical views held prior to the early modern period. Nicolas Copernicus (Mikołaj Kopernik) (1473-1543) was a Polish priest and astronomer, whose work and observations revived the heliocentric theory of the solar system and repudiated the geocentric theory that had prevailed previously. Tycho Brahe (1546-1601) was a Danish astronomer; while he rejected the Copernican hypothesis, his extremely meticulous astronomical data provided the basis for its subsequent confirmation.

was right in saying generally, as Ovid makes him say: *Morte carent animae.*[1]

90. Now as I like maxims that hold good and admit of the fewest exceptions possible, here is what has appeared to me most reasonable in every sense on this important question. I consider that souls and simple substances altogether cannot begin except by creation, or end except by annihilation. Moreover, as the formation of organic animate bodies appears explicable in the order of nature only when one assumes a *preformation* already organic, I have therefore inferred that what we call generation of an animal is only a transformation and augmentation. Thus, since the same body was already furnished with organs, it is to be supposed that it was already animate, and that it had the same soul: so I assume *vice versa*, from the conservation of the soul once it is created, that the animal is also conserved, and that apparent death is only an envelopment, there being no likelihood that in the order of nature souls exist entirely separated from all body, or that what does not begin naturally can cease through natural forces.

91. Considering that so admirable an order and rules so general are established in regard to animals, it does not appear reasonable that man should be completely excluded from that order, and that everything in relation to his soul should come about in him by miracle. Besides I have pointed out repeatedly that it is of the essence of God's wisdom that all should be harmonious in his works, and that nature should be parallel with grace. It is thus my belief that those souls that one day shall be human souls, like those of other species, have been in the seed, and in the progenitors as far back as Adam, and have consequently existed since the beginning of things, always in a kind of organic body.... This doctrine is also sufficiently confirmed by the microscope observations of M. Leeuwenhoek[2] and other good observers....

... It is not strictly true (though it appears plausible) that the benefits God imparts to the creatures who are capable of felicity tend solely to their happiness. All is connected in Nature; and if a skilled artisan, an engineer, an architect, a wise politician often makes one and the same thing serve several ends, if he

---

1 "Souls are free from death" (Ovid, *Metamorphoses* 15, 158).
2 See Appendix B.

makes a double hit with a single throw, when that can be done conveniently, one may say that God, whose wisdom and power are perfect, does so always. That is husbanding the ground, the time, the place, the material, which make up as it were his outlay. Thus God has more than one purpose in his projects. The felicity of all rational creatures is one of the aims he has in view; but it is not his whole aim, nor even his final aim. Therefore it happens that the unhappiness of some of these creatures may come about *by concomitance*, and as a result of other greater goods: this I have already explained, and M. Bayle has to some extent acknowledged it. The goods as such, considered in themselves, are the object of the antecedent will of God. God will produce as much reason and knowledge in the universe as his plan can admit. One can conceive of a mean between an antecedent will altogether pure and primitive, and a consequent and final will. The *primitive antecedent will* has as its object each good and each evil in itself, detached from all combination, and tends to advance the good and prevent the evil. The *mediate will* relates to combinations, as when one attaches a good to an evil: then the will will have some tendency towards this combination when the good exceeds the evil therein. But the *final and decisive will* results from consideration of all the goods and all the evils that enter into our deliberation; it results from a total combination. This shows that a mediate will, although it may in a sense pass as consequent in relation to a pure and primitive antecedent will, must be considered antecedent in relation to the final and decretory will. God gives reason to the human race; misfortunes arise from that by concomitance. His pure antecedent will tends towards giving reason, as a great good, and preventing the evils in question. But when it is a question of the evils that accompany this gift that God has made to us of reason, the compound, made up of the combination of reason and of these evils, will be the object of a mediate will of God, which will tend towards producing or preventing this compound, according as the good or the evil prevails therein. But even if it were shown that reason did more harm than good to men (which, however, I do not admit), whereupon the mediate will of God would discard it with all its concomitants, it might still be the case that it was more in accordance with the perfection of the universe to give reason to men, despite all the evil consequences that it might have with reference to them. Consequently, the final will or the decree of

God, resulting from all the considerations he can have, would be to give it to them. And, far from being subject to blame for this, he would be blameworthy if he did not do so. Thus the evil, or the mixture of goods and evils in which the evil prevails, happens only *by concomitance*, because it is connected with greater goods that are outside this mixture. This mixture, therefore, or this compound, is not to be conceived as a grace or as a gift from God to us; but the good that is found mingled therein will nevertheless be good. Such is God's gift of reason to those who make ill use of it. It is always a good in itself; but the combination of this good with the evils that proceed from its abuse is not a good with regard to those who in consequence of it become unhappy. Yet it comes to be by concomitance, because it serves a greater good in relation to the universe. And this is doubtless what prompted God to give reason to those who have made it an instrument of their unhappiness. Or, to put it more precisely, in accordance with my system, God, having found among the possible beings some rational creatures who misuse their reason, gave existence to those who are included in the best possible plan of the universe. Thus nothing prevents us from admitting that God grants goods that turn into evil by the fault of men, this often happening to men in just punishment of the misuse they had made of God's grace....

But to say that God should not give a good that he knows an evil will will abuse, when the general plan of things demands that he give it; or again to say that he should give certain means for preventing it, contrary to this same general order: that is to wish (as I have observed already) that God himself become blameworthy in order to prevent man from being so. To object, as people do here, that the goodness of God would be smaller than that of another benefactor who would give a more useful gift, is to overlook the fact that the goodness of a benefactor is not measured by a single benefit....

120. V. "A maleficent being is very capable of heaping magnificent gifts upon his enemies, when he knows that they will make of it a use that will destroy them. It therefore does not seem worthy of the infinitely good Being to give to creatures a free will, of which, as he knows for certain, they would make a use that would render them unhappy. Therefore if he gives them free will he combines with it the art of using it always opportunely,

and permits not that they neglect the practice of this art in any conjuncture; and if there were no sure means of determining the good use of this free will, he would rather take from them this faculty, than allow it to be the cause of their unhappiness. That is the more manifest, as free will is a grace that he has given them of his own choice and without their asking for it; so that he would be more answerable for the unhappiness it would bring upon them than if he had only granted it in response to their importunate prayers."

What was said at the end of the remark on the preceding maxim ought to be repeated here, and is sufficient to counter the present maxim. Moreover, the author is still presupposing that false maxim advanced as the third, stating that the happiness of rational creatures is the sole aim of God. If that were so, perhaps neither sin nor unhappiness would ever occur, even by concomitance. God would have chosen a sequence of possibles where all these evils would be excluded. But God would fail in what is due to the universe, that is, in what he owes to himself. If there were only spirits they would be without the required connexion, without the order of time and place. This order demands matter, movement and its laws; to adjust these to spirits in the best possible way means to return to our world. When one looks at things only in the mass, one imagines to be practicable a thousand things that cannot properly take place. To wish that God should not give free will to rational creatures is to wish that there be none of these creatures; and to wish that God should prevent them from misusing it is to wish that there be none but these creatures alone, together with what was made for them only. If God had none but these creatures in view, he would doubtless prevent them from destroying themselves. One may say in a sense, however, that God has given to these creatures the art of always making good use of their free will, for the natural light of reason is this art. But it would be necessary always to have the will to do good, and often creatures lack the means of giving themselves the will they ought to have; often they even lack the will to use those means that indirectly give a good will. Of this I have already spoken more than once. This fault must be admitted, and one must even acknowledge that God would perhaps have been able to exempt creatures from that fault, since there is nothing to prevent, so it seems, the existence of some whose nature it would be always to have good will. But I reply that it is not necessary, and that it was not feasible for all rational creatures to have so great a perfection, and such as would bring them so close to the Divinity. It may even be that this can only be made possible by a special divine grace. But in this case, would it be proper for God to grant it to all, that is, always to act miraculously in respect of all rational creatures? Nothing would be less rational than these perpetual miracles. There are degrees among creatures: the general order requires it. And it appears quite consistent with the order of divine government that the great privilege of strengthening in the good should be granted more easily to those who had a good will when they were in a more imperfect state, in the state of struggle and of pilgrimage....

130. XV. "The Being infinitely powerful, Creator of matter and of spirits, makes whatever he wills of this matter and these spirits. There is no situation or shape that he cannot communicate to spirits. If he then permitted a physical or a moral evil, this would not be for the reason that otherwise some other still greater physical or moral evil would be altogether inevitable. None of those reasons for the mixture of good and evil that are founded on the limitation of the forces of benefactors can apply to him."

It is true that God makes of matter and of spirits whatever he wills; but he is like a good sculptor, who will make from his block of marble only what he judges to be the best, and who judges well. God makes of matter the most excellent of all possible machines; he makes of spirits the most excellent of all governments conceivable; and over and above all that, he establishes for their union the most perfect of all harmonies, according to the system I have proposed. Now since physical evil and moral evil occur in this perfect work, one must conclude (contrary to M. Bayle's assurance here) that *otherwise a still greater evil would have been altogether inevitable*. This great evil would be that God would have chosen ill if he had chosen otherwise than he has chosen....

134. XIX. "Those physicians who chose, among many remedies capable of curing a sick man, of which there were several they well knew he would take with enjoyment, precisely the one that they knew he would refuse to take, would vainly urge and pray him not to refuse it; we should still have just cause for thinking that they had no desire to cure him: for if they wished to do so, they would choose for him among those good medicines one that

they knew he would willingly swallow. If, moreover, they knew that rejection of the remedy they offered him would augment his sickness to the point of making it fatal, one could not help saying that, despite all their exhortations, they must certainly be desirous of the sick man's death."

God wishes to save all men: that means he would save them if men themselves did not prevent it, and did not refuse to receive his grace; and he is not bound or prompted by reason always to overcome their evil will. He does so sometimes nevertheless, when superior reasons allow it, and when his consequent and decretory will, which results from all his reasons, makes him resolve upon the election of a certain number of men. He gives aids to all for their conversion and for perseverance, and these aids suffice in those who have good will, but they do not always suffice to give good will. Men obtain this good will either through particular aids or through circumstances that cause the success of the general aids. God cannot refrain from offering other remedies that he knows men will reject, bringing upon themselves all the greater guilt: but shall one wish that God be unjust in order that man may be less criminal? Moreover, the grace that does not serve the one may serve the other, and indeed always serves the totality of God's plan, which is the best possible in conception. Shall God not give the rain, because there are low-lying places that will be thereby incommoded? Shall the sun not shine as much as it should for the world in general, because there are places that will be too much dried up in consequence? In short, all these comparisons, spoken of in these maxims that M. Bayle has just given, of a physician, a benefactor, a minister of state, a prince, are exceedingly lame, because it is well known what their duties are and what can and ought to be the object of their cares: they have scarce more than the one affair, and they often fail therein through negligence or malice. God's object has in it something infinite, his cares embrace the universe: what we know about this is almost nothing, and we desire to gauge his wisdom and his goodness by our knowledge.... But in this we confess our ignorance of the facts, and we acknowledge, moreover, before we see it, that God does all the best possible, in accordance with the infinite wisdom that guides his actions. It is true that we have already before our eyes proofs and tests of this, when we see something entire, some whole complete in itself, and isolated, so to speak, among the works of God. Such a whole, shaped as it were by the hand of God, is a plant, an animal, a man. We cannot wonder enough at the beauty and the contrivance of its structure. But when we see some broken bone, some piece of animal's flesh, some sprig of a plant, there appears to be nothing but confusion, unless an excellent anatomist observes it: and even he would recognize nothing therein if he had not before seen like pieces attached to their whole. It is the same with the government of God: what we have been able to see until now is not a large enough piece for recognition of the beauty and the order of the whole. Thus the very nature of things implies that this order in the Divine City, which we see not yet here on Earth, should be an object of our faith, of our hope, of our confidence in God....

153. The explanation of the cause of evil by a particular principle, *per principium maleficum*,[1] is of the same nature. Evil needs no such explanation, any more than do cold and darkness: there is neither *primum frigidum*[2] nor principle of darkness. Evil itself comes only from privation; the positive enters therein only by concomitance, as the active enters by concomitance into cold. We see that water in freezing is capable of breaking a gun-barrel in which it is confined; and yet cold is a certain privation of force, as it only comes from the diminution of a movement that separates the particles of fluids. When this separating motion becomes weakened in the water by the cold, the particles of compressed air concealed in the water collect, and, becoming larger, they become more capable of acting outwards through their buoyancy. The resistance that the surfaces of the proportions of air meet in the water and that opposes the force exerted by these portions towards dilation is far less, and consequently the effect of the air greater, in large air-bubbles than in small, even if these small bubbles combined form as great a mass as the large. For the resistances, that is, the surfaces, increase by the *square*, and the forces, that is, the contents or the volumes of the spheres of compressed air, increase by the *cube*, of their diameters. Thus it is *by accident* that privation involves action and force. I have already shown how privation is enough to cause error and malice, and how God is prompted to permit them, despite there being no malignity in him. Evil comes from privation; the positive and action spring from it by accident, as force springs from cold.

---

1  "An evil principle."
2  "A first coldness."

169. The question of the *possibility of things that do not happen* has already been examined by the ancients. It appears that Epicurus, to preserve freedom and to avoid an absolute necessity, maintained, after Aristotle, that contingent futurities were not susceptible of determinate truth. For if it was true yesterday that I should write today, it could therefore not fail to happen, as it was already necessary; and, for the same reason, it was from all eternity. Thus all that happens is necessary, and it is impossible for anything different to come to pass. But since that is not so it would follow, according to him, that contingent futurities have no determinate truth. To uphold this opinion, Epicurus went so far as to deny the first and the greatest principle of the truths of reason, he denied that every assertion was either true or false. Here is the way they confounded him: "You deny that it was true yesterday that I should write today; it was therefore false." The good man, not being able to admit this conclusion, was obliged to say that it was neither true nor false. After that, he needs no refutation, and Chrysippus[1] might have spared himself the trouble he took to prove the great principle of contradictories, following the account by Cicero in his book *De Fato*: "Contendit omnes nervos Chrysippus ut persuadeat omne [Greek: axiôma] aut verum esse aut falsum. Ut enim Epicurus veretur ne si hoc concesserit, concedendum sit, fato fieri quaecunque fiant; si enim alterum ex aeternitate verum sit, esse id etiam certum; si certum, etiam necessarium; ita et necessitatem et fatum confirmari putat; sic Chrysippus metuit ne non, si non obtinuerit omne quod enuncietur aut verum esse aut falsum, omnia fato fieri possint ex causis aeternis rerum futurarum."[2] M. Bayle observes (*Dictionary*,

---

1  Chrysippus (ca. 279-206 BCE), ancient philosopher, third head of the Stoic school. See also next note.

2  "Accordingly Chrysippus exerts every effort to prove the view that every *axiôma* is either true or false. For just as Epicurus is afraid that if he admits this he will also have to admit that all events whatever are caused by fate (on the ground that if either of two alternatives is true from all eternity, that alternative is also certain, and if it is certain it is also necessary. This, he thinks, would prove both necessity and fate), similarly Chrysippus fears that if he fails to maintain that every proposition is either true or false he will not carry his point that all things happen by fate and spring from eternal causes governing future events" (Cicero, *De Fato*, ix. 21 [H. Rackham trans.]). It may be noted that Cicero's *De Fato* is the most important source for our understanding of the Stoic philosopher Chrysippus' *compatibilist* view—the earliest known articulation of this central Leibnizian position.

article "Epicurus," let. T, p. 1141) "that neither of these two great philosophers [Epicurus and Chrysippus] understood that the truth of this maxim, every proposition is true or false, is independent of what is called *fatum*: it could not therefore serve as proof of the existence of the *fatum*, as Chrysippus maintained and as Epicurus feared. Chrysippus could not have conceded, without damaging his own position, that there are propositions that are neither true nor false. But he gained nothing by asserting the contrary: for, whether there are free causes or not, it is equally true that this proposition, The Grand Mogul will go hunting tomorrow, is true or false. Men rightly regarded as ridiculous this speech of Tiresias: All that I shall say will happen or not, for great Apollo confers on me the faculty of prophesying. If, assuming the impossible, there were no God, it would yet be certain that everything the greatest fool in the world should predict would happen or would not happen. That is what neither Chrysippus nor Epicurus has taken into consideration." Cicero, lib. I, *De Nat. Deorum*, with regard to the evasions of the Epicureans expressed the sound opinion (as M. Bayle observes towards the end of the same page) that it would be much less shameful to admit that one cannot answer one's opponent, than to have recourse to such answers. Yet we shall see that M. Bayle himself confused the certain with the necessary, when he maintained that the choice of the best rendered things necessary.

... But Chrysippus and even his master Cleanthes were on that point more reasonable than is supposed. That will be seen as we proceed. It is open to question whether the past is more necessary than the future. Cleanthes held the opinion that it is. The objection is raised that it is necessary *ex hypothesi* for the future to happen, as it is necessary *ex hypothesi* for the past to have happened. But there is this difference, that it is not possible to act on the past state, that would be a contradiction; but it is possible to produce some effect on the future. Yet the hypothetical necessity of both is the same: the one cannot be changed, the other will not be; and once that is past, it will not be possible for it to be changed either.

180. I find also that M. Bayle combats admirably the opinion of those who assert that goodness and justice depend solely upon the arbitrary choice of God; who suppose, moreover, that if God had been determined by the goodness of things themselves to act, he would be entirely subjected to necessity in his actions, a

state incompatible with freedom. That is confusing metaphysical necessity with moral necessity. Here is what M. Bayle says in objection to this error (*Reply*, ch. 89, p. 203): "The consequence of this doctrine will be, that before God resolved upon creating the world he saw nothing better in virtue than in vice, and that his ideas did not show him that virtue was more worthy of his love than vice. That leaves no distinction between natural right and positive right; there will no longer be anything unalterable or inevitable in morals; it will have been just as possible for God to command people to be vicious as to command them to be virtuous; and one will have no certainty that the moral laws will not one day be abrogated, as the ceremonial laws of the Jews were. This, in a word, leads us straight to the belief that God was the free author, not only of goodness and of virtue, but also of truth and of the essence of things. That is what certain of the Cartesians assert, and I confess that their opinion (see the Continuation of *Divers Thoughts on the Comet*, p. 554) might be of some avail in certain circumstances. Yet it is open to dispute for so many reasons, and subject to consequences so troublesome (see chapter 152 of the same Continuation) that there are scarcely any extremes it would not be better to suffer rather than plunge into that one. It opens the door to the most exaggerated Pyrrhonism:[1] for it leads to the assertion that this proposition, three and three make six, is only true where and during the time when it pleases God; that it is perhaps false in some parts of the universe; and that perhaps it will be so among men in the coming year. All that depends on the free will of God could have been limited to certain places and certain times, like the Judaic ceremonies. This conclusion will be extended to all the laws of the Decalogue, if the actions they command are in their nature divested of all goodness to the same degree as the actions they forbid."

194. Yet philosophers and theologians dare to support dogmatically such a belief; and I have many times wondered that gifted and pious persons should have been capable of setting bounds to the goodness and the perfection of God. For to assert that he knows what is best, that he can do it and that he does it not, is to avow that it rested with his will only to make the world better than it is; but that is what one calls lacking goodness. It

---

1  Pyrrhonism was the ancient skeptical school.

is acting against that axiom already quoted: *Minus bonum habet rationem mali*.[1] If some adduce experience to prove that God could have done better, they set themselves up as ridiculous critics of his works. To such will be given the answer given to all those who criticize God's course of action, and who from this same assumption, that is, the alleged defects of the world, would infer that there is an evil God, or at least a God neutral between good and evil. And if we hold the same opinion as King Alfonso, we shall, I say, receive this answer: You have known the world only since the day before yesterday, you see scarce farther than your nose, and you carp at the world. Wait until you know more of the world and consider in it especially the parts that present a complete whole (as do organic bodies); and you will find there a contrivance and a beauty transcending all imagination. Let us draw conclusions from this as to the wisdom and the goodness of the author of things, even in things that we know not. We find in the universe some things that are not pleasing to us; but let us be aware that it is not made for us alone. It is nevertheless made for us if we are wise: it will serve us if we use it for our service; we shall be happy in it if we wish to be.

195. Someone will say that it is impossible to produce the best, because there is no perfect creature, and that it is always possible to produce one that would be more perfect. I answer that what can be said of a creature or of a particular substance, which can always be surpassed by another, is not to be applied to the universe, which, since it must extend through all future eternity, is an infinity. Moreover, there is an infinite number of creatures in the smallest particle of matter, because of the actual division of the *continuum* to infinity. And infinity, that is to say, the accumulation of an infinite number of substances, is, properly speaking, not a whole any more than the infinite number itself, of which one cannot say whether it is even or uneven. That is just what serves to disprove those who make of the world a God, or who think of God as the Soul of the world; for the world or the universe cannot be regarded as an animal or as a substance.

196. It is therefore not a question of a creature, but of the universe; and the adversary will be obliged to maintain that

---

1 "A lesser good counted as an evil."

one possible universe may be better than the other, to infinity; but there he would be mistaken, and this is what he cannot prove. If this opinion were true, it would follow that God had not produced any universe at all: for he is incapable of acting without reason, and that would be even acting against reason. It is as if one were to suppose that God had decreed to make a material sphere, with no reason for making it of any particular size. This decree would be useless, as it would carry with it what would prevent its effect. It would be quite another matter if God decreed to draw from a given point one straight line to another, without any determination of the angle, either in the decree or in its circumstances. For in this case the determination would spring from the nature of the thing, the line would be perpendicular, and the angle would be right, since that is all that is determined and distinguishable. It is thus that one must think of the creation of the best of all possible universes, all the more since God not only decrees to create a universe, but decrees also to create the best of all. For God decrees nothing without knowledge, and he makes no separate decrees, which would be nothing but antecedent acts of will: and these we have sufficiently explained, distinguishing them from genuine decrees.

... as all the possibles are not compatible together in one and the same world-sequence, for that very reason all the possibles cannot be produced, and it must be said that God is not forced, metaphysically speaking, into the creation of this world. One may say that as soon as God has decreed to create something there is a struggle between all the possibles, all of them laying claim to existence, and that those which, being united, produce most reality, most perfection, most significance carry the day. It is true that all this struggle can only be ideal, that is to say, it can only be a conflict of reasons in the most perfect understanding, which cannot fail to act in the most perfect way, and consequently to choose the best....

... As God can do nothing without reasons, even when he acts miraculously, it follows that he has no will about individual events but what results from some general truth or will....

208. Thus one must suppose that, among the general rules that are not absolutely necessary, God chooses those that are the most natural, the easiest to explain, and also of greatest service

for the explanation of other things. That is doubtless the conclusion most excellent and most pleasing; and even if the system of Pre-established Harmony had not been necessary otherwise, because it banishes superfluous miracles, God would have chosen it as being the most harmonious. The ways of God are those most simple and uniform: for he chooses rules that least restrict one another. They are also the most *productive* in proportion to the *simplicity of ways and means*. It is as if one said that a certain house was the best that could have been constructed at a certain cost. One may, indeed, reduce these two conditions, simplicity and productivity, to a single advantage, which is to produce as much perfection as is possible....

225. The infinity of possibles, however great it may be, is no greater than that of the wisdom of God, who knows all possibles. One may even say that if this wisdom does not exceed the possibles extensively, since the objects of the understanding cannot go beyond the possible, which in a sense is alone intelligible, it exceeds them intensively, by reason of the infinitely infinite combinations it makes of them, and its many deliberations concerning them. The wisdom of God, not content with embracing all the possibles, penetrates them, compares them, weighs them against one another, to estimate their degrees of perfection or imperfection, the strong and the weak, the good and the evil. It goes even beyond the finite combinations, making of them an infinity of infinites, that is to say, an infinity of possible sequences of the universe, each of which contains an infinity of creatures. By this means the divine wisdom distributes all the possibles it had already contemplated separately, into so many universal systems that it further compares the one with the other. The result of all these comparisons and deliberations is the choice of the best from among all these possible systems, which wisdom makes in order to satisfy goodness completely; and such is precisely the plan of the universe as it is. Moreover, all these operations of the divine understanding, although they have among them an order and a priority of nature, always take place together, no priority of time existing among them.

[...]

# ESSAYS ON THE JUSTICE OF GOD AND THE FREEDOM OF MAN IN THE ORIGIN OF EVIL

## PART THREE

[...]

282. It is therefore only necessary to understand fully some distinctions, such as that I have very often urged between the necessary and the certain, and between metaphysical necessity and moral necessity. It is the same with possibility and impossibility, since the event whose opposite is possible is contingent, even as that whose opposite is impossible is necessary. A distinction is rightly drawn also between a proximate potency and a remote potency; and, according to these different senses, one says now that a thing may be and now that it may not be. It may be said in a certain sense that it is necessary that the blessed should not sin; that the devils and the damned should sin; that God himself should choose the best; that man should follow the course that after all attracts him most. But this necessity is not opposed to contingency; it is not of the kind called logical, geometrical or metaphysical, whose opposite implies contradiction. M. Nicole[1] has made use somewhere of a comparison that is not amiss. It is considered impossible that a wise and serious magistrate, who has not taken leave of his senses, should publicly commit some outrageous action, as it would be, for instance, to run about the streets naked in order to make people laugh. It is the same, in a sense, with the blessed; they are still less capable of sinning, and the necessity that forbids them to sin is of the same kind. Finally I also hold that "will" is a term as equivocal as potency and necessity. For I have already observed that those who employ this axiom, that one does not fail to do what one wills when one can, and who infer from this that God therefore does not will the salvation of all, imply a *decretory will*. Only in that sense can one support this proposition, that wisdom never wills what it knows to be among the things that shall not happen. On the other hand, one may say, taking will in a sense more general

---

1 Pierre Nicole (1625-95), French theologian and philosopher, was the co-author, with Antoine Arnauld, of the widely-read and influential *La Logique ou l'art de penser*, otherwise known as the *Port-Royal Logic*.

and more in conformity with customary use, that the wise will is *inclined* antecedently to all good, although it *decrees* finally to do what is most fitting. Thus one would be very wrong to deny to God the serious and strong inclination to save all men, which Holy Scripture attributes to him; or even to attribute to him an original distaste that diverts him from the salvation of a number of persons, *odium antecedaneum*.[1] One should rather maintain that the wise mind tends towards all good, as good, in proportion to his knowledge and is power, but that he only produces the best that can be achieved. Those who admit that, and yet deny to God the antecedent will to save all men, are wrong only in their misuse of the term, provided that they acknowledge, besides, that God gives all help sufficient to enable them to win salvation if only they have the will to avail themselves of it.

337. The advantage of freedom that is in the creature without doubt exists to an eminent degree in God. That must be understood in so far as it is genuinely an advantage and in so far as it presupposes no imperfection. For to be able to make a mistake and go astray is a disadvantage, and to have control over the passions is in truth an advantage, but one that presupposes an imperfection, namely passion itself, of which God is incapable. Scotus[2] was justified in saying that if God were not free and exempt from necessity, no creature would be so. But God is incapable of being indeterminate in anything whatsoever: he cannot be ignorant, he cannot doubt, he cannot suspend his judgement; his will is always decided, and it can only be decided by the best. God can never have a primitive particular will, that is, independent of laws or general acts of will; such a thing would be unreasonable. He cannot determine upon Adam, Peter, Judas or any individual without the existence of a reason for this determination; and this reason leads of necessity to some general enunciation. The wise mind always acts *according to principles*; always *according to rules*, and never *according to exceptions*, save when the rules come into collision through opposing tendencies, where the strongest carries the day: or else, either they will stop one another or some third course will emerge as a result. In all

---

1 "Antecedent aversion."
2 John Duns Scotus (ca. 1265-1308), prominent Scholastic philosopher and logician.

these cases one rule serves as an exception to the other, and there are never any *original exceptions* with one who always acts in a regular way.

347. It seems, when one considers the indifference of matter to motion and to rest, that the largest body at rest could be carried along without any resistance by the smallest body in motion, in which case there would be action without reaction and an effect greater than its cause. There is also no necessity to say of the motion of a ball that runs freely on an even, horizontal plane, with a certain degree of speed, termed A, that this motion must have the properties of the motion that it would have if it were going with lesser speed in a boat, itself moving in the same direction with the residue of the speed, to ensure that the ball, seen from the bank, advance with the same degree A. For, although the same appearance of speed and of direction results through this medium of the boat, it is not because it is the same thing. Nevertheless it happens that the effects of the collision of the balls in the boat, the motion in each one separately combined with that of the boat giving the appearance of what goes on outside the boat, also give the appearance of the effects that these same balls colliding would have outside the boat. All that is admirable, but one does not see its absolute necessity. A movement on the two sides of the right-angled triangle composes a movement on the hypotenuse; but it does not follow that a ball moving on the hypotenuse must produce the effect of two balls of its own size moving on the two sides: yet that is true. Nothing is so appropriate as this result, and God has chosen the laws that produce it: but one sees no geometrical necessity in it. Yet it is this very lack of necessity that enhances the beauty of the laws that God has chosen, in which several admirable axioms exist in conjunction, and it is impossible for one to say which of them is the primary.

350. This also settles M. Bayle's difficulty, for he fears that, if God is always determinate, Nature could dispense with him and bring about that same effect that is attributed to him, through the necessity of the order of things. That would be true if the laws of motion for instance, and all the rest, had their source in the geometrical necessity of efficient causes; but in the last analysis one is obliged to resort to something depending upon final causes and upon what is fitting. This also utterly destroys the most plau-

sible reasoning of the Naturalists. Dr. Johann Joachim Becher,[1] a German physician, well known for his books on chemistry, had composed a prayer that looked like it could get him into trouble. It began: "O sancta mater natura, aeterne rerum ordo."[2] And it ended by saying that this Nature must forgive him his errors, since she herself was their cause. But the nature of things, if taken as without intelligence and without choice, has in it nothing sufficiently determinant. Herr Becher did not sufficiently take into account that the Author of things (*natura naturans*) must be good and wise, and that we can be evil without complicity on his part in our acts of wickedness. When a wicked man exists, God must have found in the region of possibles the idea of such a man forming part of that sequence of things, the choice of which was demanded by the greatest perfection of the universe, and in which errors and sins are not only punished but even repaired to greater advantage, so that they contribute to the greatest good.

360. Now that I have proved sufficiently that everything comes to pass according to determinate reasons, there cannot be any more difficulty over these principles of God's foreknowledge. Although these determinations do not compel, they cannot but be certain, and they foreshadow what shall happen. It is true that God sees all at once the whole sequence of this universe, when he chooses it, and that thus he has no need of the connexion of effects and causes in order to foresee these effects. But since his wisdom causes him to choose a sequence in perfect connexion, he cannot but see one part of the sequence in the other. It is one of the rules of my system of general harmony *that the present is big with the future*, and that he who sees all sees in that which is, that which shall be. What is more, I have proved conclusively that God sees in each portion of the universe the whole universe, owing to the perfect connexion of things. He is infinitely more discerning than Pythagoras, who judged the height of Hercules by the size of his footprint. There must therefore be no doubt that effects follow their causes determinately, in spite of contingency and even of freedom, which nevertheless exist together with certainty or determination.

---

1  Johann Joachim Becher (1635-82), German physician and chemist, advocate of the phlogiston theory of combustion.
2  "O holy Mother Nature, eternal order of things."

367. Indeed, confusion springs, more often than not, from ambiguity in terms, and from one's failure to take trouble over gaining clear ideas about them. That gives rise to these eternal, and usually mistaken, contentions on necessity and contingency, on the possible and the impossible. But provided that it is understood that necessity and possibility, taken metaphysically and strictly, depend solely upon this question, whether the object in itself or what is opposed to it implies contradiction or not; and that one takes into account that contingency is consistent with the inclinations, or reasons that contribute towards causing determination by the will; provided also that one knows how to distinguish clearly between necessity and determination or certainty, between metaphysical necessity, which admits of no choice, presenting only one single object as possible, and moral necessity, which constrains the wisest to choose the best; finally, provided that one is rid of the chimera of complete indifference, which can only be found in the books of philosophers, and on paper (for they cannot even conceive the notion in their heads, or prove its reality by an example in things) one will easily escape from a labyrinth whose unhappy Daedalus was the human mind. That labyrinth has caused infinite confusion, as much with the ancients as with those of later times, even so far as to lead men into the absurd error of the Lazy Sophism, which closely resembles fate after the Turkish fashion....

377. I think I have sufficiently proved that neither the foreknowledge nor the providence of God can impair either his justice or his goodness, or our freedom. There remains only the difficulty arising from God's co-operation with the actions of the creature, which seems to concern more closely both his goodness, in relation to our evil actions, and our freedom, in relation to good actions as well as to others. M. Bayle has brought out this also with his usual acuteness. I will endeavour to throw light upon the difficulties he puts forward, and then I shall be in a position to conclude this work. I have already proved that the co-operation of God consists in giving us continually all that is real in us and in our actions, in so far as it involves perfection; but that all that is limited and imperfect therein is a consequence of the previous limitations that are originally in the creature. Since, moreover, every action of the creature is a change of its modifications, it is obvious that action arises in the creature in relation to the limita-

tions or negations that it has within itself, and that are diversified by this change.

380. Aristotle was right in rejecting chaos: but it is not always easy to disentangle the conceptions of Plato, and such a task would be still less easy in respect of some ancient authors whose works are lost. Kepler,[1] one of the most excellent of modern mathematicians, recognized a species of imperfection in matter, even when there is no irregular motion: he calls it its "natural inertia," which gives it a resistance to motion, whereby a greater mass receives less speed from one and the same force. There is soundness in this observation, and I have used it to advantage in this work, in order to have a comparison that might illustrate how the original imperfection of the creatures sets bounds to the action of the Creator, which tends towards good. But as matter is itself of God's creation, it only furnishes a comparison and an example, and cannot be the very source of evil and of imperfection. I have already shown that this source lies in the forms or ideas of the possibles, for it must be eternal, and matter is not so. Now since God made all positive reality that is not eternal, he would have made the source of evil, if that did not rather lie in the possibility of things or forms, which alone God did not make, since he is not the author of his own understanding.

382. He places great reliance especially on that doctrine accepted of the schoolmen, that conservation is a continued creation. The conclusion to be drawn from this doctrine would seem to be that the creature never exists, that it is ever newborn and ever dying, like time, movement and other transient beings. Plato believed this of material and tangible things, saying that they are in a perpetual flux, *semper fluunt, nunquam sunt.*[2] But of immaterial substances he judged quite differently, regarding them alone as real: nor was he in that altogether mistaken. Yet continued creation applies to all creatures without distinction....

385. What can be said for certain on the present subject is that the creature depends continually upon divine operation, and

---

1  Johannes Kepler (1571-1630), German astronomer, discoverer of the laws of planetary motion.
2  "They are always flowing, they never are."

that it depends upon that no less after the time of its beginning than when it first begins. This dependence implies that it would not continue to exist if God did not continue to act; in short, that this action of God is free. For if it were a necessary emanation, like that of the properties of the circle, which issue from its essence, it must then be said that God in the beginning produced the creature by necessity; or else it must be shown how, in creating it once, he imposed upon himself the necessity of conserving it. Now there is no reason why this conserving action should not be called production, and even creation, if one will: for the dependence being as great afterwards as at the beginning, the extrinsic designation of being new or not does not change the nature of that action.

386. Let us then admit in such a sense that conservation is a continued creation, and let us see what M. Bayle seems to infer from it (p. 771) after the author of the *Reflexion on the Picture of Socinianism*, in opposition to M. Jurieu.[1] "It seems to me," this writer says, "that one must conclude that God does all, and that in all creation there are no first or second or even occasional causes, as can be easily proved. At this moment when I speak, I am such as I am, with all my circumstances, with such thought, such action, whether I sit or stand, that if God creates me in this moment such as I am, as one must of necessity say in this system, he creates me with such thought, such action, such movement and such determination. One cannot say that God creates me in the first place, and that once I am created he produces with me my movements and my determinations. That is indefensible for two reasons. The first is, that when God creates me or conserves me at this instant, he does not conserve me as a being without form, like a species, or another of the Universals of Logic. I am an individual; he creates me and conserves me as such, and as being all that I am in this instant, with all my attendant circumstances. The second reason is that if God creates me in this instant, and one says that afterwards he produces with me my actions, it will be necessary to imagine another instant for action: for before acting one must exist. Now that would be two instants where we only assume one. It is therefore certain in this hypothesis that creatures have neither more connexion

---

1   Pierre Jurieu (1637-1713), French Protestant leader and writer.

nor more relation with their actions than they had with their production at the first moment of the first creation." The author of this *Reflexion* draws from this some very harsh conclusions that one can picture for oneself; and he testifies at the end that one would be deeply indebted to any man that should teach those who approve this system how to extricate themselves from these frightful absurdities.

396. As for the souls or substantial forms, M. Bayle is right in adding: "that there is nothing more inconvenient for those who admit substantial forms than the objection which is made that they could not be produced save by an actual creation, and that the schoolmen are pitiable in their endeavours to answer this." But there is nothing more convenient for me and for my system than this same objection. For I maintain that all the souls, entelechies or primitive forces, substantial forms, simple substances, or monads, whatever name one may apply to them, can neither spring up naturally nor perish. And the qualities or derivative forces, or what are called accidental forms, I take to be modifications of the primitive entelechy, even as shapes are modifications of matter. That is why these modifications are perpetually changing, while the simple substance remains.

397. I have shown already (part I, 86 *seqq.*) that souls cannot spring up naturally, or be derived from one another, and that it is necessary that ours either be created or be pre-existent. I have even pointed out a certain middle way between a creation and an entire pre-existence. I find it appropriate to say that the soul pre-existing in the seeds from the beginning of things was only sentient, but that it was elevated to the superior degree, which is that of reason, when the man to whom this soul should belong was conceived, and when the organic body, always accompanying this soul from the beginning, but under many changes, was determined for forming the human body. I considered also that one might attribute this elevation of the sentient soul (which makes it reach a more sublime degree of being, namely reason) to the extraordinary operation of God. Nevertheless it will be well to add that I would dispense with miracles in the generating of man, as in that of the other animals. It will be possible to explain that, if one imagines that in this great number of souls and of animals, or at least of living organic bodies that are in the

seeds, those souls alone that are destined to attain one day to human nature contain the reason that shall appear therein one day, and the organic bodies of these souls alone are preformed and predisposed to assume one day the human shape, while the other small animals or seminal living beings, in which no such thing is pre-established, are essentially different from them and possessed only of an inferior nature. This production is a kind of *traduction*, but more manageable than the kind that is commonly taught: it does not derive the soul from a soul, but only the animate from an animate, and it avoids the repeated miracles of a new creation, which would cause a new and pure soul to enter a body that must corrupt it.

400. The force of these proofs, which he praises, must not be so great as he thinks, for if it were they would prove too much. They would make God the author of sin. I admit that the soul cannot stir the organs by a physical influence; for I think that the body must have been so formed beforehand that it would do in time and place what responds to the volitions of the soul, although it is true nevertheless that the soul is the principle of the operation. But if it is said that the soul does not produce its thoughts, its sensations, its feelings of pain and of pleasure, that is something for which I see no reason. In my system every simple substance (that is, every true substance) must be the true immediate cause of all its actions and inward passions; and, speaking strictly in a metaphysical sense, it has none other than those that it produces. Those who hold a different opinion, and who make God the sole agent, are needlessly becoming involved in expressions from which they will only with difficulty extricate themselves without offence against religion; moreover, they unquestionably offend against reason.

402. "To put together in few words the whole force of what I have just said to you, I will observe that it is evident to all those who go deeply into things, that the true efficient cause of an effect must know the effect, and be aware also of the way in which it must be produced. That is not necessary when one is only the instrument of the cause, or only the passive subject of its action; but one cannot conceive of it as not necessary to a true agent. Now if we examine ourselves well we shall be strongly convinced, (1) that, independently of experience, our soul is just as little aware of

what a volition is as of what an idea is; (2) that after a long experience it is no more fully aware of how volitions are formed than it was before having willed anything. What is one to conclude from that, save that the soul cannot be the efficient cause of its volitions, any more than of its ideas, and of the motion of the spirits that cause our arms to move? (Take note that no pretence is made of deciding the point here absolutely, it is only being considered in relation to the principles of the objection.)"

403. That is indeed a strange way of reasoning! What necessity is there for one always to be aware how what is done is done? Are salts, metals, plants, animals and a thousand other animate or inanimate bodies aware how what they do is done, and need they be aware? Must a drop of oil or of fat understand geometry in order to become round on the surface of water? Sewing stitches is another matter: one acts for an end, so one must be aware of the means. But we do not form our ideas because we will to do so; they form themselves within us, they form themselves through us, not in consequence of our will, but in accordance with our nature and that of things. The foetus forms itself in the animal, and a thousand other wonders of nature are produced by a certain *instinct* that God has placed there, that is by virtue of *divine preformation*, which has made these admirable automata, adapted to produce mechanically such beautiful effects. Even so it is easy to believe that the soul is a spiritual automaton still more admirable, and that it is through divine preformation that it produces these beautiful ideas, in which our will has no part and to which our art cannot attain. The operation of spiritual automata, that is of souls, is not mechanical, but it contains in the highest degree all that is beautiful in mechanism. The movements that are developed in bodies are concentrated in the soul by representation as in an ideal world, which expresses the laws of the actual world and their consequences, but with this difference from the perfect ideal world that is in God, that most of the perceptions in the other substances are only confused. For it is plain that every simple substance embraces the whole universe in its confused perceptions or sensations, and that the succession of these perceptions is regulated by the particular nature of this substance, but in a manner that always expresses all the nature in the universe; and every present perception leads to a new perception, just as every movement that it represents leads to another

movement. But it is impossible that the soul can know clearly its whole nature, and perceive how this innumerable number of small perceptions, piled up or rather concentrated together, shapes itself there: to that end it must know completely the whole universe that is embraced by them, that is, it must be a God.

[...]

## APPENDICES

## SUMMARY OF THE CONTROVERSY REDUCED TO FORMAL ARGUMENTS

[...]

Some persons of discernment have wished me to make this addition. I have the more readily deferred to their opinion, because of the opportunity thereby gained for meeting certain difficulties, and for making observations on certain matters that were not treated in sufficient detail in the work itself.

### OBJECTION I

Whoever does not choose the best course is lacking either in power, or knowledge, or goodness.

God did not choose the best course in creating this world.

Therefore God was lacking in power, or knowledge, or goodness.

### ANSWER

I deny the minor, that is to say, the second premise of this syllogism, and the opponent proves it by this

### PROSYLLOGISM

Whoever makes things in which there is evil, and which could have been made without any evil, or need not have been made at all, does not choose the best course.

God made a world in which there is evil; a world, I say, that could have been made without any evil or that need not have been made at all.

Therefore God did not choose the best course.

## ANSWER

I admit the minor of this prosyllogism: for one must confess that there is evil in this world that God has made, and that it would have been possible to make a world without evil or even not to create any world, since its creation depended upon the free will of God. But I deny the major, that is, the first of the two premises of the prosyllogism, and I might content myself with asking for its proof. In order, however, to give a clearer exposition of the matter, I would justify this denial by pointing out that the best course is not always that one that tends towards avoiding evil, since it is possible that the evil may be accompanied by a greater good. For example, the general of an army will prefer a great victory with a slight wound to a state of affairs without wound and without victory. I have proved this in further detail in this work by pointing out, through instances taken from mathematics and elsewhere, that an imperfection in the part may be required for a greater perfection in the whole. In this I have followed the opinion of St. Augustine, who said a hundred times that God permitted evil in order to derive from it a good, that is to say, a greater good; and Thomas Aquinas says (in libr. 2, *Sent. Dist.* 32, qu. 1, art. 1) that the permission of evil tends towards the good of the universe. I have shown that among older writers the fall of Adam was termed *felix culpa*, a fortunate sin, because it had been expiated with immense benefit by the incarnation of the Son of God: for he gave to the universe something more noble than anything there would otherwise have been amongst created beings. For the better understanding of the matter I added, following the example of many good authors, that it was consistent with order and the general good for God to grant to certain of his creatures the opportunity to exercise their freedom, even when he foresaw that they would turn to evil: for God could easily correct the evil, and it was not fitting that in order to prevent sin he should always act in an extraordinary way. It will therefore sufficiently refute the objection to show that a world with evil may be better than a world without evil. But I have gone still further in the work, and have even shown that this universe must be indeed better than every other possible universe.

## OBJECTION II

If there is more evil than good in intelligent creatures, there is more evil than good in all God's work.

Now there is more evil than good in intelligent creatures.

Therefore there is more evil than good in all God's work.

## ANSWER

I deny the major and the minor of this conditional syllogism. As for the major, I do not admit it because this supposed inference from the part to the whole, from intelligent creatures to all creatures, assumes tacitly and without proof that creatures devoid of reason cannot be compared or taken into account with those that have reason. But why might the surplus of good in the non-intelligent creatures that fill the world not compensate for and even exceed incomparably the surplus of evil in rational creatures? It is true that the value of the latter is greater; but by way of compensation the others are incomparably greater in number; and it may be that the proportion of number and quantity surpasses that of value and quality.

The minor also I cannot admit, namely, that there is more evil than good in intelligent creatures. One need not even agree that there is more evil than good in humankind. For it is possible, and even a very reasonable thing, that the glory and the perfection of the blessed may be incomparably greater than the misery and imperfection of the damned, and that here the excellence of the total good in the smaller number may exceed the total evil that is in the greater number. The blessed draw near to divinity through a divine Mediator, so far as can belong to these created beings, and make such progress in good as is impossible for the damned to make in evil, even though they should approach as nearly as may be the nature of demons. God is infinite, and the Devil is finite; good can and does go on *ad infinitum*, whereas evil has its bounds. It may be therefore, and it is probable, that there happens in the comparison between the blessed and the damned the opposite of what I said could happen in the comparison between the happy and the unhappy, namely that in the latter the proportion of degrees surpasses that of numbers, while in the comparison between intelligent and non-intelligent the proportion of numbers is greater than that of values. One is justified in assuming that a thing may be so as long as one does not prove that it is impossible, and indeed what is here put forward goes beyond assumption.

But secondly, even should one admit that there is more evil than good in humankind, one still has every reason for not admitting that there is more evil than good in all intelligent creatures. For there is an inconceivable number of Spirits, and perhaps of other rational creatures besides: and an opponent cannot prove that in the whole City of God, composed as much of Spirits as of rational animals without number and of endless different kinds, the evil exceeds the good. Although one need not, in order to answer an objection, prove that a thing is, when its mere possibility suffices, I have nevertheless shown in this present work that it is a result of the supreme perfection of the Sovereign of the Universe that the kingdom of God should be the most perfect of all states or governments possible, and that in consequence what little evil there is should be required to provide the full measure of the vast good existing there.

## OBJECTION III

If it is always impossible not to sin, it is always unjust to punish.

Now it is always impossible not to sin, or rather all sin is necessary.

Therefore it is always unjust to punish.

The minor of this is proved as follows.

## FIRST PROSYLLOGISM

Everything predetermined is necessary.

Every event is predetermined.

Therefore every event (and consequently sin also) is necessary.

Again this second minor is proved thus.

## SECOND PROSYLLOGISM

That which is future, that which is foreseen, that which is involved in causes is predetermined.

Every event is of this kind.

Therefore every event is predetermined.

## ANSWER

I admit in a certain sense the conclusion of the second prosyllogism, which is the minor of the first; but I shall deny the major of the first prosyllogism, namely that everything predetermined is necessary; taking "necessity," say the necessity to sin, or the impossibility of not sinning, or of not doing some action, in the sense relevant to the argument, that is, as a necessity essential and absolute, which destroys the morality of action and the justice of punishment. If anyone meant a different necessity or impossibility (that is, a necessity only moral or hypothetical, which will be explained presently), it is plain that we would deny him the major stated in the objection. We might content ourselves with this answer, and demand the proof of the proposition denied: but I am well pleased to justify my manner of procedure in the present work, in order to make the matter clear and to throw more light on this whole subject, by explaining the necessity that must be rejected and the determination that must be allowed. The truth is that the necessity contrary to morality, which must be avoided and which would render punishment unjust, is an insuperable necessity, which would render all opposition unavailing, even though one should wish with all one's heart to avoid the necessary action, and though one should make all possible efforts to that end. Now it is plain that this is not applicable to voluntary actions, since one would not do them if one did not so desire. Thus their prevision and predetermination is not absolute, but it presupposes will: if it is certain that one will do them, it is no less certain that one will will to do them. These voluntary actions and their results will not happen whatever one may do and whether one will them or not; but they will happen because one will do, and because one will will to do, what leads to them. That is involved in prevision and predetermination, and forms the reason for them. The necessity of such events is called conditional or hypothetical, or again necessity of consequence, because it presupposes the will and the other requisites. But the necessity that destroys morality, and renders punishment unjust and reward unavailing, is found in the things that will be whatever one may do and whatever one may will to do: in a word, it exists in what is essential. This is called an absolute necessity. Thus it avails nothing with regard to what is necessary absolutely to ordain interdicts or commandments, to propose penalties or prizes, to blame or to praise; it will come to pass no more and no less. In voluntary actions, on the contrary, and in what depends upon them, precepts, armed with power to punish and to reward, very often serve, and are included in the order of causes that make action exist. Thus it comes about that not only pains and effort but also prayers are effective, God having had even these prayers in mind before he ordered things, and having made due allowance for them. That is why the precept *Ora et labora* (Pray and work) remains intact. Thus not only those who (under the empty pretext of the necessity of events) maintain that one can spare oneself the pains demanded by affairs, but also those who argue against prayers, fall into what the ancients even in their time called the "Lazy Sophism." So the predetermination of events by their causes is precisely what contributes to morality instead of destroying it, and the causes incline the will without necessitating it. For this reason the determination we are concerned with is not a necessitation. It is certain (to him who knows all) that the effect will follow this inclination; but this effect does not follow from this by a consequence that is necessary, that is, whose contrary implies contradiction; and it is also by such an inward inclination that the will is determined, without the presence of necessity. Suppose that one has the greatest possible passion (for example, a great thirst), you will admit that the soul can find some reason for resisting it, even if it were only that of displaying its power. Thus though one may never have complete indifference of equipoise, and there is always a predominance of inclination for the course adopted, that predominance does not render absolutely necessary the resolution taken.

## OBJECTION IV

Whoever can prevent the sin of others and does not do so, but rather contributes to it, although he is fully apprised of it, is accessory to it.

God can prevent the sin of intelligent creatures; but he does not do so, and he rather contributes to it by his co-operation and by the opportunities he causes, although he is fully cognizant of it.

Therefore, etc.

## ANSWER

I deny the major of this syllogism. It may be that one can prevent the sin, but that one ought not to do so, because one could not do so without committing a sin oneself, or (when God is concerned) without acting unreasonably. I have given instances of that, and have applied them to God himself. It may be also that one contributes to the evil, and that one even opens the way to it sometimes, in doing things one is bound to do. And when one does one's duty, or (speaking of God) when, after full consideration, one does what reason demands, one is not responsible for events, even when one foresees them. One does not will these evils; but one is willing to permit them for a greater good, which one cannot in reason help preferring to other considerations. This is a *consequent* will, resulting from acts of *antecedent* will, in which one wills the good. I know that some people, in speaking of the antecedent and consequent will of God, have meant by the antecedent that which wills that all men be saved, and by the consequent that which wills, in consequence of persistent sin, that there be some damned, damnation being a result of sin. But these are only examples of a more general notion, and one may say with the same reason, that God wills by his antecedent will that men sin not, and that by his consequent or final and decretory will (which is always followed by its effect) he wills to permit that they sin, this permission being a result of superior reasons. One has indeed justification for saying, in general, that the antecedent will of God tends towards the production of good and the prevention of evil, each taken in itself, and as it were detached (*particulariter et secundum quid*: Thom., I, qu. 19, art. 6) according to the measure of the degree of each good or of each evil. Likewise one may say that the consequent, or final and total, divine will tends towards the production of as many goods as can be put together, whose combination thereby becomes determined, and involves also the permission of some evils and the exclusion of some goods, as the best possible plan of the universe demands. Arminius,[1] in his *Antiperkinsus*, explained very well that the will of God can be called consequent not only in relation to the action of the creature considered beforehand in the divine understanding, but also in relation to other anterior acts of divine will. But it is enough to consider the passage cited from Thomas Aquinas, and that from Scotus (I, dist. 46, qu. 11), to see that they make this distinction as I have made it here. Nevertheless if anyone will not suffer this use of the terms, let him put "previous" in place of "antecedent" will, and "final" or "decretory" in place of "consequent" will. For I do not wish to wrangle about words.

## OBJECTION V

Whoever produces all that is real in a thing is its cause.

God produces all that is real in sin.

Therefore God is the cause of sin.

## ANSWER

I might content myself with denying the major or the minor, because the term "real" admits of interpretations capable of rendering these propositions false. But in order to give a better explanation I will make a distinction. "Real" either signifies what is positive only, or else it includes also privative beings: in the first case, I deny the major and I admit the minor; in the second case, I do the opposite. I might have confined myself to that; but I was willing to go further, in order to account for this distinction. I have therefore been well pleased to point out that every purely positive or absolute reality is a perfection, and that every imperfection comes from limitation, that is, from the privative: for to limit is to withhold extension, or the more beyond. Now God is the

---

1 Jacobus Arminius (Jakob Hermandszoon) (1560-1609), Dutch theologian.

cause of all perfections, and consequently of all realities, when they are regarded as purely positive. But limitations or privations result from the original imperfection of creatures that restricts their receptivity. It is as with a laden boat, which the river carries along more slowly or less slowly in proportion to the weight that it bears: thus the speed comes from the river, but the retardation that restricts this speed comes from the load. Also I have shown in the present work how the creature, in causing sin, is a deficient cause; how errors and evil inclinations spring from privation; and how privation is efficacious accidentally. And I have justified the opinion of St. Augustine (lib. I, *Ad. Simpl.*, qu. 2) who explains (for example) how God hardens the soul, not in giving it something evil, but because the effect of the good he imprints is restricted by the resistance of the soul, and by the circumstances contributing to this resistance, so that he does not give it all the good that would overcome its evil. "Nec *(inquit)* ab illo erogatur aliquid quo homo fit deterior, sed tantum quo fit melior non erogatur."[1] But if God had willed to do more here he must have produced either fresh natures in his creatures or fresh miracles to change their natures, and this the best plan did not allow. It is just as if the current of the river must be more rapid than its slope permits or the boats themselves be less laden, if they had to be impelled at a greater speed. So the limitation or original imperfection of creatures brings it about that even the best plan of the universe cannot admit more good, and cannot be exempted from certain evils, these, however, being only of such a kind as may tend towards a greater good. There are some disorders in the parts that wonderfully enhance the beauty of the whole, just as certain dissonances, appropriately used, render harmony more beautiful. But that depends upon the answer that I have already given to the first objection.

## OBJECTION VI

Whoever punishes those who have done as well as it was in their power to do is unjust.

God does so.

---

1   "Nor (he says) is man provided by him [God] with anything by which he becomes worse, but it is only that there is not furnished that by which he becomes better."

Therefore, etc.

## ANSWER

I deny the minor of this argument. And I believe that God always gives sufficient aid and grace to those who have good will, that is to say, who do not reject this grace by a fresh sin. Thus I do not admit the damnation of children dying unbaptized or outside the Church, or the damnation of adult persons who have acted according to the light that God has given them. And I believe that, *if anyone has followed the light he had*, he will undoubtedly receive of it in greater measure as he has need, even as the late Herr Hulsemann,[1] who was celebrated as a profound theologian at Leipzig, has somewhere observed; and if such a man had failed to receive light during his life, he would receive it at least in the hour of death.

## OBJECTION VII

Whoever gives only to some, and not to all, the means of producing effectively in them good will and final saving faith has not enough goodness.

God does so.

Therefore, etc.

## ANSWER

I deny the major. It is true that God could overcome the greatest resistance of the human heart, and indeed he sometimes does so, whether by an inward grace or by the outward circumstances that can greatly influence souls; but he does not always do so. From this comes this distinction, someone will say, and why does his goodness appear to be restricted? The truth is that it would not have been in order always to act in an extraordinary way and to derange the connexion of things, as I have observed already in answering the first objection. The reasons for this connexion, whereby the one is placed in more favourable circumstances

---

1  Johann Hulsemann (1602-61), German Lutheran theologian.

than the other, are hidden in the depths of God's wisdom: they depend upon the universal harmony. The best plan of the universe, which God could not fail to choose, required this. One concludes thus from the event itself; since God made the universe, it was not possible to do better. Such management, far from being contrary to goodness, has rather been prompted by supreme goodness itself. This objection with its solution might have been inferred from what was said with regard to the first objection; but it seemed advisable to touch upon it separately.

## OBJECTION VIII

Whoever cannot fail to choose the best is not free.

God cannot fail to choose the best.

Therefore God is not free.

## ANSWER

I deny the major of this argument. Rather it is true freedom, and the most perfect, to be able to make the best use of one's free will, and always to exercise this power, without being turned aside either by outward force or by inward passions, with which the one enslaves our bodies and the other our souls. There is nothing less servile and more befitting the highest degree of freedom than to be always led towards the good, and always by one's own inclination, without any constraint and without any displeasure. And to object that God therefore had need of external things is only a sophism. He creates them freely: but when he had set before him an end, that of exercising his goodness, his wisdom determined him to choose the means most appropriate for obtaining this end. To call that a *need* is to take the term in a sense not usual, which clears it of all imperfection, somewhat as one does when speaking of the wrath of God. Seneca[1] says somewhere, that God commanded only once, but that he obeys always, because he obeys the laws that he willed to ordain for

---

1   Lucius Annaeus Seneca (ca. 5 BCE-65 CE), Roman Stoic philosopher, statesman, and playwright.

himself: *semel jussit, semper paret.*[1] But it would have been better if he had said that God always commands and that he is always obeyed: for in willing he always follows the tendency of his own nature, and all other things always follow his will. And as this will is always the same one cannot say that he obeys only that will that he formerly had. Nevertheless, although his will is always indefectible and always tends towards the best, the evil or the lesser good that he rejects will still be possible in itself. Otherwise the necessity of good would be geometrical (so to speak) or metaphysical, and altogether absolute; the contingency of things would be destroyed, and there would be no choice. But necessity of this kind, which does not destroy the possibility of the contrary, has the name by analogy only: it becomes effective not through the mere essence of things, but through what is outside them and above them, that is, through the will of God. This necessity is called moral, because for the wise what is necessary and what is owing are equivalent things; and when it is always followed by its effect, as it indeed is in the perfectly wise, that is, in God, one can say that it is a happy necessity. The more closely creatures approach this, the closer they come to perfect felicity. Moreover, necessity of this kind is not the necessity one endeavours to avoid, and which destroys morality....

---

1 "Once he commanded, always he obeys" (Seneca, *De providentia* 5.8).

# Appendix E: From David Hume, An Enquiry concerning Human Understanding (1748)[1]

[This passage from Hume's (first) *Enquiry* shows the resonance that Leibniz's conception of a pre-established harmony had in the broad European philosophical and cultural world since its appearance in Leibniz's *Theodicy* in 1710. A copy of the book, from the edition of 1720, was among the volumes in Hume's library.[2] That Hume had read it, and taken it seriously, is confirmed by a short passage in the *Abstract* of *A Treatise of Human Nature*, which Hume himself wrote, in 1740 (in the third person, and as though by an external reader) to try to advance attention to the work after its first two volumes had appeared: "The celebrated *Monsieur Leibnitz* has observed it to be a defect in the common systems of logic, that they are very copious when they explain the operations of the understanding in the forming of demonstrations, but are too concise when they treat of probabilities, and those other measures of evidence on which life and action entirely depend, and which are our guides even in most of our philosophical speculations. In this censure, he comprehends the *Essay on Human Understanding* [Locke], *Le Recherche de la verité* [Malebranche], and *L'Art de penser* [Arnauld and Nicole]. The author of the *Treatise of Human Nature* seems to have been sensible of this defect in these philosophers, and has endeavoured, as much as he can, to supply it."[3] Although Hume is being slightly ironical in the reference which he makes below to the pre-established harmony, it is to be noted both that he has

---

1   David Hume, *Enquiries concerning the Human Understanding and concerning the Principles of Morals*, ed. L.A. Selby-Bigge (Oxford: Clarendon, 1902), 2nd ed., pp. 54ff.
2   David Fate Norton and Mary J. Norton, *The David Hume Library* (Edinburgh: Edinburgh Bibliographical Society, 1996), p. 32, 109.
3   David Hume, *A Treatise of Human Nature*, ed. David Fate Norton and Mary J. Norton (Oxford: Clarendon, 2007), vol. 1, p. 408. It may be noted that Hume, or the *Abstract*'s printer, has rendered the title of Malebranche's treatise inaccurately. It should be *De la Recherche de la vérité*.

fully grasped Leibniz's conception and that his own comparable case—of an extraordinary concurrence and systematic parallel between the actual courses of nature and the psychological belief and expectation patterns and practices in human minds, in spite of an absence (Hume thinks) of any causal or rational connections between the two systems—is almost as wildly implausible as Leibniz's original. Hume also cites Leibniz in his *Dialogues concerning Natural Religion*, where he has his character Philo name Leibniz as the first philosopher of note to take the supposedly bizarre view that this is the best of all possible worlds. "That sentiment had been maintained by *Dr. King*[1] and some few others before *Leibniz*; though by none of so great a fame as that German philosopher who ventured upon so bold and paradoxical an opinion; at least, the first who made it essential to his philosophical system."[2]]

## Section V, Part II

Contiguity to home can never excite our ideas of home, unless we *believe* that it really exists. Now I assert, that this belief, where it reaches beyond the memory or senses, is of a similar nature, and arises from similar causes, with the transition of thought and vivacity of conception here explained. When I throw a piece of dry wood into a fire, my mind is immediately carried to conceive, that it augments, not extinguishes the flame. This transition of thought from the cause to the effect proceeds not from reason. It derives its origin altogether from custom and experience. And as it first begins from an object, present to the senses, it renders the idea or conception of flame more strong and lively than any loose, floating reverie of the imagination. That idea arises immediately. The thought moves instantly towards it, and conveys to it all that force of conception, which is derived from the impression present to the senses. When a sword is levelled at my breast, does not the idea of wound and pain strike me more strongly, than

---

1   William King (1650-1729), (Anglican) Archbishop of Dublin; his *De Origine Mali* [On the Origin of Evil] (1702; English trans. 1731) prompted responses by both Bayle and Leibniz. Leibniz's appeared as a fourth Appendix to the *Theodicy*.

2   David Hume, *Dialogues concerning Natural Religion and Other Writings*, ed. Dorothy Coleman (Cambridge: Cambridge UP, 2007), p. 69.

when a glass of wine is presented to me, even though by accident this idea should occur after the appearance of the latter object? But what is there in this whole matter to cause such a strong conception, except only a present object and a customary transition to the idea of another object, which we have been accustomed to conjoin with the former? This is the whole operation of the mind, in all our conclusions concerning matter of fact and existence; and it is a satisfaction to find some analogies, by which it may be explained. The transition from a present object does in all cases give strength and solidity to the related idea.

Here, then, is a kind of pre-established harmony between the course of nature and the succession of our ideas; and though the powers and forces, by which the former is governed, be wholly unknown to us; yet our thoughts and conceptions have still, we find, gone on in the same train with the other works of nature. Custom is that principle, by which this correspondence has been effected; so necessary to the subsistence of our species, and the regulation of our conduct, in every circumstance and occurrence of human life. Had not the presence of an object instantly excited the idea of those objects, commonly conjoined with it, all our knowledge must have been limited to the narrow sphere of our memory and senses; and we should never have been able to adjust means to ends, or employ our natural powers, either to the producing of good, or avoiding of evil. Those, who delight in the discovery and contemplation of *final causes*, have here ample subject to employ their wonder and admiration.

I shall add, for a further confirmation of the foregoing theory, that, as this operation of the mind, by which we infer like effects from like causes, and *vice versa*, is so essential to the subsistence of all human creatures, it is not probable, that it could be trusted to the fallacious deductions of our reason, which is slow in its operations; appears not, in any degree, during the first years of infancy; and at best is, in every age and period of human life, extremely liable to error and mistake. It is more conformable to the ordinary wisdom of nature to secure so necessary an act of the mind, by some instinct or mechanical tendency, which may be infallible in its operations, may discover itself at the first appearance of life and thought, and may be independent of all the laboured deductions of the understanding. As nature has taught us the use of our limbs, without giving us the knowledge of the muscles and nerves, by which they are actuated; so has she implanted in us an instinct, which carries forward the thought in a correspondent course to that which she has established among external objects; though we are ignorant of those powers and forces, on which this regular course and succession of objects totally depends.

# Appendix F: From Voltaire, Candide (1759)

[François-Marie Arouet de Voltaire (1694-1778) is in many respects the supreme embodiment of the European Enlightenment. Philosopher, poet, playwright, historian, wit and satirist, and activist advocate of free thought, for which he suffered extensive periods of imprisonment in the Bastille, and a beating at the hands of thugs hired by an aristocrat he had offended, Voltaire was famous, successful, and prolific. His safety at risk in more than one setting, he lived variously in France, England, Switzerland, and Prussia—the latter stay at the court and under the patronage of Frederick the Great, the grandson of one of Leibniz's "philosophical princesses." Perhaps Voltaire's still most popular, successful, and influential work is *Candide* ("*or Optimism*," to give the novel its subtitle). Prompted by specific cases of natural and moral evils of the period (e.g., the Lisbon earthquake of 1750, and the fiendishly cruel execution of Damiens, an unhinged individual who had scratched the arm of King Louis XV), Voltaire relates the wandering saga of an innocent German youth, Candide, accompanied, for most of his odyssey, by a philosopher, Dr Pangloss, described explicitly as a disciple of Leibniz. (He is not intended to be Leibniz himself, though the original domicile of the central characters is Westphalia—which is to say, in the general vicinity of Hanover.) The portrait is biting, and the consequences, for public perceptions of Leibnizian philosophy, and above all that of the *Theodicy*, probably indelible. The translation is the 1759 Nourse translation.[1]]

## CHAPTER I

In a castle of Westphalia ... lived a youth ... called *Candide*.... Pangloss, the preceptor, was the oracle of his family, and little Candide gave ear to his instructions with all the simplicity becoming his age, and natural temper of mind.

---

1 Reprinted in Voltaire, *Candide, or All for the Best*, Nourse (London) translation (1759), rev. ed. Eric Palmer (Peterborough, ON: Broadview, 2009).

Pangloss was professor of metaphysico-theologo-cosmolo-nigology. He could prove most admirably that there is no effect without a cause, and that in this world, the best of all possible worlds, the Baron's castle was the most magnificent of castles, and his lady the best of Baronesses that could possibly exist.

"It is demonstrable," said he, "that things cannot be otherwise than as they are, for all things having been created for some end, they must consequently be created for the best. Observe, that the nose is formed for spectacles, and therefore we come to wear spectacles. The legs are visibly designed for stockings, and therefore we come to wear stockings. Stones were made to be hewn, and to construct castles; therefore my lord has a magnificent castle: for the greatest baron in the province ought to be the best lodged. Swine were intended to be eaten; therefore we eat pork all the year round, and they who assert that everything is right, do not express themselves correctly; they should say that everything is for the best." [...]

## CHAPTER III

[...] There was never anything so gallant, so well accoutered, so brilliant, and so well disposed, as the two armies were. Trumpets, fifes, oboes, drums and cannon made such music as the devil himself never heard in hell. The cannonading first of all laid flat about six thousand men on each side; the musket-balls swept away out of the best of worlds nine or ten thousand ruffians that infected the surface of the earth. The bayonet was next a *sufficient reason* for the death of several thousands. The whole might amount to thirty thousand souls. [...]

## CHAPTER IV

"... In her arms I tasted the pleasure of paradise, which produced those hellish torments with which you see me devoured. She was infected with the distemper [syphilis or the pox], and perhaps she has died of it since. This present Paquette received of a learned Cordelier [Franciscan], who had traced it to the source; he was indebted for it to an old countess, who had it of a captain of horse, who had it of a marchioness, who had it of a page, who had it of a Jesuit, who in his novitiate had it in a direct line from one of the companions of Christopher Columbus. For my part I shall give it to nobody, I am dying."

"O Pangloss!" cried Candide, "what a strange genealogy! Is not the devil the original source of it?"

"Not at all," replied this great man, "it was a thing unavoidable, a necessary ingredient, in the best of worlds! For if Columbus had not landed upon an island in America, and there catched this disease—which contaminates the source of life, frequently hinders generation, and is evidently opposite to the great end of nature, we should have neither chocolate nor cochineal. We are also to observe that upon our continent this distemper is, like religious controversy, confined to a particular spot. The Turks, the Indians, the Persians, the Chinese, the Siamese, the Japanese, know nothing of it; but there is a sufficient reason to make us conclude that they will be acquainted with it in a few centuries. In the mean time, it has made prodigious havoc among us, especially in those armies composed of well-disciplined hirelings who determine the fate of nations, for we may safely affirm, that when an army of thirty thousand men fights another of an equal number, there are about twenty thousand of them poxed on each side." [...]

## CHAPTER V

[...] Pangloss endeavoured to console them by affirming that things could not be otherwise than as they were. "Because," said he, "all this is fittest and best. For if there is a volcano at Lisbon, it could be in no other spot, for it is impossible but things should be as they are, for everything is right."

Near him sat a little man dressed in black, belonging to the inquisition, who, taking him up with great complaisance, said, "Very likely, sir, you do not believe in original sin. For if everything is best and fittest, consequently there was no such thing as the fall, or punishment of man."

"I humbly ask your excellency's pardon," answered Pangloss still more politely, "for the fall and curse of man, necessarily entered into the system of the best of worlds."

"Therefore, sir," said the other, "you do not believe any such thing as liberty?"

"Your excellency will be so good as to excuse me," said Pangloss. "Liberty is consistent with absolute necessity, for it was necessary we should be free...."

# CHAPTER VI

[...] Candide, terrified and amazed at the shocking bloody scene, said to himself with some trepidation, "If this is the best of possible worlds, what must we think of the rest?" [...]

# CHAPTER XIX

[...] As they drew near the town they saw a negro stretched upon the ground, with only one moiety [half] of his habit, that is, of his blue linen drawers; the poor man had lost his left leg and his right arm. "Good God!" said Candide, in Dutch. "What art thou doing there, friend, in that shocking condition?"

"I am waiting for my master mynheer Vanderdendur, the famous merchant," answered the negro.

"Was it mynheer Vanderdendur," said Candide, "that used thee in this manner?"

"Yes, sir," said the negro, "it is the custom of our country. They give us a pair of linen drawers for our whole garment twice a year. When we work at the sugar-canes and the mill snatches hold of a finger, they cut off our hand, and when we attempt to run away, they cut off our leg. Both cases have happened to me. That is what we suffer for your eating sugar in Europe.

"Yet when my mother sold me for ten patacoons on the coast of Guinea, she said to me, 'My dear child, bless our Fetiches. Adore them forever; they will make thee live happy. Thou hast the honour of being the slave of our lords the whites, which is making the fortune of thy father and mother.' Alas! I know not whether I have made their fortune; this I know, that they have not made mine. Dogs, monkeys and parrots are a thousand times less wretched than I. The Dutch Fetiches who converted me, declare every Sunday, that we are all of us children of Adam, blacks as well as whites. I am not skilled in genealogy, but if those preachers tell the truth, we are all second cousins. Now you must allow me that it is impossible to treat one's relations in a more barbarous manner."

"O Pangloss!" cried Candide. "You never thought of this horrid scene; there is an end of the matter. I see I must renounce your doctrine at last."

"What is his doctrine?" said Cacambo.

"Alas!" said Candide, "It is the folly of maintaining that everything is right, when it is wrong!" [...]

# CHAPTER XXI

[...] "Do you believe," said Candide, "that mankind used always to cut one another's throats; that they were always liars, cheats, traitors, and ungrateful; always robbers, fools, inconstant, cowards, envious, gluttons, drunkards, misers, swayed by ambition, bloody-minded, calumniators, debauchees, fanatics, and hypocrites?"

"Do you believe," said Martin, "that hawks always eat pigeons, when these came in their way?"

"Yes, surely," said Candide.

"Well then," said Martin, "if hawks have always had the same nature, why should you pretend that mankind changed theirs?"

"Oh!" said Candide, "there is a vast deal of difference, for free-will ..." Reasoning thus they arrived at Bordeaux. [...]

# CHAPTER XXIII

[...] "You are acquainted with England. Are they as great fools in that country as in France?"

"They have a different kind of folly," said Martin. "You know that these two nations are at war, for a few acres of barren land in the neighbourhood of Canada, and that they have spent a great deal more in the prosecution of this war than all Canada is worth ..."

# CHAPTER XXVIII

[...] "Well, my dear Pangloss," said Candide to him, "when you were hanged, dissected, whipped, and tugging at the oar, did you always think that everything in this world happens for the best?"

"I am still of my first opinion," answered Pangloss. "For after all, I am a philosopher, and it does not become me to retract, especially as Leibniz could never be in the wrong and besides, the pre-established harmony is the finest thing in the world, and so is his *plenum* and *materia subtilis*."

# CHAPTER XXX

[...] "I was in hopes," said Pangloss, "that I should reason with you a little about causes and effects, about the best of possible worlds, the origin of evil, the nature of the soul, and the pre-established harmony."

[Pangloss continued,] "... there is a concatenation of events in this best of all possible worlds; for if you had not been kicked out of a magnificent castle on account of miss Cunegonde, if you had not been thrown into the inquisition, if you had not rambled all over America on foot, if you had not run the Baron through the body, if you had not lost all your fine sheep of El Dorado, you would not be here to eat preserved citrons and pistachio nuts."

"All that is very well," answered Candide, "but let us take care of our garden."

# *Appendix G: From Thomas Reid,* Essays on the Intellectual Powers of Man *(1785)*

[Scottish philosopher Thomas Reid's *Essays on the Intellectual Powers of Man* devotes an entire chapter to Leibniz, reprinted (from an 1814-15 edition[1]) below. Reid (1710-96) is particularly concerned with Leibniz's views of (sense) perception, and their implications within his system, but he presents a wider view of the whole Leibnizian system, and it is interesting to see how that system looked to the great philosopher of common sense, less than seventy years after Leibniz's death. It may be noted that Reid has consulted the *Principles of Nature and of Grace*, as well as other writings. Though he claims not to understand some parts of Leibniz's metaphysics, and is wholly dismissive of the prospects for a convincing or plausible rationale for its central doctrines, Reid does get the general structure and shape of the system, and much of its content in detail, entirely right. Most, now, would side with Leibniz against Reid (and Locke) on the intelligibility—indeed, the reality—of unconscious thought.]

## CHAPTER XV.

### ACCOUNT OF THE SYSTEM OF LEIBNITZ.[2]

There is yet another system concerning perception, of which I shall give some account, because of the fame of its author. It is the invention of the famous German philosopher Leibnitz, who, while he lived, held the first rank among the Germans in all parts of philosophy, as well as in mathematics, in jurisprudence, in the knowledge of antiquities, and in every branch both of science and of literature. He was highly respected by emperors, and by many kings and princes, who bestowed upon him singular marks

---

1   Samuel Etheridge, Jr., *The Works of Thomas Reid*, 4 vols. (Charlestown, MA, 1813-15).

2   See the Introduction, p. 10, note 1, for this alternative spelling of Leibniz's name.

of their esteem. He was a particular favourite of our Queen Caroline, consort of George II, with whom he continued his correspondence by letters, after she came to the crown of Britain, till his death.

The famous controversy between him and the British mathematicians, whether he or sir Isaac Newton was the inventor of that noble improvement in mathematics, called by Newton, *the method of fluxions*, and by Leibnitz *the differential method*, engaged the attention of the mathematicians in Europe for several years. He had likewise a controversy with the learned and judicious Dr. Samuel Clarke, about several points of the Newtonian philosophy which he disapproved. The papers which gave occasion to this controversy, with all the replies and rejoinders, had the honour to be transmitted from the one party to the other, through the hands of Queen Caroline, and were afterwards published.

His authority, in all matters of philosophy, is still so great in most parts of Germany, that they are considered as bold spirits, and a kind of heretics, who dissent from him in any thing. Wolfius,[1] the most voluminous writer in philosophy of this age, is considered as the great interpreter and advocate of the Leibnitzian system, and reveres as an oracle whatever has dropped from the pen of Leibnitz. This author [Wolfius] proposed two great works upon the mind. The first, which I have seen, he published with the title of *Psychologia empirica, seu experimentalis* [1732]. The other was to have the title of *Psychologia rationalis* [1734]; and to it he refers for his explication of the theory of Leibnitz with regard to the mind. But whether it was published I have not learned.

I must therefore take the short account I am to give of this system from the writings of Leibnitz himself, without the light which his interpreter Wolfius may have thrown upon it.

Leibnitz conceived the whole universe, bodies as well as minds, to be made up of monads, that is, simple substances, each of which is, by the Creator in the beginning of its existence, endowed with certain active and perceptive powers. A monad, therefore, is an active substance, simple, without parts or figure, which has within itself the power to produce all the changes it undergoes from the beginning of its existence to eternity. The

---

1  Christian Wolff (1679-1754), protégé and chief philosophical successor of Leibniz; the leading rationalist philosopher in Germany in the period before Kant.

changes which the monad undergoes, of what kind soever, though they may seem to us the effect of causes operating from without, yet they are only the gradual and successive evolutions of its own internal powers, which would have produced all the same changes and motions, although there had been no other being in the universe.

Every human soul is a monad joined to an organized body, which organized body consists of an infinite number of monads, each having some degree of active and of perceptive power in itself. But the whole machine of the body has a relation to that monad which we call the soul, which is, as it were, the centre of the whole.

As the universe is completely filled with monads, without any chasm or void, and thereby every body acts upon every other body, according to its vicinity or distance, and is mutually re-acted upon by every other body, it follows, says Leibnitz, that every monad is a kind of living mirror, which reflects the whole universe, according to its point of view, and represents the whole more or less distinctly.

I cannot undertake to reconcile this part of the system with what was before mentioned, to wit, that every change in a monad is the evolution of its own original powers, and would have happened though no other substance had been created. But to proceed;

There are different orders of monads, some higher, and others lower. The higher orders he calls dominant; such is the human soul. The monads that compose the organized bodies of men, animals and plants, are of a lower order, and subservient to the dominant monads. But every monad of whatever order is a complete substance in itself, indivisible, having no parts, indestructible, because, having no parts, it cannot perish by any kind of decomposition; it can only perish by annihilation, and we have no reason to believe that God will ever annihilate any of the beings which he has made.

The monads of a lower order may, by a regular evolution of their powers, rise to a higher order. They may successively be joined to organized bodies, of various forms and different degrees of perception; but they never die, nor cease to be in some degree active and percipient.

This philosopher makes a distinction between perception and what he calls *apperception*. The first is common to all monads, the last proper to the higher orders, among which are human souls.

By apperception he understands that degree of perception which reflects, as it were, upon itself; by which we are conscious of our own existence, and conscious of our perceptions; by which we can reflect upon the operations of our own minds, and can comprehend abstract truths. The mind, in many operations, he thinks, particularly in sleep, and in many actions common to us with the brutes, has not this apperception, although it is still filled with a multitude of obscure and indistinct perceptions, of which we are not conscious.

He conceives that our bodies and minds are united in such a manner, that neither has any physical influence upon the other. Each performs all its operations by its own internal springs and powers; yet the operations of one correspond exactly with those of the other, by a pre-established harmony; just as one clock may be so adjusted as to keep time with another, although each has its own moving power, and neither receives any part of its motion from the other.

So that, according to this system, all our perceptions of external objects would be the same, though external things had never existed; our perception of them would continue, although, by the power of God, they should this moment be annihilated: we do not perceive external things because they exist, but because the soul was originally so constituted as to produce in itself all its successive changes, and all its successive perceptions, independently of the external objects.

Every perception or apperception, every operation, in a word, of the soul, is a necessary consequence of the state of it immediately preceding that operation; and this state is the necessary consequence of the state preceding it; and so backward, until you come to its first formation and constitution, which produces successively, and by necessary consequence, all its successive states to the end of its existence; so that in this respect the soul, and every monad, may be compared to a watch wound up, which, having the spring of its motion in itself, by the gradual evolution of its own spring, produces all the successive motions we observe in it.

In this account of Leibnitz's system concerning monads, and the pre-established harmony, I have kept, as nearly as I could, to his own expressions, in his *new system of the nature and communication of substances, and of the union of soul and body*; and in the several illustrations of that new system which he afterwards published; and in his *principles of nature and grace founded in reason*. I shall now make a few remarks upon this system.

1. To pass over the irresistible necessity of all human actions, which makes a part of this system, that will be considered in another place, I observe first, that the distinction made between perception and apperception is obscure and unphilosophical. As far as we can discover, every operation of our mind is attended with consciousness, and particularly that which we call the perception of external objects; and to speak of a perception of which we are not conscious, is to speak without any meaning.

As consciousness is the only power by which we discern the operations of our own minds, or can form any notion of them, an operation of mind of which we are not conscious, is, we know not what; and to call such an operation by the name of perception, is an abuse of language. No man can perceive an object, without being conscious that he perceives it. No man can think, without being conscious that he thinks. What men are not conscious of, cannot therefore, without impropriety, be called either perception or thought of any kind. And if we will suppose operations of mind, of which we are not conscious, and give a name to such creatures of our imagination, that name must signify what we know nothing about.

2. To suppose bodies organized or unorganized, to be made up of indivisible monads which have no parts, is contrary to all that we know of body. It is essential to a body to have parts; and every part of a body, is a body, and has parts also. No number of parts, without extension or figure, not even an infinite number, if we may use that expression, can, by being put together, make a whole that has extension and figure, which all bodies have.

3. It is contrary to all that we know of bodies, to ascribe to the monads, of which they are supposed to be compounded, perception and active force. If a philosopher thinks proper to say, that a clod of earth both perceives and has active force, let him bring his proofs. But he ought not to expect, that men who have understanding, will so far give it up as to receive without proof whatever his imagination may suggest.

4. This system overturns all authority of our senses, and leaves not the least ground to believe the existence of the objects of sense, or the existence of any thing which depends upon the authority of our senses; for our perception of objects, according to this system, has no dependence upon any thing external, and

would be the same as it is, supposing external objects had never existed, or that they were from this moment annihilated.

It is remarkable that Leibnitz's system, that of Malebranche, and the common system of ideas, or images of external objects in the mind, do all agree in overturning all the authority of our senses; and this one thing, as long as men retain their senses, will always make all these systems truly ridiculous.

5. The last observation I shall make upon this system, which indeed is equally applicable to all the systems of perception I have mentioned, is, that it is all hypothesis, made up of conjectures and suppositions, without proof. The Peripatetics supposed sensible *species* to be sent forth by the objects of sense. The moderns suppose ideas in the brain, or in the mind. Malebranche supposed, that we perceive the ideas of the Divine mind. Leibnitz supposed monads and a pre-established harmony; and these monads being creatures of his own making, he is at liberty to give them what properties and powers his fancy may suggest. In like manner, the Indian philosopher supposed that the earth is supported by a huge elephant, and that the elephant stands on the back of a huge tortoise.

Such suppositions, while there is no proof of them offered, are nothing but the fictions of human fancy; and we ought no more to believe them, than we believe Homer's fictions of Apollo's silver bow, or Minerva's shield, or Venus's girdle. Such fictions in poetry are agreeable to the rules of art. They are intended to please, not to convince. But the philosophers would have us to believe their fictions, though the account they give of the phenomena of nature has commonly no more probability than the account that Homer gives of the plague in the Grecian camp, from Apollo taking his station on a neighbouring mountain, and from his silver bow, letting fly his swift arrows into the camp.

Men then only begin to have a true taste in philosophy, when they have learned to hold hypotheses in just contempt; and to consider them as the reveries of speculative men, which will never have any similitude to the works of God.

The Supreme Being has given us some intelligence of his works, by what our senses inform us of external things, and by what our consciousness and reflection inform us concerning the operations of our own minds. Whatever can be inferred from these common informations, by just and sound reasoning, is true and legitimate philosophy: but what we add to this from conjecture is all spurious and illegitimate.

After this long account of the theories advanced by philosophers, to account for our perception of external objects, I hope it will appear, that neither Aristotle's theory of sensible species, nor Malebranche's, of our seeing things in God, nor the common theory of our perceiving ideas in our own minds, nor Leibnitz's theory of monads, and a pre-established harmony, give any satisfying account of this power of the mind, or make it more intelligible than it is without their aid. They are conjectures, and, if they were true, would solve no difficulty, but raise many new ones. It is therefore more agreeable to good sense, and to sound philosophy, to rest satisfied with what our consciousness and attentive reflection discover to us of the nature of perception, than by inventing hypotheses, to attempt to explain things which are above the reach of human understanding. I believe no man is able to explain how we perceive external objects, any more than how we are conscious of those that are internal. Perception, consciousness, memory, and imagination, are all original and simple powers of the mind, and parts of its constitution. For this reason, though I have endeavoured to show, that the theories of philosophers on this subject are ill grounded and insufficient, I do not attempt to substitute any other theory in their place.

Every man feels that perception gives him an invincible belief of the existence of that which he perceives; and that this belief is not the effect of reasoning, but the immediate consequence of perception. When philosophers have wearied themselves and their readers with their speculations upon this subject, they can neither strengthen this belief, nor weaken it; nor can they show how it is produced. It puts the philosopher and the peasant upon a level; and neither of them can give any other reason for believing his senses, than that he finds it impossible for him to do otherwise.

# Further Reading and Select Bibliography

Adams, Robert Merrihew. *Leibniz: Determinist, Theist, Idealist.* Oxford: Oxford UP, 1994.

Antognazza, Maria Rosa. *Leibniz: An Intellectual Biography.* Cambridge: Cambridge UP, 2009.

Bolton, Martha Brandt. "Locke, Leibniz, and the Logic of Mechanism." *Journal of the History of Philosophy* 36.2 (April 1998): 189-213.

Broad, C.D. *Leibniz: An Introduction.* Cambridge: Cambridge UP, 1975.

Brown, Stuart. *Leibniz.* Minneapolis: U of Minnesota P, 1984.

Brown, Stuart, and N.J. Fox. *Historical Dictionary of Leibniz's Philosophy.* Lanham, MD: Scarecrow P, 2006.

Frankfurt, Harry G., ed. *Leibniz: A Collection of Critical Essays.* Garden City, NY: Anchor, 1972.

Garber, Daniel. *Leibniz: Body, Substance, Monad.* Oxford: Oxford UP, 2009.

Hartz, Glenn A. *Leibniz's Final System.* London: Routledge, 2007.

Hooker, Michael, ed. *Leibniz: Critical and Interpretive Essays.* Manchester: Manchester UP, 1982.

Jolley, Nicholas, ed. *The Cambridge Companion to Leibniz.* Cambridge: Cambridge UP, 1995.

Leibniz, G.W. *De Summa Rerum. Metaphysical Papers, 1675-1676.* Trans. with an introduction and notes by G.H.R. Parkinson. New Haven and London: Yale UP, 1992.

——. *The Labyrinth of the Continuum: Writings on the Continuum Problem, 1672-1686.* Trans., ed., and with an introduction by Richard Arthur. New Haven and London: Yale UP, 2001.

——. *Philosophical Essays.* Ed. Roger Ariew and Daniel Garber. Indianapolis: Hackett, 1989.

——. *Philosophical Papers and Letters.* Ed. Leroy E. Loemker. Dordrecht: Reidel, 1969.

——. *Theodicy.* Ed. Austin M. Farrer. Trans. E.M. Huggard. Routledge, 1951. New York: Cosimo, 2009.

——, and Samuel Clarke. *Correspondence.* Indianapolis: Hackett, 2000.

Lodge, Paul, ed. *Leibniz and His Correspondents.* Cambridge: Cambridge UP, 2004.

Loptson, Peter. "Leibniz, Sufficient Reason, and Possible Worlds." *Studia Leibnitiana* 17.2 (1985): 191-203.

——. "Spinozist Monism." *Philosophia* 18.1 (April 1988): 19-38.

——. "Was Leibniz an Idealist?" *Philosophy* 74 (May 1999): 361-85.

——, and R.T.W. Arthur. "Leibniz's Body Realism: Two Interpretations." *The Leibniz Review* 16 (December 2006): 1-42.

Mason, H.T., ed. and trans. *The Leibniz-Arnauld Correspondence.* Manchester: Manchester UP, 1967.

Mates, Benson. *The Philosophy of Leibniz.* Oxford: Oxford UP, 1986.

McRae, Robert. *Leibniz: Perception, Apperception, and Thought.* Toronto: U of Toronto P, 1976.

Phemister, Pauline. *Leibniz and the Natural World.* Dordrecht: Springer, 2005.

——, ed. "Rethinking Leibniz." *The Monist* 81.4 (October 1998).

Rescher, Nicholas. *G.W. Leibniz's* Monadology*: An Edition for Students.* Pittsburgh: U of Pittsburgh P, 1991.

——. *The Philosophy of Leibniz.* Englewood Cliffs, NJ: Prentice-Hall, 1967.

——. *On Leibniz.* 2nd edition. Pittsburgh: U of Pittsburgh P., 2012.

——, ed. *Leibnizian Inquiries.* Lanham, MD: UP of America, 1989.

Ross, G. MacDonald. *Leibniz.* Oxford: Oxford UP, 1984.

Russell, Bertrand. *A Critical Exposition of the Philosophy of Leibniz.* 2nd ed. London: Allen and Unwin, 1937.

Rutherford, Donald. *Leibniz and the Rational Order of Nature.* Cambridge: Cambridge UP, 1995.

——, and J.A. Cover, eds. *Leibniz: Nature and Freedom.* Oxford: Oxford UP, 2005.

Sleigh, R.C., Jr. *Leibniz & Arnauld: A Commentary on Their Correspondence.* New Haven: Yale UP, 1990.

Wilson, Catherine. *The Invisible World: Early Modern Philosophy and the Invention of the Microscope.* Princeton: Princeton UP, 1995.

——. *Leibniz's Metaphysics.* Princeton: Princeton UP, 1989.

Woolhouse, R.S., ed. *Leibniz: Metaphysics and Philosophy of Science.* Oxford: Oxford UP, 1981.

——, and Richard Francks, trans. and eds. *Leibniz's 'New System' and Associated Contemporary Texts.* Oxford: Clarendon, 1997.

# Index

absolute necessity, 157, 166, 168, 180, 188, 201, 215

*Abstract of A Treatise of Human Nature* (Hume), 209

Académie des sciences, 12n1

accidental forms, 193

*Acta eruditorum*, 11n2, 12

active force, 159, 223

adequate knowledge, 85

analytical method, 37

Anaxagoras, 35

ancient philosophy, 67-68, 83, 100, 167

animalcules, 108, 132, 144-45

animals, 32, 44, 106-07, 128. *See also* rational animals
    formation of, 158
    memory, 121
    metamorphosis in, 130-31
    organized in the seed, 148
    perceptions resembling reason, 107, 160
    souls, 96, 119

antecedent will of God, 163, 174, 202

*Antiperkinsus* (Arminius), 203

apperception or consciousness, 31, 33, 107, 119, 221-25

appetition, 34-36, 41, 105, 119, 131

appetitive faculty, 125

Aquinas, Thomas, Saint, 42, 66, 67n1, 69, 197, 203

Ariew, Roger, 46n1

Aristotelian contrast between efficient and final causes, 38

"Aristotelian" Leibniz, 44-45

Aristotle, 18, 35, 50, 88, 167, 180, 191, 225

Arminius, Jacobus, *Antiperkinsus*, 203

Arnauld, Antoine, 17, 20

Arthur, R.T.W., 50n2

Augustine, Saint, Bishop of Hippo, 92, 165, 167, 197, 204

autarkeia, 35

Averroists, 89

axioms, 37, 123

Barbarus, Hermolaus, 125

bare monads, 30, 45, 121

"basic particles," 28

Bayle, Pierre, 157, 159, 174, 177-78, 180-82, 188, 190, 192-93
    *Historical and Critical Dictionary*, 23, 119, 127, 147-53, 158

Becher, Johann Joachim, 189

Becomings, 45

being, 45, 95, 161

Beings, 45

Berkeley, George, 19n19

Berlin Society of Sciences, 12n1

Bernard, John Peter, 148

Bernoulli, Johann, 13

best of all possible worlds, 42, 109-10, 113, 161-62, 210
    Voltaire's satire, 214-17

"biologistical" thinker, 45

Birch, Thomas, 148

birth, 30, 130-31, 150

bodies, 16, 41-45, 50, 69, 96-97, 131, 149. *See also* mind-body problem; union of body and soul
    belonging to monads, 128
    intelligent cause with respect to, 84

mutual dependency of the
body and soul, 152, 172
not attached to our essences, 95
organic (*See* organic bodies)
in perpetual flux, 130
body and soul. *See* soul and body
relation
body realism (or reality of
bodies), 21, 46
Boethius, *The Consolation of
Philosophy*, 162
Boineburg, Johann Christian,
Freiherr von, 11
Brahe, Tycho, 172
Bruno, Giordano, 136
brutes. *See* animals
Burnett, Thomas, 135

calculus, 13
Calvinism, 92n1
*Candide* (Voltaire), 213-18
Caroline, Queen, consort of
George II, King of Great
Britain, 14, 220
Cartesians, 31, 107, 119, 152, 182
catoptric and dioptric laws, 82
causal relations, 21, 40
causality, 152
causes, 41, 79, 88-90, 107, 110,
118, 141, 161, 164-65, 167-70,
189, 194, 200-01, 210-11,
217, 221. *See also* efficient
causes; final causes
free, 181
God as, 73, 75, 89, 92, 94, 97,
203-04
ideal, 169
mechanical, 119
occasional, 151, 192
psychological, 42
universal, 95

chance, 80
charity, 156
Christian orthodoxy, 22-23, 35,
39-40
Chrysippus, 180-81
Cicero, 181
*De Fato*, 180
City of God, 100, 111, 133, 179, 199
Clarke, Samuel, 13, 220
common good, 156
commonwealth of learning, 10
community, 49
community of scholars, 11
compatibilist view, 180n2
composite substances, 26-28, 37,
43, 105, 128
concomitance, 174-75
consciousness. *See* apperception
or consciousness
consequent will, 163, 202
*The Consolation of Philosophy*
(Boethius), 162
contingency, 37, 71-72, 166, 168,
186, 189-90
contingent futurities, 165, 180
contingent things, 109, 161
contingent truths, 70, 125
continual dependence upon God,
35, 73, 89
continued creation, 140, 160,
164-65, 191-92. *See also* God
contradiction, principle of, 37,
72, 122, 166
Conway, Anne, 25
*Principles of the Most Ancient
and Modern Philosophy*,
135-42
Copernicus, 172
corporeal substance, 20. *See also*
bodies
created monads. *See* monads

creation of the eternal truths
(Descartes' doctrine of), 60n1
creatures
created infinite, 136-39
imperfections come from own
nature, 165
perfections from the influence
of God, 124

death, 107-08, 110, 119-20, 131,
149-50
apparent death only an envel
opment, 130, 173
decretory will, 174, 178, 186,
202-03
*De Fato* (Cicero), 180
definitions, 37-38, 85-86, 123
deism, 24n1, 26, 38-39, 50
Democritus, 35, 135
Descartes, René, 18, 35-36, 39,
76, 78, 83, 125, 132, 135, 148
doctrine of the creation of the
eternal truths, 60n1
Desmaizeaux, Pierre, 148
determinant reason, principle of,
167
determinate truth, 180
determination, 188
compatibility with contingency
and freedom, 166, 189
determinism, 24, 36, 49-50, 90-
91, 94-95, 168, 199-201, 203.
*See also* prevision and predetermination
divinely orchestrated, 42
*Dialogues concerning Natural Reli-
gion* (Hume), 210
dioptric laws, 82
*Discourse on Metaphysics* (Leibniz), 13, 17-24, 45, 59-101
Bayle's criticism of, 149-53

distinct knowledge, 85
divine agency, 29
divine creation, 39-40
divine preformation. *See* preformation
*divine wisdom. See* wisdom of
God
doctrine of reminiscence, 18, 87.
*See also* memory
dualist system, 44, 46-48

ecumenicism, 22
efficient causes, 21, 38, 41, 49,
82-83, 106, 110, 123, 131, 133-
34, 171, 188, 194-95
ego, 107
elements, 27, 117
empirical physicians, 122
empirical testing, 12
*An Enquiry concerning Human
Understanding* (Hume),
209-12
entelechies, 31, 35-36, 44, 119-20,
125, 128, 130
Epicurus, 35, 172, 180-81
epiphenomenalism, 50n1
*Essay on Human Understanding*
(Locke), 209
*Essays on the Intellectual Powers of
Man* (Reid), 219-25
eternal truths, 39, 60n1, 124-25.
*See also* necessary truths
Eugene of Savoy, François,
Prince, 26
every substance is like an entire
world and like a mirror of
God, 66-67, 73, 75
evil, 162, 174, 177, 191, 198-99, 202
cause of, 92, 106, 179
God is not the cause, 92, 165
God permits moral evil (but

doesn't will it), 158
  greater good and, 175, 189, 197
  happens only by concomi-
    tance, 174-75
  origin of, 157-58, 218

faith, 92-93, 157, 160, 179, 205
fate, 68, 170n1, 180n2, 190
feeling or sentiment, 106
felicity. *See* happiness
Fermat, Pierre de, 83
*Fiat*, 168
final causes, 18, 21, 38, 41, 49,
    82-84, 110, 123, 131, 133-35,
    171, 188, 211
  of good and evil, 106
  in physics, 79-81
final reason, 38
final reason of things (God), 109
fitness, 40, 110, 125-26, 159
free agency, 169
free will, 99, 136, 167, 175-76,
    206, 217
  of God or of creatures, 70, 72,
    99, 182
freedom, 172, 187, 189, 197, 206
  not injured by determination,
    166
futurition, 168

Galileo, 78, 160
Garber, Daniel, 46n1
  *Leibniz: Body, Substance,
    Monad*, 47n1
Gassendi, Pierre, 172
geomancy, 64
geometrical necessity, 159, 186,
    188, 207
geometry, 64, 69-70, 72, 79, 87,
    107, 157
  eternal truths of, 60

George II, King of Great Britain,
    14, 220
God, 15, 17, 22, 30, 36-37, 40-
    41, 49, 59, 79, 95, 152, 224-25
  absolute monarch of the most
    perfect city, 70, 97-98, 111,
    133
  all other substances depend
    upon, 94, 97
  architect of the machine of the
    universe, 133
  best possible universe, 61-62,
    64, 71, 80, 94, 161-63, 167,
    178, 206 (*See also* best of
    all possible worlds)
  cause of all perfections, 165,
    203-04
  creative God of theism, 24
  Divine Goodness and Wisdom,
    136
  final reason of things, 109, 160
  first free decree of, 72
  glory of, 67, 74, 94, 133, 156
  God could have done better
    argument, 60, 182-83,
    196-97
  God created man as a sinner
    argument, 164
  God must exist if he is pos-
    sible, 124
  God's actions
    distinguishing from those
      of his creatures, 65
  grace of, 92-93, 133, 169
  grandeur of, 127
  greatest and wisest of spirits, 98
  infallibility, 166, 168
  infinitely powerful, 137-38
  intimately united to all created
    things, 94
  justice, 100, 109

knowledge of all, 111
as legislator, 133
love of God, 112-13, 134, 156
miraculous intervention (*See*
   miracles)
moral quality of, 99
more than one purpose in his
   projects, 174
most complete of all spirits, 97
most free agent, 136-37
necessary being, 39, 138
the only immediate external
   object, 89
the only original simple substance, 29, 125
ordained that spirits alone
   shall live forever, 99
orders all things at once beforehand, 159
perfection of, 16, 18, 38, 40,
   59, 62, 94, 109, 112, 124
perfect (*See* perfection of God)
permits sin and misery, 158, 197
power of, 39-40, 125, 133,
   138-40, 157, 174, 196
preserves life of man before
   that of animals, 98
proof of existence, 38, 110,
   125, 161, 167
reasons for choices unknown
   to mortals, 94
social relations, 99
source of essences, 124
spirits alone are made in his
   image, 99
sun and the light of souls, 84, 89
supportive maintenance, 35,
   73, 89
supreme substance, 123
very special monad, 27

wholly without body, 130
workman, 82
good and bad actions, 169
good will on the part of men, 100
goodness, 137-38, 161
   of God's work, 59, 61, 128
   principles of, 60

*hæcceity* (thisness), 66
Hansch, M.G., 55
happiness, 99-100, 111-13, 134, 173
   God's aim or purposes, 63,
      98, 176
   joys that God has laid up for
      those who love him, 101
harmony, 133, 173, 177. *See also*
   pre-established harmony
   between physical realm of
      nature and the moral realm
      of grace, 133
   general harmony that con-
      nects present, future, and
      past, 110, 120, 159, 189
   principle of, 170
   universal harmony, 24n2, 98,
      127, 156, 206
   of the universe, 61, 63
Hartsoeker, Nicolas, 149
Heliodorus of Larissa, 83
Heraclitus, 45
Hippocrates, 128
*Historical and Critical Dictionary*
   (Bayle), 23
Hobbes, Thomas, 23n1
Holy Scriptures, 59, 61, 89, 187
Hoole, Samuel, 144
Huggard, E.M., 155
Hulsemann, Johann, 205
human nature, 72, 108, 132, 194
human responsibility, 42

Hume, David
    *Abstract of A Treatise of Human Nature*, 209
    *Dialogues concerning Natural Religion*, 210
    *An Enquiry concerning Human Understanding*, 209-12
hypothetical necessity, 166, 201

"I," 37, 97, 122
idealism, 19-20, 22, 43, 46-47, 51, 88
imagination, 225
immortality, 96-97, 107, 142, 173n1
imperfections. *See also* evil
    from creature's own nature, 124
impiety, 84
Incarnation, 99n1
incorporeal natures, 68, 84
indifference of will, 136-37. *See also* free will
infinite divisibility of everything into ever smaller parts, 141
infinity, 27, 183
    of possibles, 185
intelligent souls, 97
    open to chastisement or recompense, 70, 97
    other creatures should serve, 70
intelligent substances
    difference from others, 98
intuitive knowledge, 85

James, William, 23n1
Jesus Christ, 100, 155
*Journal des savants*, 11n2, 143, 148
Judas, 90-91
Julius Caesar, 152-53
Jurieu, Pierre, 192
justice, 60, 137, 157

goodness in conformity with wisdom, 109
of punishment, 200-01, 204
    (*See also* punishment)
supreme justice in God, 40, 100, 109
universal law of, 142

Kant, Immanuel, 49
Kepler, Johannes, 191
King, William, 210
kingdom of heaven. *See* City of God
knowledge, 40, 59, 85-86, 97, 109, 122, 156
    adequate, 85
    God's, 39, 71, 111, 125, 164
    intuitive, 85
    reflective, 107
Köhler, Heinrich, 25n3, 55

Latta, Robert, 55
laws of motion, 81, 110, 159
laws of nature, 76, 79, 81, 84
"Lazy Reason," 157
Lazy Sophism, 190, 201
learned societies and associations, 10, 12
Leeuwenhoek, Antonie van, 143-45, 149n1, 173
Leibniz, Gottfried Wilhelm, 148, 151-52, 210
    Aristotelian view, 45, 47
    body realism, 46
    calculus, 13
    Christian orthodoxy, 22-23, 39-40
    chronology, 53-54
    controversy with Newton, 220
    correspondence with Arnauld, 20

correspondence with Johann Bernoulli, 13

correspondence with Samuel Clarke, 13, 220

as deist, 24n1, 26, 38-39, 50

determinism, 24

*Discourse on Metaphysics*, 13, 17-24, 45, 59-101

doctrine of the absence of causal interaction between created monads, 40

dualist, 44, 46-48

early life, 9-11

formal career, 10-11

idealism, 43, 46-47

intellectual culture of Europe and, 10

as mathematician, 11, 13

*Metaphysical Disputation on the Principle of Individuation*, 25n2

metaphysical system, 14-51

*Monadology*, 13, 18, 24-27, 29, 32, 34, 37, 41, 43-44, 117-34, 143, 147, 155

*New Essays Concerning Human Understanding*, 23n2

"New System of Nature and of the Communications of Substances," 149

personal life and later years, 13-14

Platonistic view, 18, 23, 45, 46n2

*The Principles of Nature and of Grace*, 13, 18, 24-27, 34, 36, 40, 43-44, 105-13, 219, 223

Reid's criticism, 219-25

*Summa Rerum*, 15n1

*Theodicy*, 13, 17, 25, 155-85, 209

*The Leibniz-Arnauld Correspondence*, 20n2

*Leibniz: Body, Substance, Monad* (Garber), 47n1

*Leipzig Journal*, 160

*Leibniz: Philosophical Essays* (Ariew and Garber), 46n1

"Leibniz's Body Realism" (Loptson), 50n2

Lewis, C.I., 38n1

liberty, 61, 70, 94. *See also* freedom

consistency with absolute necessity, 215

"little animals." *See* animalcules

living and non-living divide, 32

living being, 44, 128

location, 33

Locke, John, 36, 219

*Essay on Human Understanding*, 209

Lockman, John, 148

logic, 38n1, 107, 209

Universals of, 192

Loptson, Peter, "Leibniz's Body Realism," 50n2

Lutheranism, 22

Magliabechi, Antonio, 144

Malebranche, Nicolas, 90n1, 224-25

*De la Recherche de la vérité*, 149, 209

Malpighi, Marcello, 149

Mason, H.T., *The Leibniz-Arnauld Correspondence*, 20n2

Masson, Samuel, 46

Material nature, philosophy of, 16

material necessity, 80

mathematical concepts, 37

mathematicians, 123

mathematics, 10, 84

mechanical philosophy, 79, 84

mediate will, 174

medicine, 21, 82

memory, 96-97, 106, 120, 225
    consecutiveness that imitates-
        reason, 121
    of facts, 107

*Meno* (Plato), 18, 87

mental or next-to-mental states,
    32-33

mentalistic terms, 34

metamorphosis, 108, 130-31

(metaphysical) atoms of the
    world, 15

*Metaphysical Disputation on the
    Principle of Individuation* (Leib-
    niz), 25n2

metaphysical necessity, 182, 186,
    190

metaphysical points, 50

metaphysics, 19, 68, 79, 108
    eternal truths of, 19
    reconciling the language of
        metaphysics with that of
        practical life, 19, 74

metempsychosis, 108, 130

microbiology, 143

microscope observations, Leeu-
    wenhoek's, 143-45, 173

mind-body problem, 41-42

minds, 31-32, 42, 87, 132

miracles, 64, 75, 152, 169, 177, 193

modern thinkers. *See* new
    philosophers

*Monadology* (Leibniz), 13, 18, 24-27,
    29, 32, 34, 37, 41, 43-44,
        117-34, 143, 147, 155

monads, 26-31, 34, 42-43,
    125, 220-21. *See also* simple
        substances
    Anne Conway's use of term, 136
    bare monads, 30, 45

begin by creation and end by
    annihilation, 117

with the capacity for reason,
    29-30, 37 (*See also* spirits)

changes proceed from an in-
    ternal principle, 118-19

do not need anything to main-
    tain their existence, 35

each different from every
    other, 118

each monad is a living mirror, 106

every created monad represents
    the entire universe, 128

have body, 44

have imaginations, think by
    association, and form
        habits, 37

hierarchical gradation among,
    36

infinity of degrees among, 106

influence on one another (only
    through intervention of
        God), 126

Leibniz's source for, 136

Leibniz's use of term, 24-25

multiplicity in, 119

Reid's account of, 220-25

simple substances or monads,
    15, 26, 28, 64-65, 105, 117-
        19, 172
    argument for the existence
        of, 27
    begin by creation and end
        by annihilation, 117, 173
    express the world, not God,
        97, 99
    includes everything that
        can happen to them, 70
    internal activities of, 119
    living mirror of the universe,
        127

must be true immediate cause of all its actions, 194

never act upon another particular substance, 74

simplicity (partlessness and indivisibility), 34

sources of their own actions, 35

spirit monads, 49

*monas*, 105

Montgomery, George R., 55

moral agents, 49

moral necessity, 182, 186, 190, 207

moral psychology, 41

moral quality of God, 99

More, Henry, 25, 135-36

mortality of the soul, belief in, 119

motion, principles of, 79

motions, 106, 109

movement, general law of, 163

mutual dependency of the body and soul, 152, 172

naked monads. *See* bare monads

natural inertia, 191

Naturalists, reasoning of, 189

naturalizing of thought, 31

necessary substances, 38

necessary truths, 37, 70, 72, 96, 107, 122, 161, 166. *See also* eternal truths

necessity, 37, 110, 188, 190

material necessity, 80

metaphysical necessity, 182, 186, 190

moral necessity, 182, 186, 190, 207

"neighbourhood," 33-34

neighbourhood-apparent-relatedness, 33, 45

*New Essays Concerning Human Understanding* (Leibniz), 23n2

new philosophers, 18, 67, 76-77, 86

Newton, Isaac, 13, 220

Nicole, Pierre, 186

nominal definition, 85-86

nothing happens without sufficient reason (principle), 108

numbers, 59, 71-72, 107, 112, 199

Oldenburg, Henry, 143

organic bodies, 41, 105, 129-30, 159, 173, 193-94. *See also* bodies

of animals, 158

organism, 128, 158-59

original sin, 92, 215

orthodox Christianity. *See* Christian orthodoxy

Ovid, 173

parallelism, 42

Parmenides, 45

Paul, Saint, 94

pendulum, 77, 150-51

perception, 31, 33-37, 105-07, 119-21

inexplicable by mechanical causes, 119

Reid's view of, 219, 221, 223-25

perceptions of our senses, 88, 96

perceptive faculty, 125

perfect being (God), 15, 156

perfect government, 133

perfection, 35, 38-39, 59-62, 98-99, 124, 127

of God. *See* God, perfection of

principle of, 15-16

perfect order established in the universe, 113

perfect or essential definition, 86

perfect republic of spirits. *See* City
of God
Peripatetics, 78, 224
*Phaedo* (Plato), 34, 81
*Philosophical Transactions of the
Royal Society of London*, 11n2, 143
physicists, 68, 108
physics, 21, 27, 67, 69, 82, 84
piety, 94
of the ancients, 67, 79-80
love of God, 156
plagiarism, 13
Plato, 19, 23, 45, 50, 135, 167, 191
doctrine of reminiscence, 87
*Meno*, 18, 87
*Phaedo*, 34, 81
Platonistic view, 46n2, 47
"Platonist" Leibniz, 45
Platonists, 165
plenum, 105-06, 118, 128
Poiret, Pierre, 125
postulates, 16, 18, 37-38, 123
power, 36, 59, 74-75, 90-92, 109,
126, 156, 161, 171, 211-12,
219-25
of God. *See* God, power of
practical canons, 37
prayers, 162, 169, 176, 201
predicate is in the subject (or *in
esse*), 66, 71
pre-established harmony, 16,
41-42, 49, 106, 152, 159, 170-72,
185, 209-11, 217-18, 222,
224-25
among all substances, 131
between the realms of nature
and grace, 112
preformation, 130, 159, 173, 195
in the seeds of the bodies, 158,
170
pre-formed seeds, 108

prevision and predetermination,
200-01. *See also* determinism
primary principles, 123
"principle of the best," 159
*The Principles of Nature and of
Grace* (Leibniz), 13, 18, 24-27,
34, 36, 38, 40, 43-44,
105-13, 219, 223
*Principles of the Most Ancient and
Modern Philosophy* (Conway),
135-42
psychological causes, 42
psychological theory (Leibnizian), 37
psycho-physical parallelism, 42
Ptolemy, 172
public service
equivalent to worship of God,
24n2
punishment, 97, 111, 133, 142,
169, 215
justice of, 200-01, 204
Pyrrhonism, 182
Pythagoras, 172, 189

rational agency, 50-51
rational animals (whose souls are
called spirits), 107
rational inquiry, 37
rational soul (spirit), 111, 122
real definition, 85-86
reality of bodies, 21, 46
reason, 107, 122, 193-94
soul elevated to, 106
*La Recherche de la vérité* (Malebranche), 149, 209
recompense. *See* reward
reflection, 80, 224-25
acts of, 37, 107, 122
reflective knowledge, 107
*Reflexion on the Picture of
Socinianism*, 192-93

refraction, 83

Régis, Pierre-Sylvain, 149

Reid, Thomas, *Essays on the Intellectual Powers of Man*, 219-25

representing, 31-32, 34

reward, 97, 111, 133, 142, 169

Rorarius, Hieronymus, 147n1

"Rorarius" article, 119, 127, 147-48, 158

Royal Society (London), 12n1, 143

S5 modal principle, 38, 124n4

salvation of men, 156-57, 178, 187

Schmuck, Catharina, 10

scholastic philosophers, 68-69, 89, 170

schoolmen, 68, 118, 136, 148, 163, 167, 193

sciences, 10-12, 107, 111, 122

Scotus, John Duns, 187, 203

secularism, 12

self-conscious perceptions, 32-33. *See also* apperception or consciousness

self-sufficiency, 35, 84

Seneca, 206

sensuous pleasures, 112

simple or primitive ideas and propositions, 37

simple substances. *See* monads

sin, 75, 91-92, 163-64, 194, 202-03

  God not the cause of, 165

  original sin, 92, 215

  permitted by God, 158

  sins carry their punishment within them, 133

  world could have been without sin argument, 162

skepticism, 147

Snellius, Willebrord, 83

Socrates, 81

Sophia, Electress, consort of Ernest Augustus, Elector of Hanover, 14

Sophie Charlotte, Queen, consort of Frederick I, King of Prussia, 14

souls, 36, 41-42, 44, 69, 105-07, 120, 128, 149

  act according to laws of final causes, 131

  beauty of the universe in each soul, 110

  begin by creation and end by annihilation, 148, 173, 193

  body and soul relation, 95, 132, 152, 158-59, 172, 222

  blank tablets view, 18, 88

  dependence upon body and senses, 172

  each soul knows the infinite, but confusedly, 111, 171

  express God and the universe and all essences as well as all existences, 87

  God inclines our souls without necessitating them, 90

  human souls, 100, 142, 173, 221

  immortality, 107

  independence, 171

  more than a mere monad, 120

  nature of, 218

  pre-existing in the seeds from the beginning, 90, 95, 173, 193

  principle of action in, 160

  rational, 111, 122

  simple and indivisible, 152

  souls of the righteous, 100

  transmigration, 130, 149-50

speculative theorems, 37-38

spermatic animals, 108, 131
Spinoza, Benedictus de, 23n1,
    38-39, 50, 60n1, 143, 159
spirit of man, 141, 171
spirits, 37, 84, 105-07, 122
    capable of perfection, 98
    differences from other sub-
        stances, souls or substantial
        forms, 96, 98-99
    express God rather than the
        world, 97, 99
    God prefers them to other
        creatures, 97
    image of the divinity, 111
    made in God's image, 99
    members of the City of God, 111
    mirror of universe of crea-
        tures, 111
    open to rewards and punish-
        ments, 100
    preserve forever their moral
        quality, 100
    rational souls, 132
    society with God, 98, 111, 132
spontaneity, 94, 152, 157, 170-71
Stoics, 112
substantial forms, 67-69, 96
sufficient reason, 40, 108, 214
    for contingent truths, 123
    for the existence of the uni-
        verse, 109
    God as, 123
    for God's choices, 126
    principle of, 15-16, 28, 37-38
supernatural, 75, 76, 169
supralapsarian view, 92
Supreme Reason, 156
supreme substance (God), 38, 123
Swammerdam, Jan, 149
swoons, 97, 106, 120
    confusing with death, 107

theism, 22, 42
theistic philosophy, 50
theodicy, 17
*Theodicy* (Leibniz), 13, 17, 25,
    155-85, 209
theologians, 68-69, 164, 182
theology, 10, 30, 40, 67-68, 99n1
thinking, 19, 31-32, 34
thisness, 66n1
Thomasius, Jakob, 25n2, 136
toleration, 12
transformation or metamorpho-
    sis, 44, 108, 130, 150, 173
transmigration of souls, 130,
    149-50
truths, 86, 161
    contingent truths, 70, 125
    of fact, 122-23
    of reasoning, 122

unconscious perception, 36, 219
understanding, 161
unhappiness, 174-76. *See also* evil
union of body and soul, 95, 131,
    152, 158-59, 222
universal harmony, 98, 127, 156,
    206
universal truths, 96

Van Helmont, Francis Mercury,
    135
virtue, 111, 151, 156, 182
Voltaire, *Candide*, 213-18

"Why is there something rather
    than nothing?," 38, 108
wickedness. *See* evil
will, 109, 138, 161, 163, 186-87
    action of God upon the hu-
        man will, 90
    antecedent will of God, 174, 202

consequent will, 163, 202

decretory will, 186

final and decisive will, 174

good will on the part of men, 100

mediate will, 174

primitive antecedent will, 174

will of God, 40, 125, 134, 156

William of Saint Amour, 89

windowless monads, 29

wisdom, 59, 110, 126, 137, 159, 161

of God, 67, 81, 92, 136, 170, 173, 185

wise will inclined antecedently to all good, 187

Wolff, Christian, *Psychologia empirica, seu experimentalis*, 220

world could have been without sin argument, 162

The production of this title on Rolland Enviro 100 Print paper
instead of virgin fibres paper reduces your ecological footprint by :

Tree(s) : 2
Solid waste : 127 kg

Water : 8393 L
Air emissions : 330 kg

Printed by Marquis Book Printing. The interior of this book is printed on Rolland Enviro 100,
containing 100% post-consumer recycled fibers, Eco-Logo certified, processed without chlorinate,
FSC ® Recycled and manufactured using biogaz energy.